The Poet's Freedom

SUSAN STEWART

The Poet's Freedom

A NOTEBOOK ON MAKING

The University of Chicago Press Chicago and London

SUSAN STEWART is the Avalon Foundation University Professor in the Humanities and director of the Society of Fellows in the Liberal Arts at Princeton University. A former MacArthur fellow, she is the author of five earlier critical studies, including *Poetry and the Fate of the Senses* (2002), winner of the Christian Gauss award of the Phi Beta Kappa Society and the Truman Capote Award. She is also the author of five books of poems, most recently of *Red Rover* (2008) and *Columbarium* (2003), winner of the National Book Critics Circle Award. These titles, along with *The Open Studio* (2005) and *The Forest* (1995), are all published by the University of Chicago Press.

The University of Chicago Press, Chicago 60637
The University of Chicago Press, Ltd., London

Published 2011.
Printed in the United States of America

20 19 18 17 16 15 14 13 12 11 1 2 3 4 5

ISBN-13: 978-0-226-77386-5 (cloth)
ISBN-13: 978-0-226-77387-2 (paper)
ISBN-10: 0-226-77386-8 (cloth)
ISBN-10: 0-226-77387-6 (paper)

Library of Congress Cataloging-in-Publication Data

Stewart, Susan (Susan A.), 1952–
The poet's freedom : a notebook on making / Susan Stewart.
p. cm.
Includes bibliographical references and index.
ISBN-13: 978-0-226-77386-5 (cloth : alk. paper)
ISBN-10: 0-226-77386-8 (cloth : alk. paper)
ISBN-13: 978-0-226-77387-2 (pbk. : alk. paper)
ISBN-10: 0-226-77387-6 (pbk. : alk. paper)
1. Freedom and art. 2. Poetry—Authorship. 3. Creative writing. I. Title.
PN1031.S835 2011
808.1—dc23

2011018308

♾ This paper meets the requirements of ANSI/NISO Z39.48-1992 (Permanence of Paper).

To be alive—is Power—
Existence—in itself—
Without a further function—
Omnipotence—Enough—

To be alive—and will!
'Tis able as a God—
The Maker—of Ourselves—be what—
Such being Finitude!

EMILY DICKINSON

CONTENTS

ACKNOWLEDGMENTS

I quote several poems in full: I thank Srs. Philippa and Benedicta at Stanbrook Abbey, and Louise Anson, Helen Waddell's great-great-niece, for permission to quote Helen Waddell's translation of *Dies irae*, "The Day of Wrath"; from K. Foster and F. Boyde's edition and translation of Dante Alighieri, *Dante's Lyric Poetry*, I quote "Dante da Maiano to Various Makers of Rhyme," © 1967 Oxford University Press; "I am not one of those who left the land" from *Poems of Akhmatova*, selected, translated, and introduced by Stanley Kunitz, with Max Hayward, © 1967, 1968, 1972, 1973 by Stanley Kunitz and Max Hayward, originally published by Little, Brown and currently available from Mariner Books; Robert Tracy's translation of Mandelstam's "Epigram to Stalin" from *Osip Mandelstam's Stone*, © 1981 Princeton University Press, reprinted by permission of Princeton University Press; Donald Davie's translations of Mandelstam's "Octet 73" and "Octet 75" originally appeared in *Agenda* 14:2 (1976), and I thank Michael Schmidt and Carcanet Press Limited for permission to reproduce these octets here.

Versions and portions of the following sections of this book were delivered or published as follows:

from 1: "Freedom of the Poet," public lecture at the School of Criticism and Theory at Cornell University, June 2009.

from 2: "What Praise Poems Are For," *PMLA* 120, no. 1 (Winter 2004–5): 235–45. Reprinted by permission of the copyright owner, The Modern Language Association of America.

from 3: "Poetry and the Feeling of a Thought," keynote address at "Poetry, Music, and the Senses," École des hautes études en sciences sociales, Paris, June 2005; University of Michigan, September 2006; "Beginning a Poem," Pennsylvania Academy of the Fine Arts, Philadelphia, September 2006; "Convergence in Poetry," Stanford University interdisciplinary conference "Convergence," Palo Alto, August 2006.

from 4: "Freedom from Imagination," Conference on Philosophy and Literature, Temple University, Philadelphia, March 2008; Centre for Literary Study, University of Western Sydney, Australia, July 2008; Dean's Lecture, Radcliffe Institute, Cambridge, Massachusetts, May 2009; Princeton Society of Fellows, Princeton, May 2009.

from 6: "Rhyme and Freedom," in *The Sound of Poetry / The Poetry of Sound*, ed. Marjorie Perloff and Craig Dworkin (Chicago: University of Chicago Press, 2009).

from 7: "Dante and the Poetry of Meeting," a conference in honor of Rachel Jacoff, "Dante Vivo," Wellesley College, September 2005; *American Poetry Review* 35, no. 4 (July-August 2006): 39–42. "Anna Akhmatova: Poet of the Future," public lecture for Poets House and Poetry Society of America, New York, April 2007, also delivered for the public series "Branching Out" at the Kansas City Public Library and Fresno Public Library, May 2006; and Hartford Public Library, March 2008.

"The Sand Castle" appeared in *Chicago Review*, Spring 2010, and in *Poetry Daily*, July 4, 2010.

* * *

I am grateful to the Humanities Council at Princeton University, which granted me an Old Dominion Fellowship in 2009–10, enabling me to finish this book. Many friends and colleagues contributed to my work, among them Robert Harrison, Daniel Heller-Roazen, Susan Howe, James Longenbach, Giuseppe Mazzotta, Mark Payne, Marjorie Perloff, Alan Singer, Michael Wood, and Froma Zeitlin. My editors at the University of Chicago Press, Alan Thomas and Randy Petilos, were unstinting in their support of the project, and I owe a great debt to Ann Hamilton—not only for her conversation and insights but also for her thoughtful contribution to the book's cover. And to my family of thinkers, tinkerers, and makers—Daniel Halevy, Jacob Stewart-Halevy, and Sam Stewart-Halevy—more thanks than words can say.

On the Method of This "Notebook"

This book bears the subtitle *A Notebook on Making* because I have written it out of concerns that have unfolded over time—the concerns of a poet with a vivid interest in other art forms. I therefore hope my words will be of use to makers of many kinds, but I should say from the outset that my world of examples and references necessarily reflects my own practice and predilections. Another book entirely could have been written on these concerns by a composer of music or prose fictions, for example, and yet the "otherwise" remains our common resource.

I have framed the parts of this book as "entries" and provided some room at the end for readers' notes. And although I have spoken to those readers as if they will turn the pages continuously from start to finish, I imagine, and hope, I have made a book for perusing from time to time. I have not unwound a single story or hammered a final argument into place, for this is a book about the pleasures of making and thinking as unfinished, ongoing, means of life. My aim has been to set forward some ideas about the freedom artists have—the deep past of that freedom, and its future.

A SAND CASTLE

I don't remember where, which coast, or which sea, but one late summer afternoon I was reading under a beach umbrella, and beyond the periphery of its oblong shadow, I could catch sight of a boy, maybe eight, maybe nine years old, who was building an elaborate sand castle: turrets, moats, interior walls, indentations carved by a spoon's edge to show where the windows would be. His blunter instruments, shovels and buckets, were thrown aside, for his work had reached the point of minor additions and deletions, revisions made with the tips of his fingers. He had chosen his site carefully as well—even as the tide came in his castle would be safe, and unless in the dark a drunk or a pair of lovers stumbled across it, or a patrolling jeep wheeled over it, it would be there tomorrow.

Meanwhile, strips of red, orange, then darker blue, darker than the sky, streaked the horizon. Sunbathers shook out their towels and spilled the day's find of shells and bony driftwood into emptied buckets; smaller children began to whine for their supper; and still the boy worked on.

Then he stood, smacked his hands together, turned, ran back a few yards, stopped, turned again, and raced back to his castle. Reaching it, he kicked with all his might, his arms and legs flailing like a gritty whirligig as the castle's sandy walls and towers became barely distinguishable from the sand surrounding them, then not distinguishable at all.

Startled, feeling that something beautiful had, as we say, "come to grief," I thought of the end of Shelley's "Ozymandias": "the lone and level sands stretch far away." But the boy was delighted—he grinned (to himself, to me, I couldn't tell) and skipped off to wherever he was going next.

Since then, that boy has represented for me a certain relation we have to making. Without the freedom of reversibility enacted in unmaking, or at least always present as the potential for unmaking, we cannot give value to our making. Was his castle a work of craft rather than art—one he felt could be replaced easily? Did this object that implied, but could not realize, an interior acquire an interiority in being a memory alone?

By destroying the mere thing, and using all his physical might to do so, the boy seemed to be returning the power of the form back into himself, as if what he had been practicing all along was a mode of memorization or, better, learning. Once the skills used in making the castle in its entirety were internalized, they were ready to be used again. Unwilling or unable to be the curator of his creation, the boy swiftly returned it to its elements, that is, to its pure potential.

The dark side of the news he brought is that our desire to destroy what we have made often overcomes our respect for the formal finitude of made things—there is no such thing as a precision bomb, or even the precision destruction of a sand castle. Care in destruction is a form of self-deception, and fury is blind.

1 / BEGINNING

A genuine Transcendence is more than a limit concept: it is a *presence* which brings about a true revolution in the theory of subjectivity. It introduces into it a radically new dimension, the *poetic* dimension. At least such limit concepts complete the determination of a freedom which is human and *not* divine, of a freedom which does not posit itself absolutely because it *is not* Transcendence. To will is not to create.

—PAUL RICOEUR, *Philosophie de la volonté*[1]

Initium . . . ut esset, creatus est homo, ante quem nullus fuit.

—AUGUSTINE, *City of God* 12.20[2]

I The Freedom of the Maker

How free is the artist in making? And why is the artist, at least in Western culture, but surely in some others as well, a figure of freedom? How is it that artists create their own rules, and how might such self-legislation serve humankind in other spheres of life? When we consider these perennial questions, we are confronted with a pair of inevitable, interwoven, truths: first, freedom is necessary for making—at least for making anything that is actualized beyond mere repetition—and second, freedom is both inalienable to human life and itself something that we make or actualize.

To begin to think about freedom is to think about causality, for if nature is the outcome of an endless series of causal forces, our human being is only partially bound by such natural laws. Even the most cursory review of the intellectual history of the idea of freedom reveals a concept çontinually shaped within the tension between natural law and human will. In the *Nicomachean Ethics* (3.6), for example, Aristotle suggests that whereas the nonhuman universe is ruled by material and teleological necessity, human events are contingent and underdetermined. Further, he holds that the ends we place in store for ourselves are determined by the kind of person we are; he finds an intrinsic connection between our character and what we bring about in the world. Particularly concerned with the problem of our responsibility for our actions, Aristotle also realizes that such responsibility can be damaged by ignorance or violence.

Medieval Christian concepts of freedom, embedded in problems of theodicy, are similarly concerned with the relations between freedom and action and are perhaps most succinctly framed by Augustine's insistence that the will, under the weight of divine love, may be inclined toward the good, but human action is performed freely. More continuous in Western thought than discontinuous, this emphasis upon human freedom and human powers of self-fashioning, even within a divinely planned world, culminates in Renaissance humanism. The most well-known proclamation of that movement, Pico della Mirandola's "Oration on the Dignity of Man" of 1486 establishes an analogy between the free making of the Hebrew god, who is a "supreme Architect" (*il Sommo Padre, Dio architetto*) and "Artisan" (*l'Artifice*) creating by "the sublime laws of His ineffable Mind," and the free choosing of human beings, who must establish for themselves the "limits and bounds" of their nature. Pico declares to his fellow human beings: "With free choice and dignity, you may fashion yourself into whatever form you choose." The Neoplatonic frame of Pico's thinking emphasizes humanity's ascent from plant and animal nature to the powers of a contemplative intelligence, where each man and woman is a "divinity clothed in flesh." Yet in line with his just as strongly held occultism, Pico concludes that human beings should disdain both earthly things and "the things of heaven." Humans do not hold a "lower place" than angelic creatures, he contends, but rather one close to God, whose choices in making include endowing them with choices in making.[3]

Eventually a paradox emerges in thinking about the causal conditions of freedom: if natural laws account for all changes and events in the world, then human choices cannot be free. But if human actions are not only exercised freely but also capable of bringing about changes in the natural world, then not every action is subject to purely physical laws and universal determinism cannot hold. The emerging modern revelations that the laws of nature are subject to vagaries of perception, that the laws of physics are thereby contingent, and that the task of knowing nature may never be completed, led, on the one hand, to Descartes's separation of mind and matter and Kant's separation of the world of freedom from the world of nature and, on the other, to the determinist claims of Spinoza, Leibniz, and Hume, who wrote that we may think our acts are free, but this is because their determining causes elude us. Hegel and Marx in turn pursue dialectical answers to the problem of material and willed causes. Seeking freedom through processes of externalization and expression, they look toward the future and the problem of ends. For Hegel, freedom has a political character and finds its end in the state. For Marx, freedom is realized through a reordering of the terms and conditions of existence itself as human agents discover and shape their common interests.

Yet the concept of freedom is of course not merely a matter of philosophical debate. It is an idea that we feel and pursue. We recognize, and at times are forced to recognize, that our behavior is not consonant with our desires and motivations. Our capacities for self-consciousness and self-deception, our abilities to deliberate, reflect, and judge, all open our existence beyond the panoply of contingent and necessary forces that shape us. We live, like the rest of nature, in the present; and we live as well, unlike the rest of nature, beyond the discernible horizon. We are able to speculate about the sources of things and on into futures of imagined possibilities; so far as we know, we are the only beings who can form their own desires, withdraw at will, and suffer regret. The concept of freedom continually invites us to initiate, to choose, and to judge.

Freedom thus in many ways is tied to issues of beginnings, and where we begin when we conceive of it makes all the difference in our relation not only to its causes but also to its consequences. It is a commonplace of the philosophical discourse on freedom to distinguish, for example, between negative and positive freedoms. Negative freedoms, or freedoms *from*, rely on prior causes and involve independence from existing powers, whether such powers stem from the divine, the state, or elsewhere. Under this paradigm, being free is expressed as becoming free or breaking free, casting off fetters or overcoming limitations.[4] When we conceive of negative freedom, we thereby begin, like the partisans of any liberation movement, in situations that determine the shape and direction of whatever freedom might be exercised; by definition, negative freedoms are concrete and reactive. Indeed, arguments about negative freedom, with their inherent tensions between "external" forces and "internal" desires, tend to restrict our concerns and hopes to the limits of our bodies. Such negative freedoms grant from the outset that power is something that must be wrested away from what is outside of our bodies and the limits of our bodily extension.

Positive freedoms, however, involve acts of affirmation—they are experienced not as away from but as toward. The prevailing theme of negative freedom is our mortality; that of positive freedom, our decision to live. This notion of positive freedom has been popularized by the Cold War writings of Isaiah Berlin,[5] but its most forceful statement could be said to have come more than a century and a half earlier, in the discussion of teleological thinking at the close of Immanuel Kant's *Critique of the Power of Judgment*. There Kant emphasizes that whereas there are some facts, such as things or objects of nature, that can be established by means of experience, and other facts, such as mathematical ideas of magnitude or geometry, that can be established by being presented to the reason, only one fact, as an "idea of reason," bridges the relation between experience and reason itself—the fact of freedom. Kant remarks that it "is quite remarkable [that] there is even one idea of reason (which is in itself incapable of any presentation in intuition, thus incapable of theoretical proof of its possibility) among the facts, and that is the idea of freedom. . . . It is the only one among all the ideas of pure reason whose object is a fact and which must be counted among the *scibilia* [knowable things]."[6] Thus for Kant, our freedom, inalienable and intrinsic to our human being, is not an object derived from what we think of as "external" experience. As a nonmaterial idea with a "particular kind of causality," it is manifested or exercised through actions and intelligible in that world of space, time, and indeed causality that we inhabit. Poised between natural causality and this causality of "a particular kind," human freedom becomes, in Kant's thought, the link between nature and the moral laws we create through our practical judgments. We in turn could say, in line with such a notion of positive freedom, that freedom is exercised or played upon the world rather than wrested from it.

In Kant's writings, our practical freedom involves independence from determination by particular sensuous impulses that we might have or—to come closer to their effects—that might occupy us at any given moment. But from Kant's perspective this independence is not asserted, as it might at first seem, as a negative freedom. Once the will is able to act spontaneously and autonomously, that is, without dependence on some antecedent and external cause, our capacity for transcendental freedom is absolute and positive; through it, we are able to issue actions and events from ourselves, to be self-legislating.

Human beings thereby are able to evade the determinacy that rules the empirical world, not merely because we act according to principles but also because we always can choose to do otherwise, and the choices we make in turn are subjected to further judgments of praise and blame. Our freedom is bound to the fact of our status as living beings; the open decision to act in one way rather than another is rooted existentially in the always prior and fundamental decision to continue to live. In the realm of moral choices, such a capacity for transcendental freedom becomes a precondition for practical freedom, and not the other way around.[7] At least since the slave Epictetus's claim that "if you will, you are free," a transcendental freedom is the Stoic's birthright.[8] If for later thinkers, such as Hannah Arendt, "inner freedom" was a retreat from the world consequent to the denial of external, negative freedoms,[9] in this contrary tradition running from the Stoics to Kant, freedom is present whenever human beings think of themselves as living, willing intelligences.

Kant's concerns with the cosmological and positive dimensions of human freedom are carried forward in a number of otherwise often incommensurable later philosophies. To choose some representative voices: Friedrich Schelling, Martin Heidegger, Arendt, and Stuart Hampshire have each proposed concepts of freedom inextricably linked to issues of causality, self-determination, acting, and making. Schelling's 1809 *Philosophical Investigations into the Essence of Human Freedom and Related Matters* takes up the question of freedom not only in relation to human actions but also within a more general concern with issues of theodicy. In contrast to Kant, Schelling views the fundamental condition of freedom not as reason liberated from its ground in the sensuous but as action willed from necessity; humans exercise this will in a process of becoming that is inseparable from other natural processes. Like Aristotle, Schelling emphasizes the force of personality as a consciousness emerging in nature; prior to existence proper, human self-creation is infused with a "lively feeling" of freedom that is inherently capable of good and evil. Schelling introduces a felt sense of peril into his account of human freedom as he describes the free person as a dizzy man poised on a precipice who has a desire to jump into the abyss.

More than a century before Freud's writings on the death instinct, Schelling writes of the analogous urge to withdraw from our powers: "The fear of life itself drives man out of the center in which he was created; for this center is, as the purest essence of all will, a consuming fire for every particular will; in order to be able to live in it man must be mortified in all his ownhood, for which reason he must almost necessarily attempt to step out of it and into the periphery, in order to seek rest there for his selfhood." In the end, Schelling's theology of freedom holds that God is "not a system, but a life" that can incorporate, in a continual process of overcoming, both personal existence and the ground or condition against which that existence comes into relief. Schelling holds that humans are creatures who cannot integrate the conditions or ground of existence into such an absolute personality; we are finite, and in that finitude, like the finitude of all natural beings, we suffer the melancholy of our incapacity to overcome ourselves. Yet he also emphasizes that, unlike other natural beings, humans are continually becoming conscious. He concludes that in Christianity human existence finds its value "as the beginning of a new covenant" wherein humanity mediates the relation between God and nature: "since man himself is combined with God, God . . . also assumes nature and integrates it *into himself*. Thus man is the redeemer of nature, and all its prototypes point toward him."[10] In Schelling's philosophy, as in Pico's "Oration," human beings find their freedom within the precarious, indeterminate, and yet finite situation that characterizes their existence between natural causes and near-divine powers of self-making and self-comprehension.

In his Freiburg lectures delivered in 1930–32, as he took up the terms of those arguments regarding freedom that he had found in Kant and Schelling, Martin Heidegger, too, emphasizes that human beings are uniquely capable of understanding their freedom. Heidegger concludes in a transposition of Kant's arguments about freedom: "Freedom must itself, in its essence, be more primordial than man. Man is only an administrator of freedom." The problem of beginning and absolute beginnings continues in Heidegger's writings as well to be an intrinsic feature of thought about freedom. Freedom is revealed as a power of self-origination and hence must somehow precede human being.

Hannah Arendt, who had been Heidegger's student, sees the administration of freedom as embedded in means of social relations that are unpredictable and indeterminate. The Stoics had imagined such bonds to other persons as in truth not the fruit of human freedom but rather as the web that entangles humans in relations of violence, submission, and obligation. Arendt, to the contrary, breaks freedom away from determination by necessity. She contends that freedom need not be tied to sovereignty and that a notion of action as open-ended process can enable us "to begin something new . . . of not being able to control or foretell its consequences." Our faculties of forgiving and promising, the first overriding the past and the second actively shaping the future, help us create a free relation to time that—rather than being rooted in regulation and domination—emerges, she argues, in the actual forging of social relations. These faculties are exercised in free will and turn out to have a binding power necessary to action.[11]

More recently, Stuart Hampshire has explored the relation between self-legislation and the creation of human desires. For Hampshire we are not the products of our desires so much as the makers of them. He writes, "Desires do not only occur; they may also be formed, and formed as the outcome of a process of criticism . . . if a man can identify his desires to act in certain ways as satisfying certain descriptions, and can therefore reflect upon them, he may also evaluate and criticise them. They are his, in a strong sense of authorship, and he may take responsibility for them." In Hampshire's account, whatever is volitional in our existence is linked intrinsically to our powers to reflect, to "make up our minds";—to discover or come to know, and to communicate with ourselves as well as others.[12]

Why be interested, as I am, in these accounts of freedom from the viewpoint of the philosophy of art, with its concerns with artistic production, and aesthetics, with its concerns with art reception? After all, in Kant's larger system aesthetic judgments are merely a subtype of reflective judgments—those that do not apply existing categories of the understanding. Reflective judgments either modify the understanding's categories, as in the case of science, or suspend or block them, as in the respective experiences of beauty and sublimity. And reflective judgments are in turn only one of a number of types of judgment that Kant analyzes. Hence aesthetic experiences of nature and, to an even lesser extent, of works of art are hardly fundamental to his arguments regarding freedom. Nevertheless, Kant sets up a comparison between aesthetic experiences and other experiences, most suggestively in the relation between moral feelings and the experience of beauty. Later Romantic thinkers, including Schelling and Samuel Taylor Coleridge, will place art making in a far more powerful role, imagining human freedom and self-formation to be vitally rooted in artistic processes, including symbol making.

As early as the discussion of metaphor in Aristotle's *Poetics*, the intuitions of genius are set into tension with learning, and insight is linked to a transforming perspectivalism that moves between recognition and estrangement. Aristotle writes, "The greatest thing by far is to be a master of metaphor. It is the one thing that cannot be learnt from others; and it is also a sign of genius, since a good metaphor implies an intuitive perception of the similarity in dissimilars."[13] Similarly, just as Kant's notions of both practical and transcendental freedom depend upon the application of maxims, or the meeting of experience with such maxims, and so the binding of moral decisions to rules, so does his aesthetics depend upon the ongoing practice of art making as self-authorizing and self-legislating.

In his passages on the "aesthetic power of judgment" in his *Critique of the Power of Judgment*, Kant writes, "Genius is the talent (natural gift) that gives the rule to art . . . a talent for producing that for which no determinate rule can be given, not a predisposition of skill for that which can be learned in accordance with some rule, consequently that originality must be its primary characteristic."[14] As we have seen, Kant contends that we cannot know how freedom and natural causality fit together, but as members of the noumenal world we nevertheless have a capacity for self-legislation. Freedom lies thereby in giving one's self one's own law out of one's own essence. Analogously, as the maker or genius gives the rules to art, he or she is enjoying positive freedom in conditions of unusual intensity. Such autotelic activity creates another nature out of the material that actual nature provides, and despite the preservation of a noumenal world unintelligible to human concerns, the Kantian system tends to anthropomorphize all phenomena, suggesting the sovereignty of the human reason over them. Even the experience of the sublime in Kant's system ultimately rests not in the powers of a dynamic nature or mathematical infinity, as we might first conclude, but rather in the intuition of the reason.

Even so, as Kant makes the case for art making as an actualized and actualizing practice of freedom, we also can argue that any artist who dedicates his or her life to making things—things that, certainly from the perspective of poets, have varying degrees of "thingness"—must at some point, or perhaps all along, explore the fundamental qualities of what he or she is doing, the broader traditions from which the work derives, and the work's consequences or aims. Artworks have a saturated value far beyond their materiality and use value. They are an exaggerated example of the phenomenon of desirable objects described by Georg Simmel in his treatise *The Philosophy of Money*. Simmel writes that we only desire objects that "are not immediately given to us for our use and enjoyment, that is, to the extent to which they resist our desire. The content of our desire becomes an object as soon as it is opposed to us, not only in the sense of being impervious to us, but also in terms of its distance as something not yet enjoyed."[15] Although Simmel himself goes on to quote Kant regarding the relation between sense impressions and objects of understanding, we could say, in counterpoint, that objects of desire do not present themselves to the understanding but rather resist any ready hermeneusis. This resistance is part of their attraction to us and why they live in the future as much as in the present; we save them for that future, which extends beyond our own lived horizons.

Artworks are not merely superestimated commodities that reify the cultural causes of value. Although precious materials bear some relation to precious objects, it is the interiorization of skill and thought in the artwork that figures its worth. Alfred Gell writes with regard to Simmel's arguments about value that "the resistance which [artworks] offer, and which creates and sustains this desire [to make and obtain them], is to being possessed in an intellectual rather than a material sense, the difficulty I have in mentally encompassing their coming-into-being as objects in the world accessible to me by a technical process which, since it transcends my understanding, I am forced to construe as magical."[16] It may be that the technical process at times leads to stupefaction in the viewer, but in fact technical processes can be taught and repeated; it seems far more likely that we construe the magical in an artwork when, despite our best efforts, we cannot imagine the maker's intention or the origin of the concept. We may conclude that the artwork is overdetermined, but it is the mind of another that overwhelms us with its plenitude.

In our own time we are undergoing a crisis about made things. What is essential to our lives, and at what scale and multitude? What must be renewed, and what deserves the continuity of curating and other processes of care? At what cost to the continuity of the natural world do we pursue such aims of creating and maintaining objects? It is difficult, certainly, to argue for making more things. If we have an environmentalist's conscience, restraint and even withdrawal seem the most moral responses to the natural world. At the same time, we constantly feel the pressure of the need to make new art. We never say "We have enough art and now we'll simply take care of what we have." Indeed, every generation seems to have an obligation to the future not only to represent its thinking in created forms but also to use created forms as a means of thought itself. The necessity of starting out, of new beginnings, is as central to our existence as life itself—the very nature of our vitality.

To assume that art making is a practice indicates from the outset that the long historical task of art is unfinished. Individual works will necessarily exhibit formal closure, but the task of art in general is incomplete and drives this process of continual beginnings. Something continues to call for art, something in the experience of those who make it and something in the experience of those who seek to apprehend it. Nature produces beauty without human intervention, but nature does not produce works of art, and no artwork can be completed without reception.

Our metaphors for these recurring openings to art as a summons to apprehension—*to call, to speak, to hear, to touch*—reveal the etymology of aesthetics in sense experiences. Whether we are reflecting on our own artistic practice or the works of others, our freedom in aesthetic activity is exercised as well in the interpretive task of receiving finite forms and imputing intention and purposiveness to them. Such experiences call for intersubjective apprehension, an apprehension that most often proceeds along the lines of face-to-face encounters with other persons.[17]

Each of us has immediate knowledge of our free spontaneity, yet just as self-legislation has no power over any natural laws, no natural law has power over our capacity for self-legislation. The artwork is created by means of voluntary acts of beginning. Its form speaks to a set of abandoned alternatives: it might not have been conceived; it could have been left unfinished; it might have been, and still might be, destroyed. The same dimensions of the otherwise trace the work's reception, for no one is obliged to attend, care for, or keep it. But because we do so voluntarily, hence endowing works of art with the value of our labor and our concern, art continues to be a domain of valued, even treasured, things. The usefulness of these things does not become absorbed into the world, and when an artwork is lost, it cannot be replaced.

Aesthetics proper is an eighteenth-century invention, a breakthrough in deliberations regarding sense apprehension by German Pietist theologians and the study of the relations between common sense and taste by early eighteenth-century philosophers. Alexander Baumgarten is often thought to have been the first, in his reflections on poetry from 1735, to transpose the meaning of *aesthesis* from sense impression per se to taste with regard to beauty. Yet Baumgarten was well aware of the word's Greek etymology, and recent research by the historian Simon Grote has shown that Pietist theologians had been using *aesthetics* in the context of debates over moral education for several decades and that the concept was central to views on art, the notion of beauty, and sense perception in the views of Anthony Ashley Cooper, the third Earl of Shaftesbury, Francis Hutcheson, and others.[18]

Moral reflections on freedom in art making and reception arise as well among ancient thinkers. They can be found specifically in certain passages on the relations between willing and making in Plato and in the account of the poet/maker's relation to natural processes in the thought of Aristotle. In book 10 of the *Republic*, as well as the dialogues *Ion*, *Gorgias*, and *Phaedrus*, Plato condemns the poet who arouses, nourishes, and strengthens the passions at the expense of reason. Yet in his work as a whole, Plato leaves a quite contradictory and confusing picture of his view of poetry as an art form, and it is difficult to make claims about the particulars of any "Platonic" position. For example, in *Ion*'s attack on the poet who cannot participate in any form of knowledge like that of generals or doctors or charioteers, poetry is separated from crafts. And in *Phaedrus* Plato elaborates: "If any man come to the gates of poetry without the madness of the Muses, persuaded that *technê* alone will make him a good poet, then shall he and his works of sanity be brought to naught by the poetry of madness, and behold, their place is nowhere to be found."

In *Gorgias* poetry is a practice that requires not *technê* but something like an intuitive facility designed to please: *empeiria*. According to the argument against rhetoric in this dialogue, any rhetorical composition, including tragedy and poetry, cannot meet the requirement that produces good results. But in his *Symposium*, Plato suggests as well something integral and pervasive about the poet as maker: "Everything that is responsible for creating something out of nothing is a kind of poetry and all the creations of every craft and profession are themselves a kind of poetry, and everyone who practices a craft is a poet."[19] Although Plato contends that any art form suffers from being two degrees removed from the true and abstract reality of ideal forms, he also argues that what is known by the mind rather than the senses is free of contradictions and has an unchanging stability, and hence leads the way toward the beautiful and the good.

Even so, Platonism, Neoplatonism, and other idealist systems like the later monism of Spinoza have in their impersonality very little room for notions of either freedom or creation. And it is difficult to conclude that Plato makes any claims at all about art as we know it, including poetry. In Plato's discourse, poetry is framed within discussions of rhetoric and craft as a matter of know-how. This is a know-how of craftsmanship and replication—not one that has as its end a unique object that is the outcome of individual creation. As the historian of religion Claude Tresmontant has explained, because such systems have no doctrine of creation, they also have no concept of "creative uncreated liberty."[20] Everything proceeds eternally as emanation from The One, the point of origin, which is a self-contained Absolute.

Aristotle, however, roots his philosophy in experience; the later motto of the existentialists, that existence precedes essence, is Aristotelian in this regard and follows from Aristotle's sense that no distinction separates the particular from the universal, that we come to know essences through the forms in which and by means of which they are manifested. As we have glimpsed in his comments on metaphor, Aristotle is far more interested in change than in absolutes, and thus his various comments on art engage practices of making and the existential conditions under which making proceeds. In the *Nicomachean Ethics* he writes, "All art is concerned with the realm of coming-to-be, i.e., with contriving and studying how something that is capable both of being and not being may come into existence, a thing whose starting point or source is in the producer and not in the thing produced. For art is concerned neither with things that exist or come into being by necessity, nor with things produced by nature; these have their source of motion within themselves." For Aristotle, the work of artists from the outset involves making something that might or might not exist, and he expands on this point by arguing that art is not necessary or instrumental. In his *Physics* he argues that the maker partly imitates nature and partly carries to completion what nature has left incomplete. He further argues that the artist sometimes "errs voluntarily" and that such willed errors are preferable to those made involuntarily; in this regard, artistic decisions are the opposite of ethical decisions, where to err voluntarily is a serious offense and involuntarily a lesser one. Addressing error, Aristotle thereby prepares the ground for an argument that the consequences of art making should be distinguished from those of ethics and that artistic freedom, self-governed by its own open conditions of proceeding, includes the freedom to err and begin again. The Aristotelian tradition lays the foundation for an argument that art is a means of discovery regarding nature and human nature within it. Rather than an imitation of an imitation, art is, for Aristotle, a perfected form—an improvement upon nature that penetrates to the principles of nature.[21]

Indeed, when we picture the scene of art making, we can follow a progression from spontaneity to determination. In the act of composition, many forces are at work, some conscious, others unconscious, some available to analysis and others not, or perhaps not yet. At the start, all the elements are assembled—say, the initial phrase or rhyme or stanza scheme for a poem, or perhaps the rudimentary palette of colors, brushes of various shapes and sizes, and prepared surface for a painting. Until a mark is made, and then the next and the next, the form is replete with any number of choices, and each choice then exercised is dense with its relation to what could have been otherwise. Each determination, like the trail of filings left by a burin, leaves behind a trace of what might have been. Furthermore, because actions have shapes and consequences, they admit of the possibility of going astray, of being mis-taken. The otherwise can in this sense beckon so much as it falls away, and not only the materials of the work but also the process itself resist domination. As all these successive determinations develop into a finite form, the maker may experience frustration, blockage, release, insight, and a diminishment or intensification of powers of judgment. The psychological valence of the process is no more ends-defined than any other aspect of it. Absorption promises only a release from any prior sense of personality or reified style—not a realization of it. In the end, the only two possibilities are the extreme binaries of acceptance and destruction—and as the sand castle maker perhaps knew, acceptance is no guarantee against the world's destruction. Conversely, the receiver of the artwork who traces the maker's steps follows this experience back to the conditions of origin where everything is pure potential.

Whatever freedom the will might possess is available in this process of possibility without resolution. As the etymological connection between *technê* and *birth* indicates, the onset of art making can be seen as an imitation of birth, just as finality of form is an imitation of death. Yet here birth and death are posed in undertakings that continually open to a sense of alternatives. Until reaching the brink of realized form, the maker proceeds by gestures of free choosing and free willing that find their motives and explanations only retrospectively.

II The Creator in Genesis

Western philosophers of art emphasize the creation of something out of "nothing"—or if not nothing, then out of other things, such as the Greek Chaos, of no significance. And such thinkers put forward as well the creation of positive forms against a backdrop of the otherwise that remains unrealized and unrealizable. Yet the fact remains that nature has no gaps. Everywhere there is something, instead of nothing.[22] This truth of our apprehension of the world means that nature appears to us as an integral, ever-changing, and self-forming form. Nature is something not only created but also constantly creating, and creating itself, as we know from the long Aristotelian tradition, clarified by Spinoza, of the relation between *natura naturans*, an acting and creating nature, and *natura naturata*, a created nature. In its Aristotelian frame nature is always inventing, and *natura naturans* becomes the paradigm for any producing activity that involves self-regulation and self-forming.

Because we are part of nature's open totality, we have both a particular, felt relation to it and an inability to grasp it in its entirety; indeed, our sense of that entirety is intuitive and resembles the way we experience the myriad complexity of our own bodies and have difficulty imagining their individual finitude. It is we who are the authors of nothingness; like Schelling's figure on the edge of the abyss, we teeter at the edge of an openness that is an artifact of our own freedom—the ever-unfolding, nontotalizable realm of human signs and meanings. Meanwhile, our dual relation to nature, embedded and individuated at once, involves this kind of shift of perspective, which we practice all the time as the difference between the first-person and third-person point of view—between an embedded subjectivity and an ever-expanding reflexive outlook tied to the far-flung operations of metaphor. At perhaps its most primitive and sublime level, the third-person perspective requires the invention of divinities who might embody a comprehensive yet humanly unintelligible view. By endowing these divinities with powers of both creation and destruction, we can also place ourselves within an economy of making and sacrifice that serves as a foundation of all other value.

The lineage of the philosophy of art and aesthetics that we follow through neoclassicism's revival of ancient Greek texts has often overlooked another strain of influence on our traditions of art making—that of the Hebrew scriptures.[23] Perhaps because of the scriptures' relation to the prohibition on images of the divine, and the consequent tormented history of iconoclasm and iconophilia that still informs much of our attitude to art today, this influence has gone more or less unconsidered. Yet as Pico's "Oration" emphasizes, the story of creation by the monotheistic god in the first book of the Hebrew scriptures sets out a certain paradigm for creation that we continue to carry over, perhaps unwittingly, into the conditions and consequences for making art.

Genesis is of course only one of the extant, and myriad, world creation stories, and such stories bear certain typical characteristics.[24] By definition, they narrate a formal account of any notion of "beginning" and explain how the inanimate world became hospitable to forms of life, including humans as living beings. Such stories distinguish the time of beginnings from human chronology, and mythical time often serves as a ground for human time. In contrast, mythical space—the vast spaces of heavens and paradises—is often unintelligible and thereby offers a backdrop to the measurable and traversable spaces of human existence. Whereas human ancestors are characterized by their mortality, the gods are most often extraordinary in power and size. Such myths go on to establish hierarchies between men and women, and set forward other social values—for example, ranks or distinctions between those who respect the order of the gods and those who violate it. Suffering most often ensues for the transgressors.

Some myths pose autochthonous origins, others birth from elemental parents, others reproduction out of the self-splitting of primordial entities, ranging from the particularity of atoms to the inchoate frame of Chaos. Hesiod's *Theogony*, which most likely dates to the late eighth century BCE, is one such tale of the self-splitting of Chaos. Four centuries later, in Plato's *Timaeus*, composed around 360 BCE, a great Demiurge or Divine Craftsman endows the imperfect initial state of chaos with qualities of wholeness, proportion, and goodness borrowed from the eternal world of ideal forms.[25] As we have seen earlier in Platonic accounts, the living world is secondary to that ideal one, and in the *Timaeus* the craftsman creates not out of nothing but out of a flux of all elements.

The Western myth of origins told in the Hebrew scriptures, which scholars trace to the tenth century BCE, however, strikingly emphasizes that the beginning of the world is the consequence of acts of intellection on the part of a single being.[26] This is the first quality of the Hebrew creation myth we might consider—that a divine being creates via acts of mind that have no intrinsic relation to experience or to the god's individual biography. As he makes, the Hebrew god encounters no subjective limit. Nor does the god disappear after his task is completed; instead he is portrayed as continuously active, engaged in holding things in being. Like the *Timaeus*, cosmologies before the Hebrew scriptures suggest that matter, even chaotic matter, is present at the god's founding gestures, and the god therefore intervenes and has a narrative or biography attached to him or her. The Hebrew god, however, is an absolute point of origin and has no anthropomorphic divine counterpart.[27] When later in the scriptures the god makes singular human beings in his own image and goes on to condemn them to work and pain in childbirth, he is both defining their relation to their ground, that clay of which they are made, and endowing them with the freely spontaneous will that characterizes his own initial gestures of making. In his sovereign freedom, the Hebrew god continues to stand apart from creation. Thus, unlike other prior and contemporary deities who are characters in their own cosmogonies, this god possesses transcendental majesty and claims absolute power over the created world.[28]

What is the beginning of this story of beginning? The Hebrew title of the first book, *be-re'shit*, is also the first word of the book; it is often translated as "in the beginning" or "in beginning," but it has no definite article.[29] It therefore functions as a dependent temporal clause. It is followed by a parenthetical clause, indicating "the earth being then a formless waste," and then the verb stem *b-r-* (*bara'*), signifying "created." This is a word used only for divine creativity. It indicates a thing that is completed solely because of the god's action and not the material of which it is made.[30] The notion that this creation is ex nihilo is not remarked upon directly and consequently becomes a great source of debate for theologians. Nevertheless, in 2 Maccabees 7:28 we find the commands "Look up to heaven and earth and see all that is therein and know that the god made them out of things that did not exist by the time of the Second Temple," suggesting such a creation was out of nothing.[31] The theological problem remains that if what ensued at the onset of creation was a chaos needing to be remedied, the Creator would have made an inadequate start. Yet the scriptures emphasize initiating activity over the state of origin, and what is modeled is not the loss and replacement of worlds but the means and order of their invention.

The dynamic, dialectical progress of the god's creative activity in speech and acts of making is therefore a second aspect of the Genesis story that we might emphasize. We are told that the initial spaces of heavens, earth, and waters are formless and depthless and that as the breath of the god "moves over the face of the waters," the deity initiates a series of speech acts with the pronouncement "Let there be light."[32] The consequence of this pronouncement is manifestation: once light exists, it can be separated from darkness, and each term is then ascribed to a set of additional names—day/night, evening/morning—and a relation between them: one day.

We might expect the myth to continue as an account of creation by the fiat of successive speech acts.[33] Indeed, after we find this initial pronouncement of light in verse 3, we read of the command to gather the waters and let land appear in verse 9, and the command that the earth bring forth vegetation in verse 11. In these instances, saying so does make it so.[34] From the making of the firmament and separation of the waters in verse 7 forward, the deity turns not to actions that are mere statements but instead to actions of making and separating.

These passages distinguish between the verb form *bara'* (created) and the verb *'asa* (made).[35] The deity makes, rather than states the existence of, the sun, moon, and stars, the fish and birds, and the animals and serpents. The two accounts of the creation of humankind in Genesis particularly emphasize this duality between speaking and making. The first account, at 1:26, comes from the Priestly source text of the sixth to fifth centuries BCE. In this account "Let us make man in our image," the creation of human beings, is performed by word; the god speaks and his command is realized. The second account, at chapter 2:4, is drawn from what is called the J source, dating to the tenth to ninth centuries BCE.[36] These verses tell how the god formed man from clay and woman from man's rib. This older J account seems to be drawn from the motif in Sumerian and Babylonian mythology of a creator shaping man from mud, clay, or dust and breathing life into him.[37] We find a similar duality in the Psalms: in Psalm 8, for example, verse 3 mentions "thy heavens, the work of thy fingers," and verse 6 "the works of thy hand"; in Psalm 136, however, verse 5 speaks of the one "who by understanding made the heavens."

In these distinctions between speech acts and acts of making, tasks of the intellect and tasks of the hands, thus lies something of the difference between magic and work, yet the switch from pronouncement to material intervention also emphasizes the reflexive and dialectical quality of the creating god's sequential acts.[38] We might wonder why the god makes things happen one after another, rather than making everything exist at once. The logic of sequence here allows for growth and change. The god is alone and then, as a consequence of pronouncing and naming, the world is filled; being is a process of becoming informed literally by separation, branching, and transformation. Later, the Gospel of John, with its emphasis on beginning in the Word, similarly yokes an initial conceptualism to the ultimate manifestation of divinity in flesh—the figure of the simultaneously historical and divine Jesus.

Although Genesis does not tell us how the god went about his divine making, we cannot fail to notice the parallels between, on the one hand, the god's instantaneous spells of making by speech acts and the passive reception of paradise when Adam and Eve are placed in the garden, and, on the other, the god's acts of material forming and Adam and Eve's later existence under a mandate "to work the soil" and suffer in childbirth. In Genesis 2:4–9, the god does not simply declare the existence of organic life, including human beings, but also goes about creating according to a certain sequence that repeatedly emphasizes humankind's earthbound situation and tasks. In the King James translation: "The LORD God had not caused it to rain upon the *earth*, and there was not a man *to till the ground*. But there went up a mist *from the ground* and watered the whole *face of the ground*. And the LORD God formed man of the dust *of the ground*, and breathed into his nostrils the breath of life; and man became a living soul. And the LORD God planted a garden eastward in Eden; and there he put the man whom he had formed. And *out of the ground* made the LORD God to grow every tree that is pleasant to the sight, and good for food; the tree of life also in the midst of the garden, and the tree of knowledge of good and evil."[39]

In this emphasis on both the resistance of the ground—that dry land, needing to be worked, that is the habitat of humankind—and the resistance offered by this first intimation of theodicy, we glimpse the impediments to human success and succession. If reality is absolutely good, the manifestation of the god's goodness, evil is found on a moral rather than mythological plane. Here is a precedent for the spatial requirements of an area or reserve of freedom that Isaiah Berlin traced in arguments regarding negative freedom he found in treatises by John Locke, John Stuart Mill, and others. It is also a notion underlying Maurice Merleau-Ponty's mid-twentieth-century contention that "if freedom is to have *room* in which to move, if it is to be describable as freedom, there must be something to hold it away from its objectives, it must have a *field*, which means that there must be for it special possibilities, or realities which tend to cling to being."[40] The need for a realizable field where freedom can appear similarly led Jean-Paul Sartre to observe that dreaming is incompatible with freedom because dreaming leaves us with no sphere of action.[41] Of course the most fundamental threat to freedom is the threat of death and death itself, and this fact lends significance to the finality of form that is any individual life. Life presents a canvas, as the cliché goes, and that canvas has a frame. Yet the relation art making bears to resistance, work, and suffering is often far less abstract than such analogies suggest. Indeed as physical suffering leads us to recoil from sensual immediacy, we often overcome such painful states by reassimilating ourselves to the natural world via the sensual pleasures of making.[42]

Even so, in Genesis pronouncing and making are not the endpoints of creation—the end lies in judgment and blessing. This is therefore a third quality of the Genesis myth to which we might attend as a paradigm for the philosophy of art in the West: the god's final proclamation that his artifacts are good. The god sees that vegetable growth is good, that the sun, moon, and stars are good, that the fish and birds are good, and blesses them; he sees that the animals and serpents are good and, using the first-person plural in his command, makes men and women in his image and blesses them. The dynamic between judging and blessing is one that indicates a difference between particular and overall forms of apprehension, and the sequence is fixed: goodness precedes blessing and is thereby intrinsic to the phenomenon before its retrospective apprehension. The Hebrew sense of good here has a broader range than its English equivalent, and the phrase, which can be translated literally as "saw that it was good" or "saw how good it was," becomes a refrain as the account proceeds.[43]

Does the proclamation "it is good" indicate a kind of divine anthropomorphism—one that suggests things could be otherwise, that the god could make anything other than something good?[44] This announcement instead indicates a judgment regarding the temporal completion of the work and its spatial integrity. The proclamation of something's goodness indicates it is time to stop making. Until the broken covenants recounted in the stories of the expulsion, the flood, the golden calf, and more, all of which interrupt the perfection of creation, there is no indication that the god has made anything that is not good. At the same time, we cannot help but notice that human beings, the masterpieces of the god's creation and divine self-portraits insofar as they are made in his image, are characterized by their freedom—even at the expense of their goodness. As Schelling wrote in his 1809 essay on the essence of human freedom, "The procession [*Folge*] of things from God is a self-revelation of God. But God can only reveal himself to himself in what is like him, in free beings acting on their own, for whose Being there is no ground other than God but who are as God is."[45]

Informed by their sense of goodness as success or completion, the writers of the Hebrew scriptures borrow from the Akkadian verb *šuteṣbû*, which indicates "to inspect and approve." It is a word applied to the work of craftsmen such as the masons in section 233 of the Code of Hammurabi. The translator of the Babylonian Genesis translates the phrasing "It was good" as "It was declared finished." The editor of the *Anchor Bible* prefers "brought to a gratifying close."[46] "It was good" also proclaims that because the divine creative work is finished, the fundamental structures and elements within the cosmos do not have to be created anew.[47] What is ensured as well by the determination of goodness is the necessity to praise the creating god.

This emphasis on the maker's judgment further indicates the need for creation to exist not merely within the sphere of intention but also in the sphere of reception. Without finality of form and reception, there would be only process and no perspective upon it. By declaring that the work is finished, by establishing the Sabbath as a day of nonmaking, or rest, and perhaps above all by admitting the possibility of destruction—by flood or other means—the exercise of judgment commits itself to the future, the very possibility of a future for a creation whose teleology is otherwise concealed.

This emphasis on finishing and concluding also underscores the volitional dimension of creation. In Greek thought the world's existence is coeternal with the god and has no beginning or end; the forms of things within the world can either be or not be, and were begun and ended. The world could not be otherwise. But the Hebrew notion of creation, with its temporal beginning of the world, emphasizes the work of a contingent will.[48] We, too, can always interrupt our making or leave it unfinished—the possibility of stopping is linked equivocally to both error and success; we thereby have domains of practice, happily saturated with the wayward and bracketed from constraints of finish or polish. And we have domains of ease that repel us and make the work not worth completing, for, once again, the work may not offer the resistance that freedom requires. In either case, stopping is linked metonymically to starting again.

In sum, framing creation with language and narrating the myth from the point of view of retrospection, the writers of the Hebrew scriptures establish a particular mimetic bond between god and humankind that emphasizes all the more the belatedness of the human point of view. The god in turn commands that Adam and Eve themselves begin to create—that they go forth and multiply, and that they till and tend. Later, as they exercise their human freedom by disobeying the god's interdiction, the terms become more difficult. They no longer have access to the easily tended *pardês* (*paradeisos* in the Septuagint) that is Eden, and they must work and labor to bring forth their future.

What are the lessons of this account of creation? Whatever relation speaking has to making, we inevitably must acknowledge that the language we use preexists us and that ours are Adamic powers to name, categorize, and know—if we do not create a new nature entirely, we do anthropomorphize ourselves and we change our language each time we use it. Creation ex nihilo is of course impossible to us, who are always later. It remains a vanishing point, forever deferred by our own point of beginning, which is inevitably embedded in time and space. If in imagining negative freedoms we are bound all the more to powers of prior cause—picturing ourselves as free of the world or the gods, a becoming free rather than being free—the very fact of turning away and turning against in such negating speaks to our sense of an autonomy of which we have been deprived or robbed. It is to counter the absurdity of this position that Arendt imagines the activities of promising and forgiving as binding gestures that remedy what would otherwise be a freedom of empty sovereignty. The history of a religion of covenants and forgiveness lies behind her insight, as does the story of the dominion of an intellect that plunges into the openness of a creation that manifests its own will.

Freedom's relation to negation is a theme that is tied thereby not only to the eventual succession of broken covenants in the Hebrew scriptures but also to the story of the merely negating slave in Hegel's *Phenomenology* and, in our own time, the story of an avant-garde bound to repeat the terms of what it refuses. If Aristotle is correct and erring voluntarily is intrinsic to the creation of works of both art and craft, such unwitting mistakes may seem to require more radical forms of beginning anew—rethinking all assumptions under an artistic skepticism that will rearrange the very terms of art. But skepticism will remain bound to what it negates, and such an art will be doomed to allegory by its predetermined goals.

Yet in positive freedom—that affirmative freedom involving making without prior rules—we find an always-potential state of being poised to start. Belatedness creates the conditions for venturing out into a field and shaping it. The purpose not yet in evidence, we find ourselves open, considering, and about to act in relation to a domain that, even as we become aware of its limits, we define as we go. Because the exercise of positive freedom does not depend upon experience, such freedoms are prior to us, and prior even to the laws of nature—they re-create the cosmological situation of a world that issues from itself.

So let us consider these three qualities of making as we have inherited them from Genesis a bit further. We are not gods, and this story we tell ourselves about the origin of creation tells us something about our own anthropomorphic powers, or at least how we envision them on what we hope is the path to realizing them. First, making is not dependent upon a prior narrative, including the biography of the maker. To claim this independence from experience makes no particular experience or quality of person necessary for art making and as well means that the artist has no particular or necessary obligation to what he or she has thus far known. In this claim we are perhaps not so much denying experience as recognizing, as Kant did before us, that even if all knowledge and insight begins with, or is prompted by, experience of the natural world, it cannot be said that our knowledge and insight are derived from the natural world. We have cognitive means for recognizing phenomena, and we create forms for presenting them to ourselves and making them truly ours.

Such making requires a dynamic exchange between conceptualizing and material intervention in nature. Divine speech works by proclamation, but we post-Adamic beings must speak and make intersubjectively. Hence for us the realms of conceptualization and making by physical means are far closer. Like the early Renaissance painter described in Leon Battista Alberti's *Della pittura* who sets to work by establishing the lines of perspective as he pleases, the god of Genesis can begin wherever he likes.[49] We human makers confront the arbitrary nature of our own signs and the necessity of constantly reinvesting them, and remaking them, under terms that are intelligible to others. In doing so, we discover the nonarbitrary—the iron laws of convention and history—that our free making, viewed retrospectively, will literally reform or transform. No thought, including an unspoken thought, emerges without language, and the realization of ideas in the shared, endlessly accommodating space of intelligibility is necessary to the creation of any work—whether verbal, visual, auditory, or tactile—designed to be received.

Furthermore, making compels judgment, just as, in turn, judgment is necessary for closure. Indeed, judgment is an intrinsic part of the process of making from the outset—the completion of the work begins as soon as the first choice is made regarding its materials and the first action extended toward its form, and such judging continues until the point of finality or abandonment. Every choice, every act, is shaped by myriad considerations intrinsic to the work and entering from beyond the work—yet the interpretive task of grasping those considerations is a project of reception that is as ongoing as all future encounters with the work.

One way to understand the implications of these three qualities of the Hebrew myth of creation is to imagine what it would be like to have an aesthetics based on reversing them. We could, for example, have traditions of making that had an absolute obligation to the experience of the maker; in such a hyperrealist aesthetics, artists would be bound to represent their experience, and art would always be turning necessarily toward the past for its content. Or we could have an aesthetics based completely upon conceptualization or its opposite: an aesthetics based upon material intervention. The first would necessarily be something like a Hegelian art of absolute spirit—an art of pure concept that, lacking actualization, would remain privative, if not, thanks to language, unintelligible. The second would resemble the transmission of somatic skills alone—a pure craftsmanship that, lacking concepts, would be perpetually, often naively, repeated. Such an entirely nonreflexive art practice would be inseparable from nature—an endlessly productive/reproductive practice driven by the circumstances that surround and determine it, and so like the making of ants or bees.

In truth, each of these imaginary scenarios has its realization in some moment of art history—strains of realism, conceptualism, the imitation of mechanical reproduction, and the arts of the everyday would overlap with these positions. And each would have its own claim of resistance: the realist in a critique of imagination, the conceptualist in a critique of materialism, the materialist in a critique of hyperintellectualism, the artist of the everyday in a critique of self-consciousness. Yet, for obvious and self-contradictory reasons, these approaches to art making are defined by negative freedoms—they are driven by freedoms *from*. Bound by definition to those practices they deny, they cannot overcome their secondariness.

Why should that matter? It matters because, as Paul Ricoeur indicates in his discussion of the voluntary that serves as my epigraph, art has an intrinsic utopian potential—a pure, unforeseen, and inexhaustible potential that keeps it ahead of other domains of culture. It is not simply that the positive freedom of making within the field of art negates the problematic secondariness of negative freedoms. It is also that the artist's positive freedom of making, and the face-to-face encounters between persons that follow from it, are, as we shall explore, the foundation for the meetings of free and freely creating persons in free associations—those ideal meetings where persons sustain a mutual respect toward one another's intentions as they move toward an open future.

2 / PRAISING

I The Thought of Thankfulness

The point in question in the Creation is not the truth and reality of the World, but the truth and reality of personality, of subjectivity in distinction from the world. . . . The true principle of creation is the self-affirmation of subjectivity.

—LUDWIG FEUERBACH, *The Essence of Christianity*[1]

Our human values regarding making rely on creation myths that we ourselves have created, and Feuerbach's well-known disenchantment with religion was destined to become a kind of reenchantment with human powers. Yet even as we may dream of a magical making by pure intellection, the central fact of the Hebrew origin myth remains the distinction between the god's making out of nothing and the inherently received quality of our world. We human makers find ourselves in the midst of nature, the source of all materials. Our making takes place and proceeds within nature's dispensation; with these resources already present to hand, we make things that are also forms, and the material world becomes a resource for and, inevitably, an impediment to, our form making, for we are part of nature and finite within its infinity. Our secondariness thereby both evokes our wonder and compels our powers of judgment, binding us to the obligations—at times sacrifices—of praise.

No more beautiful and succinct summary of these issues could be found than this passage in Rainer Maria Rilke's "Ninth Duino Elegy," here in Stephen Mitchell's translation:

> . . . Between the hammers our heart
> endures, just as the tongue does
> between the teeth and, despite that,
> still is able to praise.

Praise this world to the angel, not the unsayable one,
you can't impress *him* with glorious emotion; in the universe
where he feels more powerfully, you are a novice. So show him
something simple which, formed over generations,
lives as our own, near our hand and within our gaze.
Tell him of Things. He will stand astonished; as *you* stood
by the rope-maker in Rome or the potter along the Nile. . . .[2]

The first lines cited, with the parallel but inverted phrase "Zwischen den Hämmern besteht / unser Herz, wie die Zunge / zwischen den Zähnen," bring forward the invisible work of the body's tools of life and speech: the heart survives its hammering force as the tongue survives the motion of the teeth. The plosive phrases "die doch, / dennoch, die preisende bleibt" sound like these hammering motions but change them, somewhat stuttering in their reversal toward the point of all this motion: not merely endurance but the praise that transcends it.

Rilke emphasizes the work, the truly man-made quality, of praise and in the next stanza further explains how praise is made. We send our praise to the angel and not to the Creator, whose name, according to Hebrew tradition, may not be pronounced. Human praise cannot approach the scale of the gods, but humans can praise with things they have made—things that are an accomplishment of generations who have practiced and refined their mastery over materials. These generations themselves are the made structure of kinship—that succession, both biological and elective, that compensates for the interruptions of mortality. The god's astonishment indicates a free human making, undetermined by prior divine plan, and we ourselves stand analogously thunderstruck before such ancient crafts as those of the rope-maker and potter. The simple, elegant everyday objects these craftspersons make are devices of yoking, binding, and containing—devices that run through all weaving, printing, painting, molding, and sculpting. These objects thereby hold the forces of heart, tongue, hand, and eye that were involved in their own making. As Rilke writes in one of the "Sonnets to Orpheus" (1.7), "Rühmen, das ists!" (Praising is what matters), and Orpheus is the one who holds a bowl of ripe fruit "worthy of praise" "far into the doors of the dead."[3]

In the tradition of the Hebrew scriptures, human making mirrors and reverses the making of the god, for the story of creation is one, as we know, of successive separations: of light from darkness, of land from water, of the heavens from the earth, and onward. But the story of human making is one of combinations and applications "near our hand and within our gaze." And as we have seen, when the Hebrew scriptures recount how the god regards his individual acts of creation, concluding that each is "good," the implication is that each is "done well." The integrity of the thing is not a self-evident aspect of its form but rather a quality discerned at some aesthetic distance; completion is therefore determined, not simply reached as a point of arrival. The judgment that something is "good" indicates that it is true, just, appropriate, or whole. Judgment involves separation and determination: as man's task of naming ensues, kinds of things might be compared and human judgment arises in its own sphere. And both divine and human judgment of completion and integrity involve retrospection—thought that is not swept up in the ongoing labor of making and so can look back on experiences. Leisure and respite, one kind of Sabbath or another, are needed for judgment to have its day.

The historical progress of praise travels from praising specific objects in their respective milieus to praising creation itself by means, eventually, of forms and modes of praise that will praise the praiser—the one who has mastered these epideictic forms. A certain relation between making and being follows this reflexive turn from the qualities of objects to the qualities of expression. We can see a parallel to the ancient Greek idea of the *eudaimon*, that felicitous spirit inhabiting the well-done act and the well-conducted life. For the Greeks, all appearances demand not only our perceptual attention as sentient beings but also our recognition and praise, increasing our own powers of apprehension.[4] To have some sense of what is at stake in praising, we might consider for a moment the corresponding negative history of the curse. The curse travels along the lines of context specificity; it is uttered particularly, and the one who utters it may be powerful within such a restricted context, but he or she remains, as we know from many a fairy tale, a marginal and often alienated figure. If blessings have the generality of the eudaimonic and the just, curses have all the specificity and limitations of revenge.[5] No speech is more enslaved than the blessing or curse made under the pressure of violence; no speech is more free than the blessing arising from pure volition.

Surrounded not by nothing, but by the replete world of creation, human beings begin in response, and the most fundamental, preliminary act of willed response is the expression of wonder. What follows such awe is praise's articulating and articulated forms. As such form gives shape to nature and time, so does praise endow its objects with value. Praise is tied to those phenomena that evoke it, but as we shall see, it is destined to circulate and enter into a general economy of human values. The heresy of idolatry, for example, is that instead of worshiping what has made them, humans worship what they have themselves made; praise offered toward the given or received world, the giving of thanks, is a prophylactic against this ungrateful mistake.[6]

We could thereby say that the most fundamental act of artistic making is the act of creating value by praising, for in praising creation we also set out a field of discrete choices and combinations that are necessary to human thought and making. As Heidegger indicated in his book-length essay of 1954 *Was Heisst Denken?* (translated as *What Is Called Thinking*, although the title can also be translated as "What calls for thinking?"), giving thanks is as well a means of thinking—a connection exaggerated by the proximate, if controversial, etymologies between both the German *danken* and *denken* and the English *thanking* and *thinking*. The genitive case *thanks*, from the Middle English *thankes*, for example, literally means "of thought" or "of goodwill" and signifies something done voluntarily or willingly.[7]

Heidegger suggests that thinking is at once given to human consciousness and the means by which the given can be apprehended and appreciated; ever-deferred, ever untotalized, thinking characterizes the protean process of remembering, gathering, and becoming as it thinks itself into being. In turn, to thank is to specify and recognize, to make something "count" while maintaining an aesthetic distance—we think what we value and, in valuing it, value thinking. As any reader of Heidegger's essay will discover, this dynamic process never rests. More recently Gilles Deleuze similarly has described how thinking involves continually emerging formations—the creation of concepts along what he calls a "plane of immanence." Deleuze argues that "thought demands 'only' movement that might be carved into infinity."[8] As concepts are created and then transformed by ensuing concepts, whatever is determined in thought depends upon the temporal unfolding of this plane. If "plane" is here a metaphor, it is one that shares in the human situation of traversing landscapes bounded by horizons. We cannot create an image of thought without its consequent transformation—and even, at times, erasure—by the progress of thought.

Unmotivated praise involves a pure judgment of the integrity of form, a response, quite literally, of appreciation that follows from contemplation. Such praising has all the qualities that Enlightenment aestheticians demanded of aesthetic judgments: it is not linked to deliberative thought or appetite or other desires to possess and consume; it takes for granted the universality of its claims; its object is formed by the very act of apprehension as it articulates the features and limits of the phenomenon. Praise addresses and frames phenomena—as we say in English, something or someone is "singled out for praise."

Praise in this sense has something like a cognitive function—a capacious one that calls on more than either reasoning or the application of prior terms and values. The dialectic between abstraction and analysis in praise is far more complex than any matter of grasping alone, and perhaps stems from the encounter between the enormity of the source of the given—be it the perceptual manifold or nature itself—and the limiting and separating powers of the human intellect. This contrast is evident as the naming and articulating powers of Adam are compared to the world-forming activities of the Hebrew god. Or we can find it in Wallace Stevens's pronouncement in a poem about poetry from his 1942 book *Parts of a World*, that "we think / without the labor of thought, in that element" of the "bright scienza" of poetry—"a gaiety, that is being, not merely knowing."[9] Indeed, in states of joy or gratitude it is specific powers of mind that often are surrendered to the enormity of such feeling.

Even so, one of the most fundamental aspects of our human condition is that we must judge what is finished and what is unfinished, what is and what might be, within a constant flux of becoming. As Aristotle emphasizes the made as what otherwise might not have been, the human maker is poised to act, and to act is to act upon, for whatever gesture we make, whatever form we create, is an intervention in the world as we have received it. Addressing this given, we acknowledge and speak to the value of made things as we also praise their makers. The dynamic between speech and hand and eye that I noted as characteristic of the god's creative activity in Genesis I is here transposed. The god sees that his creations are good, and declares them good. Humans, who give names to things, also have at their command the powers of speech. Praise, organized in finite passages that can be transported, cited, and carried far from their original speakers, has no limit of application or context.

Praise is offered, then, but what kind of offering is it? In many cultures praising, praying, and ritual are simultaneous and interrelated practices, yet the open economy of praise stands in vivid contrast to the restricted economy of sacrifice. In the religious practices of ancient Greece and Rome, sacrifice is manifested in material forms—in so many hecatombs of animals, or parts of animals, fish or fruit, grains, or libations such as wine, honey, water, oil, or milk. Humans have an obligation to surrender a material portion and will often partake of the very same substance offered to the gods. The apportionment of sacrifice is underlined by the specific rules for counting and framing the sacrificial items; what is surrendered has been wrested from external nature and is put under humanly intelligible terms of distribution. As Joan Breton Connelly writes, "At the very core of Greek worship was the act of animal sacrifice. Once the procession had arrived at the sanctuary the formal rites of dedication and consecration took place. These are followed by lustration, the throwing of barley groats, and prayer. The culminating moment was the slaughter of the victim, which was inspected for omens, cut up in pieces and placed on the altar fire." The meat was then distributed to divinities and worshipers alike, with the divinities receiving the bones and inedible portions and the humans taking the succulent meat and viscera.[10] Ancient Greek and Roman blood sacrifice, for example, involved both killing and the taking in of the blood by the devotee.[11]

The transference of meaning along with the sacrificial material is underlined by the relation that sacrificial ritual has to the future. Denis

Feeney has contended in relation to Roman practices that it is a mistake to consider ritual outside of the reciprocal exchange of meanings between the highly differentiated positions of gods and human beings. Feeney writes, "If ritual is a language and means something to an audience, we must remember that the notional audience is the gods. They are the exegetes of the texts of ritual. . . . The Romans [and, as we have seen, the Greeks] distinguished clearly between the two communicative systems operating between humans and gods. The gods send *auspicia* down to us and we send *sacra* up to them; if we are the ones who interpret the *auspicia* then they are the ones who can interpret the *sacra*."[12] What is striking in this formulation is indeed the fact that for human beings origin alone is not explanation—to the contrary, origin requires interpretation. The sources of the *auspicia* are precisely where we cannot turn to understand their meaning and destiny. It is in their reception, a reception requiring renewal and reinterpretation, that their significance is generated as an ongoing open practice—*sacra* are the engine of signs. There is never an end to the practice of sacrifice of this kind; it is administered punctually and continually. The completion of one sacrifice is never the completion of sacrifice itself.

Praising, praying, and ritual have quite different economies, and the offering of praise is of an entirely different form of materiality than that of these practices of sacrifice. As Rilke described the work of the hammering heart and tongue, praise is not wrested from the world but drawn from within. Since it is given, it also may be withheld: human beings feel obligations to praise and may meet those obligations or not, for their own volition is the source and means of the sacrifice. Praise given under the threat of force is merely utterance; praise given idly is merely "going through the motions." As we know from the Hebrew psalms, what is surrendered in praise is sound—praise is sounded by speech and singing, by the "joyful noises" of lyres, timbals, and drums, and by the human drums of clapping and rhythmic shouting.[13] Such sounding emphasizes all the more that there are no restrictions on praise's production and no restrictions on its distribution. What is sent out returns not only concretely but also in multiple form. As the psalmist declares in Psalm 34, "Oh taste and see that the LORD is good." The metaphysical expenditure of praise brings tangible benefits directly back to the speaker. Such an uneven reciprocity is underlined in Psalm 7's prayer for judgment: "The LORD judges the peoples; judge me, O LORD, according to my righteousness, and according to the integrity that is in me."

The analogy between offering up praise and offering sacrifices is clarified by their existence as parallel but separate acts—if smoke enters the air, obscuring and overwhelming, praise takes wing on specificity and elation. Praise is indeed a kind of expense, an expense of spirit and something offered, but the Hebrew psalms, for example, make a clear temporal distinction between the sacrifice of praise and the animal sacrifice of burnt offerings, and some members of the congregation hold hereditary roles regarding their performance. The foremost scholar of the Hebrew scriptures, Nahum Sarna, whose writings on Genesis informed my earlier discussion of creation, notes that "the elaborate rules and regulations for the sacrificial rituals as laid down in the Torah are all but silent about accompanying prayer or music, while the headings to the psalms have nothing to say about any sacrificial association. The sacrificial ritual is the responsibility and prerogative of the priesthood; the recitative and musical components of the official worship are a Levitical franchise."[14] The human speaker of Psalm 5 says, "O LORD, in the morning thou dost hear my voice; in the morning I prepare a sacrifice for thee, and watch." In Psalm 50 the voice of God declares, "I do not reprove you for your sacrifices; your burnt offerings are continually before me. I will accept no bull from your house, nor he-goat from your folds . . ." The divine voice explains that because "the world and all that is in it is mine," such offerings are redundant, and suggests, "Offer to God a sacrifice of thanksgiving." In Psalm 51 the human speaker has internalized this lesson and recognizes that "thou hast no delight" in the sacrifice of burnt offerings. In Psalm 54 the human speaker says, "With a freewill offering I will sacrifice to thee; I will give thanks to thy name."[15]

The noncontingent nature of praise's sacrifice is emphasized repeatedly by this tradition. The volitional nature of praise lies in its being freely, liberally, and continually offered and drawn from the energies of the person who praises. In Jewish tradition, holy days require the recital of "The Hallel" or "The Praise," that section of Psalms from 113 to 118. And the offering of praise indeed punctuates the experience and expression of suffering—this is just as evident in the continual return to praise in the laments and requests of the Psalms as it is in the role of the kaddish, or hymn of praise to God. A particular version of this prayer, the mourner's kaddish, is central to the Hebrew funeral rite. Here is the mourner's text in a contemporary English translation:

> Exalted and hallowed be His great name [congregation: Amen].
>
> Throughout the world which He has created according to His will. May He establish His kingship, bring forth his redemption and hasten the coming of His Mashiach [cong.: Amen] in your lifetime and in your days and in the lifetime of the entire House of Israel, speedily and soon, and say Amen.
>
> [cong.: Amen. May His great Name be blessed forever and to all eternity. Blessed.]
>
> May His great Name be blessed forever and to all eternity.
>
> Blessed and praised, glorified, and exhaled and extolled, honored, adored and lauded by the Name of the Holy One, blessed be He [cong.: Amen], beyond all the blessings, hymns, praises and consolations that are uttered in the world; and say Amen [cong.: Amen].
>
> Upon Israel and upon our Sages and upon their disciples, and upon all the disciples of their disciples, and upon all those who occupy themselves with the Torah, here or in any other place, upon them and upon you, may there be abundant peace, grace, kindness, compassion, long life, ample sustenance and deliverance, from their Father in heaven; and say Amen [cong.: Amen].
>
> May there be abundant peace from heaven, and a good life for us and for all Israel; and say, Amen [cong.: Amen].
>
> He who makes peace [during the Ten Days of Penitence say: the peace] in His heavens may He make peace for us and for all Israel: and say, Amen [cong.: Amen].

Among the many remarkable qualities of this prayer, perhaps foremost is what it leaves unspoken: any reference to the funereal context or death itself. Instead, the prayer is marked by an intense redundancy: the multiplication of synonymous terms, the distribution of reciprocal blessings, the literal disembodiment of the human voice in space and time—from creation to the end of time; from this world to heaven. The mourner's words create a surplus where death had brought a lack; he or she rushes in to fill a singular absence with a repetitive abundance. One of the most sustained meditations on the qualities of this prayer is Allen Ginsberg's book-length elegy of the same name, *Kaddish*, written after the death of his mother Naomi in 1956. There Ginsberg writes in the shadow of the mourner's prayer:

> Nameless, One Faced, Forever beyond me, beginningless, endless,
> Father in death. Tho I am not there for this Prophecy, I am unmarried,
> I'm hymnless, I'm Heavenless, headless in blisshood I would still adore
> Thee, Heaven, after Death, only One blessed in Nothingness, not
> light or darkness, Dayless Eternity—
> Take this, this Psalm, from me, burst from my hand in a day, some
> of my Time, now given to Nothing—to praise Thee—But Death—[16]

Ginsberg brilliantly weaves the querying, death-obsessed thoughts of the mourner into the dignified unfolding lines of the prayer until the prayer seems to speak as the voiceover that the lyric "I" once was. The incongruity of the mourner's kaddish, like the punctuation of experience and suffering exemplified in the progress of the Psalms, returns us to the sheer *inutility* of praise—its freedom from the very realities from which it arises. Those who offer up praise, even such a hymn to loss and Nothingness, are increased by their own donation.

What are the implications of this presentation or declaration of praise that, even when parallel to acts of sacrifice, is not subsumed within them? If praise, as I have suggested, is not offered within a "restrictive economy" but instead within a "general economy"—the former being finite and the second endlessly open—then praise, like thinking, is a kind of giving up that replenishes itself. I borrow these terms, without a clear intent to repay them, from the early twentieth-century anthropological theorist Georges Bataille. Bataille recognized that only loss, and consequently scarcity, creates value. Any spectacle of production for its own sake, or of the bare accumulation of things, returns such things to their pure or "merely" material state. As it is only death that gives shape to lived existence, so the rhythm of forming, losing, and reforming creates patterns of value. Yet the specter of loss can arise only within the finite context of a restrictive economy: loss is an event within that frame. Beyond such a boundary lie the endlessly emerging and returning possibilities of the general economy—the economic as a mode that continually replenishes itself. This general economy lies behind and beyond the operation of the restricted economies as language lies beyond the finite terms of speech.

Bataille explained in his 1949 book *La part maudite* (translated by Robert Hurley as *The Accursed Share*) : "Changing from the perspectives of a *restrictive* economy to those of a *general* economy actually accomplishes a Copernican transformation: a reversal of thinking—and of ethics. If a part of wealth (subject to a rough estimate) is doomed to destruction or at least to unproductive use without any possible profit, it is logical, even *inescapable*, to surrender commodities without return."[17] The "part maudite" is an excessive, never-recoverable part of any economy that is spent luxuriously and without any particular reciprocity. Whereas Georg Simmel saw highly valued objects like artworks as thwarting or resisting our desire, and Albert Gell pictured them as magical in their opacity, for Bataille art is only one of several spheres of inestimable expenditure: others include sex without procreation, spectacles, sumptuary objects, and monuments. Bataille held that without such expenditure, humankind would invariably turn to a sacrificial logic, in the form of war or other acts of pure destruction.

Although Bataille does not emphasize praise and is far more concerned with traditions of materialism and gift-giving than I am here, praise can be brought under his economic thinking as the ultimate example of expenditure without limit; even Bataille's enthusiasm for the general economy is based on an acknowledgment of the endless human capacity for creating, destroying, and re-creating value up against the finitude of nature. In turn, the more praise is given, the more value is invested in the objects of praise, and the more benefit ensues not only to the one who praises but also to the human community at large.

Psalm 22, for example, expresses the triadic nature of praising that circulates among human speaker, divine listener, and "congregation." Beginning with the anguished solo cry "My God, my God, why hast thou forsaken me? / Why are thou so far from helping me, from the words of my groaning? / O my God, I cry by day, but thou dost not answer; and by night, but find no rest," the speaker goes on to recite his afflictions and then turns to the congregation to offer praise, declaring, in verse 24, that "he has not hid his face from him, but has heard, when he cried to him." "From thee comes my praise in the great congregation." Psalm 22 thereby succinctly illustrates the process of generalization that intensifies and gathers response. A solo speaker has no force when enveloped in pain; by means of the recitation and mastery of praise, the psalmist incrementally summons the full support of his audience. As poetic utterances shape the language, they enter back into it and their parlance is chanted by "the great congregation." Traditions of praising a Creator thereby intensify and multiply the gifts of creation. Like the proverbial ever more detailed map of a coastline that poses the possibility of infinity, the specifying act of praise enriches the manifold of the world. "I will praise; I will magnify," claims the speaker in Psalm 69—to praise is to enlarge.[18]

II The Birth of a New Song

> . . . then a singer,
> the servant of the Muses, sings of the famous deeds of men of old
> and of the blessed gods who dwell in Olympus.[19]

So writes Hesiod in his *Theogony* at lines 99–101. Here is the traditional role of the Western poet—to serve the Muses in the context of praising both the gods and those human actors who deserve such attention. The poet is a messenger between the divine and sacred realms, at once outside and above time and within the community that hears his words. Thus far we have considered praise offered to celebrate and call upon the god, and praise of the gods, but praise of human achievement has its own distinctive genres, and the relation between passivity and activity, control, loss, and renewal in praise is as fluid and rhythmic as the forms in which such approaches are expressed. What we might call secular praise follows from sacred paradigms. In the Hebrew scriptures, Ecclesiastes and the Song of Songs bring praise into an anthropocentric sphere, and the book of Job especially speaks with a certain querying skepticism. In the secular domain, praise is an act of living speech that has as its aim contagion, fame, or reputation. Like proverbs and aphorisms, the genres of praise are meant to be circulated, and as we have seen, praise involves both singling out and creating phrases that can be detached and repeated. Even in the most archaic extant examples of hymns and praise poems, it is difficult to determine when a work is part of a historical ritual context and when it represents or indicates one by means of fiction.[20]

Dating from the eighth to the sixth centuries BCE,[21] the Homeric hymns are the prototype for praise poems in the West. They offer embedded narratives that appear to be intended as offerings to those gods or goddesses whose attributes they honor and celebrate. These hymns tell the god or goddess things he or she presumably already knows. By this very structure the hymns indicate the speaker's knowledge of the divinity, and often the more specific knowledge of the divinity's cults as they also bring their human listeners into that knowledge. They magnify and extend the circle of devotees even in those instances, like the Homeric "Hymn to Demeter," where occult knowledge and solutions to riddles are merely indicated.

In form the Homeric hymns follow a ring structure, often using the name of the god or goddess who is to be addressed as the very first word. This opening and the hymn's closing also employ the epithets of the divinity. Between beginning and ending, a narrative or narratives are recounted to explain the powers and merits of the addressee. With their three parts arranged in sequence—exordium, exposition, then peroration—the hymns enact an approach by a human speaker, who refers to himself or herself in the first person, to the god, who is called upon, praised, and asked for favor, including above all the favor of his or her return and presence. The hymns themselves end with a return to the circumstances of the god's conception, offering an envoi and, like so many of the Hebrew psalms, promising another song to come. The twelve-line Homeric hymn to Hermes, for example, has the following structure: two lines identifying the god by epithet and territory, seven lines recounting the circumstances of his conception, and a three-line conclusion, the latter here in the translation of Apostolos N. Athanassakis: "So Hail, son of Zeus and Maia / I began with you, but I will now turn to another hymn. / Hail, Hermes, guide and giver of things graceful and good."[22]

Many scholars believe that the Homeric hymns were written to be performed at ritual feasts; others contend they were part of poetic contests where they served as *prooimia* or preludes to longer epic poems; still others argue that the hymns survive from archaic times and that only a few were definitively composed for cult performances in honor of their addressees. On internal evidence alone, many of the hymns narrate the origins of phenomena, origins tied to events that occur after the reign of Zeus but before the earth has acquired its familiar forms. The "Hymn to Apollo," "Hymn to Hermes," and "Hymn to Dionysus" all recount the births of their respective subjects. But as early as the third-century rhetorician Menander, critics have noted that all genealogies and hymns with genealogical themes contain mythic elements, but not all mythic hymns use genealogies.[23]

The Homeric "Hymn to Demeter" is a good example of the dynamic relation between praising, knowing, and economy that characterizes these works. The hymn narrates an origin full of redundancies and overdeterminations. There a god (Demeter) gives the means (agriculture) by which men make sacrifices to the gods. Demeter, in other words, does not do so directly, on behalf of man, but stands as the agent behind human offerings to the divine realm to which she herself belongs. And the myth as well relates the crisis that results from the redundancy that is incest: Zeus, father of Persephone by his sister Demeter, gives the pubescent girl to his brother, Hades, who is also of course the girl's uncle. The problem underlying the "Hymn to Demeter" is literally one of sacrificial economy, for Hades's appropriation of Persephone causes the loss of a daughter to Demeter—in consequence, Demeter roams the earth, looking for the girl and seeking her return. Demeter will not allow the crops to grow, and this disruption has halted the ability of humans to sacrifice to the gods. The problem is solved by sharing not crops but the body of Persephone between her uncle/husband, Hades, and the grieving mother: she will spend the winter season with one and the summer season with the other.

Nevertheless, the knowledge we could consider to be hidden in the hymn is not the literal knowledge of distribution but rather the hidden knowledge of reproduction. The force of reproduction, represented by Demeter, must be given its due in relation to the forces of death and the underworld represented by Hades. The hymn ends not only with the new distribution of Persephone's body and the restoration of the sacrificial offerings to the gods but also with the institution of the cult of Demeter and its concomitant balance between secrets and praise. Indeed secrets, rather than the more obvious cursing, are in this instance the antithesis of praise: their scarcity is the counterpoint to praise's bounty, a sign that the initiates understand the value of what the knowledge of praise has revealed. After Demeter teaches her mysteries, described as "holy rites that are not to be transgressed, nor pried into, nor divulged," the hymnist explains, "For a great awe of the gods stops the voice." He or she requests in the hymn's last lines that "for my song grant gladly a living that warms the heart. / And I shall remember you and a new song as well."[24]

The very fact of telling the god something he or she already knows is evidence of a shift to the performative and of an audience that appreciates the speaker's skill. And it is striking that early examples of praise poetry after the Homeric hymns, such as Sappho's "Hymn to Aphrodite" and many of the Hebrew psalms, take the possibilities of citation all the way to the presumption of quoting the divinity herself or himself.[25] As Sappho entreats Aphrodite in this hymn to become her ally in procuring and sustaining human love, she says, in Anne Carson's translation:

> But you, O blessed one,
> smiled in your deathless face
> and asked what (now again) I have suffered and why
> (now again) I am calling out
>
> and what I want to happen most of all
> in my crazy heart. Whom should I persuade (now again)
> to lead you back into her love? Who, O
> Sappho, is wronging you?[26]

The appearance of Sappho's proper name in her own mouth as she ventriloquizes the goddess is not only surprising but also a vivid, literal embodiment of the fact that language belongs to others before we speak it and that as we speak, we change it—making it our own and inserting ourselves into its history.

In Psalm 30, the human being's very existence is justified by his function in praising God:

What profit is there in my death,
  if I go down to the Pit?
Will the dust praise thee?
  Will it tell of thy faithfulness?
Hear, O LORD, and be gracious to me!
O LORD, be thou my helper!

An implicit equivalence weighs the human's obligatory praise against the bestowal of the god's favor.[27] In contrast, Psalm 91 is a small symphony of intermingled voices: the third-person psalmist; the praising devotee who is protected by God in all circumstances; and, as the psalm closes, once again, the quoted, responding divinity:

Because he cleaves to me in love, I will deliver him;
  I will protect him, because he knows my name.
When he calls to me, I will answer him;
  I will be with him in trouble,
  I will rescue him and honor him.
With long life I will satisfy him,
  and show him my salvation.

What is remarkable about these quotations of the divinity is also their return to a human scale; the one who offers a generic praise is answered particularly.

Throughout the classical tradition, the poetic speaker of hymns and odes expends praise as a gift or implicit sacrifice offered by an individual out of positions ranging from designated authority to abject supplication. Although the god's benefaction can be gained through sacrificial offerings, song, often itself represented as an offering, has a special status as a means of securing favor. In the "Hymn to Hermes" and "Hymn to Apollo" of Sappho's contemporary Alcaeus, for example, the poet states this license quite strongly. Alcaeus begins the hymn to

Hermes by hailing the god and saying he is singing of him because he wants to: "Greetings, lord of Kyllene: you are the one / my heart desires to sing of. . . ."[28] Hermes has not demanded the sacrifice of this song: it is driven by the poet's own needs.

The hymns of the later Hellenistic poet Callimachus have a great deal of rhetorical ornament and frequently display not only their artifice but also their worldly erudition. In Hymn 4, for example, at lines 165–66, Callimachus lavishly praises his patron Ptolemy Philadelphus as he also displays his secular knowledge and power. He makes the Greek god of jealousy and envy, Phthonos, a character in his "Hymn to Apollo." Phthonos whispers a criticism of the hymn within the hymn, saying that the poet cannot sing as well as the sea. But Apollo gives Phthonos a push with his foot and replies that the Assyrian River, despite its size, cannot compete with the fine mist arising from the pure spring where bees gather water for Demeter. In the end, Apollo seems to spurn his fellow god because he is more pleased with Callimachus's song of praise.

In this self-referential moment, Callimachus foregrounds his skill at refining lyrics from the larger stream of Homeric epic—hence the fine mist's triumph. This turn to esteeming quality over quantity, precision over expansion, is not merely a claim for the merits of lyric as opposed to epic but also a claim for the skill of the poet, whose powers of judgment hold their own against those, including immortals, who envy their creativity.[29]

The speaker/singers of hymns to the gods seem to enjoy particular freedom of expression. Callimachus develops a high level of artifice in his hymns, often by inserting details from the present in what we might call "cameo roles" as he recounts passages of myth. In "To Apollo," for example, he adds his native Kyrene to the list of cities blessed by the gods. His contemporary the Stoic Cleanthes also emphasizes human values. In his only surviving work, "Hymn to Zeus," he praises the god in language that seems to derive from inference more than religious formulas. Cleanthes writes that humans "yield / Glad homage to the god if they are by reason guided."[30]

The sacred hymn brings reverence for the god into the common light; it not only congregates but also yokes the human and divine realms. If, as the structuralist classicist Jean-Pierre Vernant has noted, the Olympian pantheon codified by poets presents "a system of classification, a way of giving order to, and conceptualizing the universe by clarifying its powers and forces,"[31] the hymn proceeds by a vertical axis of prayer that not surprisingly is typical for a culture that places its gods in the sky. To look, for a moment, ahead more than two thousand years, the vertical function of the hymn is similarly expressed, and with the utmost simplicity, in the well-known Protestant doxology written in 1674 by Thomas Ken:

> Praise God, from Whom all blessings flow;
> Praise Him, all creatures here below;
> Praise Him above, ye Heavenly Host;
> Praise Father, Son, and Holy Ghost. Amen.

Or we might remember John Dryden's tribute to St. Cecilia, the patron of music, in his 1697 "Alexander's Feast": "He raised a mortal to the skies / She dreamed an angel down." Up and down; above and below—these are cosmological distances in need of overcoming or bridging. The long Western sequence of human separation from the gods—the theft of Prometheus, the succession of ages to our age of iron, "the fall" of humankind—in fact makes an approach to the gods possible. In writing about such an "ascensional dynamics," the philosopher of aesthetics Jean-Marie Schaeffer has emphasized their relation to a sublation of the sensuous to the intelligible. At the heart of any Platonic or Neoplatonic theory of the symbol, he contends, is "the idea of an inadequation between the intelligible and the sensuous that the symbol abolishes by spiritualizing it."[32] In the hymn of praise the ascensional dynamic finds a symbolic mode of sacrifice commensurate to its spiritual aims.

As the most common medium of praise in the West is speech, and its joyful noises, the major early forms of Western praise that have survived are not only such hymns, however, but also the ode to the victorious athlete, who, like the dancers performing in his honor, represents an incarnate freedom—the grace of a harmony between the body and the mind's intentions. In contrast to the abstracting verticality of the sacred hymn, the classical ode celebrating such human achievements often proceeds by paths and byways, following a horizontal axis that emphasizes the idea of turns or revisions and their consequences. Only four Pindaric books survive in manuscript—indeed, they are among the very few examples of Greek lyric in manuscript; the rest of the corpus exists in papyrus fragments and citations in other texts. Yet from Pindar's odes to athletic champions, with their frequent praise of heroic actions in general, we can detect certain conventions of secular praise. The ode to the victor goes out onto the wind and is as well a matter of public acknowledgment. The ancient Greek *kudos*—the acknowledgment of fame or renown that will spread across the land and sea—begins in the odist's acts of praise.

Written by individuals and performed by a chorus, from their first emergence they manifest the process of transmission from lip to lip and ear to ear that is their reason to exist. Pindar's *Nemean* V begins with the hopeful command to its own composition: "on board every ship / and in every boat, sweet song, / go forth from Aigina and spread the news."[33] For the odist who is doing the praising, his expenditure will be rewarded not only by forms of grace or blessedness but also by the furthering of his own reputation as a maker; from Simonides and Pindar forward, the odist is more often than not paid for his work and thanked for his gift.

Expressing praise, the odist displays a mastery over lack or suffering by transposing a focus upon the self to an orientation outward toward an object. If the hymnist's praise involves approaching, addressing, and retreating from the divine, the odist's praise involves dance motions of turning, counter-turning, and standing. When Pindar announces at the beginning of *Nemean* V, "I am not a sculptor," he is saying something particular about the odist's work and its relation to figuration. He describes how statues stand on fixed bases, whereas his own song will, once again, sail forth to spread its news.[34] If sculptures are made of earth and stand on earth, odes are made of sound and go forward as sound. In the ode, enjambment and surprise create effects of motion. Sculptures have edges; they emerge toward fixity, and one can get behind and around them. Sculpture cannot animate, because it defines and separates the form from the surrounding material. Foursquare or in the round, sculpture distributes space around its presence. But the ode gathers an accumulating knowledge in time; it makes absent things present by recalling them rather than by manifesting them.

So long as the ode is set in motion, however, it will not fix or define, and as *Nemean* V states, within the ode's boundaries it is up to the poet to decide what to include and what to omit. For example, as Pindar begins to provide a genealogy of the people of Aigina who have produced the victor Pytheas, he reaches the story of the murder of Phokos and explains, "I will halt, for not every exact truth / is better for showing its face, / and silence is often the wisest thing / for a man to observe."[35] And so he changes the subject: "But if it is decided to praise happiness, strength of hands / or steel-clad war, let someone dig for me / a jumping pit far from this point, / for I have a light spring in my knees and eagles leap even beyond the sea."[36] Similarly, in *Olympian* XIII, when the moment approaches to tell of Bellerophon's doom, he says, "I will keep silent." There is a difference between such replete silences and an empty silence, as there is a difference between conscious withdrawal and mere avoidance. Here the poet is capable of what we call "pregnant silences," and whenever there is a rhythm or form or other matrix determining an emergent art, those beats that are unmet, or those spaces that emerge as negative space rather than nothing, acquire the force of consequence. The decision is made by the poet in the present with regard to the theme of ancestors and the inherited pattern of the ode itself.

These displays of Pindar's self-mastery are thereby also more general displays of mastery. The poet is obliged to his patron, but his tongue can send the news as praise or calumny. In the conclusion to *Pythian* III, an ode written for the military autocrat Hieron of Siracusa in celebration of the horse race he won in 476 BCE, Pindar reflects upon the conditions of his work and the work of odists more generally, saying, in the translation of C. M. Bowra, "I will be little when little is my circumstance / And great when it is great." A few lines later he adds a comment about the intertwined economies of fame: "If God should give me the luxury of wealth / I think surely I would know / Thenceforth the heights of fame, / Of Nestor and the Lykian Sarpedon / Those household names / The loud lines speak, which craftsmen built with skill, / And thence we know them. / Greatness in noble songs / Endures through time; but to win this, few find easy."[37]

Odes have outlines and gaps, leaps, and intense substitutions of terms before they arrive at such concluding "stands."[38] Even so, by the time of Pindar's compositions, the structure of the epinician ode was fixed by tradition; it was designed to include such elements as praising the gods, naming and elaborating on its human subject and his genealogy, and finding an analogue in myth with appropriate observations drawn from maxims according to its subject. But like a comedian who teases his audience by delaying his beginning or digressing without promise of return, Pindar continually, at least in those poems of his that we have, exercises his control over the progress of his art. As he chooses his patron, he chooses his sequence, and goes ahead to say so.

Here in the world of fifth-century Greece before the Christian era, we already encounter the issues of rule-giving and rule-breaking, spontaneity, and the representation of spontaneity, that will continue to haunt Western art down to the present. Whereas epinician poetry was performed orally and in public, by the time of Pindar it was composed in private. Pindar's work plays upon this immediacy with frequent deictic gestures: "Take down the Dorian lyre from its peg," in *Olympian* I, for example, or *Pythian* IV's literally ecstatic opening, "Today, Muse, you must stand by the side of a friend, / By the King of Kyrene." In the opening to the antistrophe of *Nemean* I, Pindar declares, "I have taken my stand at the courtyard-gate / Of a man who welcomes strangers / And sweet is my song."[39] These imaginative acts play against the audience's knowledge of reality and assert the poet's powers of transport and self-determination. Even, or perhaps especially, when telling a familiar narrative, only the poet knows what, exactly, will come next—by stages that knowledge becomes a kind of self-surprise.[40] Pindar controls and shapes the flow of speech and maintains his status as its source.[41]

The odist is controlling not only information, knowledge, and the depiction of context but also time. Pindar's odes are punctuated literally with the expression καὶ νῦν—indicating "and now," "now for," "even now."[42] The odist in all these ways emphasizes the importance of the present; those myths and genealogies that are recounted end, by means of a loop structure, in the exigencies of singing the praises of the athlete's recent victory. The present and, even more exaggeratedly, the future have no shape and content without these gestures, from the kairotic to the merely attentive, that mark the now. And the expanding, contracting, leaping, and lingering techniques of the odist link the poet's breathing efforts to the athlete's feats. Yet it is praise that will amplify the present, ensuring the continuity of its object into at least the near future, for in odes and hymns the Greek sense of the past is no longer under the epic ethos that gives the past priority over the present; whatever feats have been accomplished are destined to meet with new occasions and new celebrations. There is no sense of tragedy in this, but rather a considerable confidence in what is permanent—the poet's abilities to enlarge and lend significance.[43]

In the Hebrew psalms a dynamic relation between anticipation and announcement likewise places an emphasis on the new as something waiting to be made.[44] The aesthetic condition of producing something that will be received, a call waiting for a response, is analogous to the psalmist's repeated expressions of longing on the one hand—"But thou, O LORD—how long? / Turn, O LORD, save my life" (Psalm 6) and "How long, O LORD? Wilt thou hide thyself for ever?" (Psalm 89)—and a promised breakthrough in expression on the other: "O sing to the LORD a new song; sing to the LORD, all the earth!" (Psalm 96); "O sing to the LORD a new song, for he has done marvelous things!" (Psalm 98); "I will sing a new song to thee, O God; upon a ten-stringed harp I will play to thee" (Psalm 144); "Praise the LORD! Sing to the LORD a new song, his praise in the assembly of the faithful!" (Psalm 149). The psalmist continually asks the divine figure to turn, to be face to face, to end his hiding, to reveal his face—as in Psalms 13, 27, 30, 31, 51, 69, 89, and 104. And as the Homeric hymns end by turning to new songs, and the "Hymn to Demeter" in particular brings forward the theme of childbirth, a number of Pindarics touch as well on the themes of birth and unusual births. Nemean VII, for example, to Sogenes of Aigina, winner of the Boys' Pentathlon, is particularly notable for its apostrophe to Eileithyia, goddess of childbirth.[45]

Throughout its history this genre of affirmation, surplus, and esoteric knowledge has been devoted to themes of birth, rebirth, and the life after death promised by reputation on earth or redemption elsewhere.[46] The first English ode to use Pindaric turns, translating the strophe, antistrophe, and epode into "turn," "counter-turn," and "stand," is Ben Jonson's "To the Immortal Memory and Friendship of that Noble Pair, Sir Lucius Cary and Sir H. Morison," an elegy that begins with the story of the birth of a newborn who then crawls back into the womb. From this poem and Jonson's Horatian "Ode on Himself" forward, the ode also becomes a form associated with transforming or reevaluating perspectives upon the self. Milton's "Hymn on the Morning of Christ's Nativity" marks the death of the pagan gods and proleptically reads the sacrifice of the new god into the account of his birth. And the long tradition of St. Cecilia odes, which we encountered earlier through the work of Dryden, celebrates, in language that approximates music, the ascent into heaven of a woman who twice died and twice was reborn.[47] Thus, at the general level of occasion, an imperative of overcoming finality of all kinds becomes the paradoxical task of a carefully composed literary form. Especially as they come under the influence of Abraham Cowley's experiments with Pindarics and William Collins's transformations of the Horatian, English odists tend to combine psychological and public themes on the one hand and an overall irregularity with local patterning of stanza shapes on the other.[48]

Praise, the child of wonder, is thereby the parent of exaltation, but all praise results in a kind of evaporation. Language that goes out into the world as fame or reputation does not necessarily maintain its initial form, as anyone who has ever played "Whisper Down the Lane" knows well.[49] In a particularly insightful passage of his *Aesthetics*, Hegel gets to the point of why praise per se does not result in a finite form. He writes, with reference to the Hebrew psalms, that "ecstasy intensifies . . . into a purely vague enthusiasm which struggles to bring to feeling and contemplation what cannot be consciously expressed in words. Caught in this vagueness, the subjective inner life cannot portray its unattainable object to itself in peaceful beauty or enjoy its self-expression in a work of art."[50] The speaker of praise, in awe of the referent, longs for the creation of new forms, and the fluid—expanding, contracting, expanding—forms of hymns and odes prove endlessly adaptable to such needs.

As the eighteenth-century and Romantic odists met with religious enthusiasm and a Romantic aesthetic of emotional expression, they frequently use the form not only to praise but also to self-scrutinize, as the period's numerous odes to such emotions as Fear, Pity, and Dejection attest. Hegel describes how the odist comes to master his or her own subjective enthusiasm. The weight of the topic is ultimately pitted against the poet's subjective freedom, and Hegel says that "it is . . . the pressure of this opposition that necessitates the swing and boldness of languages and images, the apparent absence of rule in the structure and course of the poem, the digressions, gaps, sudden transitions, etc.; and the loftiness of the poet's genius is preserved by the mastery displayed in his continual ability to resolve this discord by perfect art and to produce a whole completely united in itself, which, by being his work, raises him above the greatness of his subject-matter."[51] For Hegel, any ode has an underlying narrative that shapes it and as well becomes a driving impulse within it. Encountering greatness as an obstacle to his powers of apprehension and representation, the odist works without rules to create an art of perfected unity—one that consequently reflects back upon those very powers. Thus the very obligation to phenomena opens the praising poet's field of naming, judging, withholding, and giving.

3 / FREEDOM FROM MOOD

My thoughts were often in creative vision during factory work. I've put in years at machines—dreaming aesthetic ends—one never becomes oblivious to the surrounding order—in concentrated work alone under ideal conditions—outside vistas intrude like sex—hungers and assorted fears, fear in survival—lonesomeness for my children—many waves intrude during the most ideal set up. One works with one's nature—sets his own equilibrium, develops his resources, evens up his rage. . . . When elements like noise, others, dirt, grease enter the procedure, they are but elements in nature more easily transposed than intruding mental props . . .

—DAVID SMITH, *Report on Voltri*[1]

I A Sympathetic Nature

Our attempts to understand, or even to begin to shape our understanding of, the role of our emotions when we are creating artworks stand in sharp contrast to the repeatable, objective procedures we use in scientific method and other predetermined means of ratiocination. Enlightenment- and Romantic-era hymns and odes that turn toward subjective states for their themes remind us that poetic making of all kinds is informed by more than reason and the will: our motives and choices in making works of art are often revealed to us, if at all, only partially and almost entirely after the work is completed. In making art, we act and later understand; if we understood from the beginning, there would be, indeed, no reason to act.

We speak of being "in a poetic mood," yet like any mood, a poetic one is absorbing, and the only certain thing we can know about it is that it is not certain we can "know" it. We fall into, awaken from, or "snap out of" moods: if we can write about a mood, we are out of the mood. A mood's will is not at work in the light. If in praise poetry the abstraction of wonder leads to the context-free particulars of praise, other kinds of poetry—nocturnes, meditations, laments, complaints, for example—

are rooted in the obscurity that is their subject. As Keats famously wrote of the poet's "negative capability" as a capacity to remain in doubts, hesitations, and uncertainties, any artist is suspended within, and must inevitably endure, states where certainty not only is deferred but also must be made. It is not that an artistic mood is mere anxiety, for the racing mind will never acquire a referent. Only immersion in temporality emerges into form.[2] Indeed, as we will see, the musicality that characterizes poetic moods is the call of a structure that is the very antithesis of anxiety's abysmal emptiness. The poet who succumbs to a musical mood will follow its internal rhythms and dynamics; the poet who resists such a mood will still be subject to it by negation.

Philosophers have brought the same ambivalence to moods that they often bring to poetry itself. For Søren Kierkegaard, for example, moods of anxiety, ironic awareness, melancholy, and despair draw us away from an encounter with our own interiority and the necessity to decide our beliefs. Heidegger thought of moods as characterizing not individual psychology so much as ages—as when we speak of "the restless mood of the '60s" or, say, "the acquisitive mood of the '80s." He therefore argues that we are always in a mood or always have a mood, and that moods call us back to the being of the world. Heidegger takes the impenetrability of mood by cognition to be a productive aspect of the capacity of moods to disclose existence at a deeper and more original level. In his treatise on the concept of mind, Gilbert Ryle similarly suggested that moods are frames of mind or temporary conditions that collect events and are not themselves events; they are, for Ryle, propositions, not acts or states.[3] A mood, once initiated, is already on its way. Enveloping emotions of this kind are like the haze from which Venus appears in all her glory: the best outcome is beauty and an intervening grace; the worst mere power exercised in obscurity.

In beginning to make a poem, we claim some measure of freedom from the context of the situation—that is, the situation itself is undetermined, ineffable, a feeling or ambience tied to the absence of intention or purpose. To make the work is to free such making from the very context that proposes it. As any Romantic theory of art, even those that get waylaid by notions of individual expression, will suggest, a work of art does not communicate something that is already understood. The work is a determined outcome built from an inchoate, merely suggestive, beginning. Just as beauty appears to us as somehow artful, works of art come to be by fulfilling or manifesting their own initiating nature.

We have seen how knowledge is a consequence, rather than a cause, of the specifying particulars of praising. In his 1965 study *The Arts of the Beautiful*, Étienne Gilson similarly criticizes the tendency of philosophers to think of art making as based in the manifestation of an already-existing cognition. "No doubt knowledge always accompanies creation," he writes, "but in the complex interaction of knowledge and artistic production, knowledge does not produce. It would be more correct to say that knowledge is at the service of production. The will to make comes first; only afterwards does a man [or woman] ask himself [or herself]: What am I going to make?"[4] Gilson's argument, which makes content emergent in a practice of form, ups the ante of Romanticism's earlier wresting of art from practices of imitation to practices of expression.

Yet the most radical, and perhaps most eloquent, spokesperson for the moment of compulsive, noncognizable will inaugurating a work arrives more than a century earlier in Percy Shelley's 1821 tract "A Defence of Poetry":

> Poetry is not like reasoning, a power to be exerted according to the determination of the will. A man cannot say, "I will compose poetry." The greatest poet even cannot say it: for the mind in creation is as a fading coal which some invisible influence, like an inconstant wind, awakens to transitory brightness: this power arises from within, like the colour of a flower which fades and changes as it is developed, and the conscious portions of our natures are unprophetic either of its approach or its departure. . . . When composition begins, inspiration is already on the decline, and the most glorious poetry that has ever been communicated to the world is probably a feeble shadow of the original conception of the poet.[5]

Shelley's insights in this famous passage regarding the force of intuition, which is nothing more or less than the response of our nature to nature, are convincing, but his further claim that a great and unarticulated poetry lies whole at the moment of conception seems a gesture of mystification that lands us in the fallen world of things as they are. Like Coleridge in his account of the composition of "Kubla Khan," where the poet describes an interruption that diminishes the always deferred, always displaced, original conception of the poem to the state of the fragment we read as "Kubla Khan" the extant poem, Shelley frames the work as diminished in order to glorify the qualities of the poetic mind.[6]

Even so, Shelley is surely right that too much determination, what he calls "labor and study," have a chilling effect on inspiration. What is needed as a precondition of art making seems to be something like an atmosphere of spontaneity—a situation of beginning to begin that can repeat itself without ever repeating the same consequences. At the onset of making a work of art, a free mood, a state of preconceptual intent, prevails. If we lack, if I lack, a vocabulary to describe this state, the most simple term—a sense of *liveliness*, of life responding to life, vibration to vibration, rhythm to rhythm—might be, as Shelley indicates, the most promising one.

We may be skeptical of a notion of sympathetic nature, thinking it is a projection of the poet's subjectivity across the noumenal divide, but we might also remember that we often frame the poet's moods as passive and open, with nature as well projecting its feelings upon the human agent, who is after all a part of nature. Perhaps as a legacy of art making's early connections to those practices of prayer and sacrifice that I have been exploring, we anthropomorphize inspiration, ascribing it to muses or gods or, more often for male poets, goddesses who deign to visit and fill the maker with their breath, providing the means of inspiration through direct in-spiration. That this image involves a change in pattern, a re-regulation or alteration of our usual breathing rhythm, is a constant theme, as is the notion of taking dictation, of having words emerge from somewhere other than the conscious reason, and hence from somewhere other than the discursive production of syntax.[7]

Discursive is a fashionable word in contemporary art making, as if artists working in any medium could mark their success by how much talk their work generates. Yet perhaps this trend is merely a result of celebrity culture, which lacks any confidence in firsthand experience. Susanne Langer, for one, has eloquently made the case for the nondiscursive aspect of art making and its relation to rhythm. She writes:

"Non-discursive form in art has a different office [from the creation of significance], namely to articulate knowledge that cannot be rendered discursively because it concerns experiences that are not *formally* amenable to the discursive projection. Such experiences are the rhythms of life, organic, emotional and mental (the rhythm of attention is an interesting link among them all), which are not simply periodic, but endlessly complex, and sensitive to any sort of influence. All together they compose the dynamic pattern of feeling. It is this pattern that only non-discursive symbolic forms can present, and that is the point and purpose of artistic construction."[8] Following out this argument, we need not claim that rhythm represents a kind of knowledge, especially when we think of rhythms as embodied and preceding any thought about them. And unless we assume, in a somewhat paranoid way, that nature has singular intentions of which we are not aware, there is no reason why rhythms need to be purposeful. Yet Langer usefully gives a sense of the myriad interconnections between such patterns of feelings. And in suggesting that attention itself has a rhythm, she indicates not only the dynamic between absorption and distraction but also the scales of intensity involved.

Here we return to the differences between contemplative and deliberative thought and the dynamic between wonder and the hortative in the ecstatic practices of praise. As Paul Valéry famously described being seized by a rhythm as the paradigmatic instantiation of a poetic mood,[9] the rhythms to which we succumb, by which we are swept, are not so much "outside" us as intending subjects as coursing through us, deliberately suppressed in those moments when we seek a particular outcome, but otherwise in force and linking us to life. The experience of rhythm offers what Emmanuel Levinas has called a "reversed intentionality": "We cannot speak of consent, assumption, initiative or freedom, because the subject is caught up and carried away. . . . We have really an exteriority of the inward. It is surprising that phenomenological analysis never tried to apply this fundamental paradox of rhythm and dream, which describes a sphere situated outside of the conscious and the unconscious, a sphere whose role in its ecstatic rites has been shown by ethnography."[10] Certainly Levinas is right to conceive of the state of being caught up in rhythm as something that cannot be intended or willed, yet to be taken in this way is not simply to be passive but also to be receptive—alert to something in the circumstances of the present without quite knowing what will happen next. Consider one of the most well-known poems of sympathetic nature—here a human nature in sympathy with an external nature, and vice versa, and all without "reason":

"Il pleure dans mon coeur."

Il pleut doucement sur la ville.

—Arthur Rimbaud

Il pleure dans mon coeur
Comme il pleut sur la ville;
Quelle est cette langueur
Qui pénètre mon coeur?

Ô bruit doux de la pluie
Par terre et sur les toits!
Pour un coeur qui s'ennuie
Ô le chant de la pluie!

Il pleure sans raison
Dans ce coeur qui s'écoeure.
Quoi! nulle trahison? . . .
Ce deuil est sans raison.

C'est bien la pire peine
De ne savoir pourquoi
Sans amour et sans haine
Mon coeur a tant de peine!

Verlaine's lyric, from his *Romances sans paroles* of 1874, indeed emphasizes the paradoxical idea of being without words; the poem's rhyme scheme, *abaa*, suggests by the second stanza, with the slight echo of "ville" and "pluie," that rain and solitude are in fact a kind of rhyme, and the last single *b* term—"pourquoi"—resonates beyond the close. The poem also plays beautifully with a set of prepositions that emphasize the poem's many themes of heartbeat and rainbeat, of inner isolation brought into consonance with external sound: *dans*, *sur*, *par*, *sur*, *dans*, *pour, sans, dans, sans, sans*. Things that "penetrate," that are within, upon, beside, and without, arrive by the steady rhythm of the rain's fall.

Thus the poem both follows and critiques Rimbaud's claim that the rain falls softly on the town. The epigraph, like all epigraphs, is stranded. But this line has a particular history of being abandoned, for it seems to have belonged to a very early poem that Rimbaud gave to his schoolmate Labarrière, who lost it but continued to remember this line: "Il pleut doucement sur la plaine." Verlaine in turn was writing in London during days of winter rain and fog, desolate that Rimbaud had left him for a month-long period.[11] This brief lyric's claim nevertheless is an objective one, and we are made quite conscious of the difference between the tradition of the stanzaic poem, which must parse out its tones and feelings incrementally, and the strophic poem with its outpourings. Verlaine's lyric answers Rimbaud's in subjective terms entirely; it brings forward his languor, boredom, senselessness, and pain. Verlaine seems to suggest that our moods exist to balk at nature and the natures of others, or perhaps we discover hardness only in the presence of softness, pain in the presence of sweetness, our mood in the presence of another who shares our weather but not our state of mind.

In his magisterial study of the implications of the German word *Stimmung*, or "attunement," Leo Spitzer explores the unity of such feelings between persons and their environments. He writes, "Stimmung is fused with the landscape, which in turn is animated by the feeling of man—it is an indissoluble unit into which man and nature are integrated. In German you can say [both] 'the Stimmung of a landscape' and 'my Stimmung.' There is a relation also with 'gestimmt sein,' 'to be tuned.'" Spitzer points out that the English idea of "state of mind" is too independent in its internalization to quite match this notion, and he emphasizes that the environment is not only spatial but also temporal—that a sense of *Stimmung* arises often from the moment to hand.[12]

Ancient and medieval thinkers held that such notions of attunement and harmony were extended to universal concepts of world harmony, a musical harmony that human ears could catch in part through their own music, accessible as well to human reason to the extent that such thought was ruled by numbers. In *Protagoras*, Plato has Protagoras argue that the teaching of music particularly will instill self-control in young people and turn them away from evil, via different forms of rhythm and *harmonia*, "so that they may be more gentle, and by becoming better attuned and more rhythmical may be useful in speech and action; for the whole life of man needs rhythm and attunement. " As these pupils become *euarmostoteroi*, or "well-tuned," their musical skills will extend as well to speaking and doing.[13] Especially for the Pythagoreans, the human lute responded to the music of the stars, imitating the playing of the god Apollo. For Heraclitus, the lute and the arrow, dual attributes of Apollo, are alike in form and indicate how strife (the arrow) can turn into harmony: the name of the bow (Bios) is also the name of life (Bios), and its work is death.[14] Spitzer records how the intertwining of mood, attunement, and concepts of world harmony leads to a dual sense, a kind of thinking together, of the universe as endowed with human feeling and of sympathy for other human beings aligned with the revolving motion of the stars.

The concept of *Stimmung* continues, then, to run a parallel course with the idea of world harmony; by the late medieval period, Spitzer concludes, St. Ambrose has done the most for the notion of world harmony and his acolyte St. Augustine the most for *Stimmung*. Even so, notions of the two are difficult to separate, since the immediacy of attunement in the time and space at hand is linked musically to the perfection of the universe and the harmony of the spheres. Spitzer finds that the unification of the concepts, an exemplification in fact of the ideology they propose, continues to the time of Luther, and then gradually the world-harmony dimension continues under a displacement. "It is no chance," he writes, that "the eighteenth century, when German *Stimmung* was lexicologically constituted, was among other things the period of a pietism of the *schöne Seele*, which ultimately harks back to Augustinianism. Nor is the Ambrosian world harmony dead today: if the man of the nineteenth century leaves behind the cell of his *Stimmung*, he may perhaps see a *Stimmung* on the top of a mountain, at a seashore, or when he bathes in the waves of music (in Wagner). Only the immediate life around him, his environment, has become unpoetic; it is only *ambiente*, a *milieu*, an *Umwelt*, spatial, yes, but narrow and not pervaded by the Idea of God."[15]

Using similarly passionate tones, Spitzer deduces that the mechanistic spirit of the eighteenth century "robbed" *Stimmung* of "its blossoming life."[16] Within the framework of literary history we sometimes frame this receptiveness in terms of literary influence alone, but Spitzer provides us with a sense of the long and complex history of the notion of influence, from the theories of humoral psychology to philosophies such as that of Averroës, which held that concepts of the world soul are communicated to individual souls by the rays of the stars. In such a vibrating universe, every part shares in, and is moved by, the sensitivity of the whole.[17]

In the first volume of *The World as Will and Idea*, Arthur Schopenhauer described at length a "lyrical state of mind" that similarly arose from its environment. He writes of such a state of mind as "a pure knowing," going on to contend that "in the lyric and the lyrical mood, desire (the personal interest of the ends), and pure perception of the surrounding presented, are wonderfully mingled with each other; connections between them are sought for and imagined; the subjective disposition, the affection, the affection of the will, imparts its own hue to the perceived surrounding and, conversely, the surroundings communicate the reflex of their colour to the will."[18] Among Schopenhauer's examples of these lyrics responsive to their circumstances are the folkloric songs of the "Wunderhorn" gathered or composed by Achim von Arnim and Clemens Brentano at the beginning of the nineteenth century. Schopenhauer particularly praises this little song, "O Bremen, now I must leave thee!"[19]

Abschied von Bremen
Mündlich

O Bremen, ich muß dich nun lassen,
O du wunderschöne Stadt,
Und darinnen muß ich lassen
Meinen allerschönsten Schatz.

Wir haben oft beisamm gesessen,
Manche schöne Monden-Nacht,
Manchen Schlaf zusamm vergessen,
Und die Zeit so zugebracht.

Mein Koffer rollt, der Morgen kühlet,
Ach, die Straßen sind so still,
Und was da mein Herze fühlet,
Nimmermehr ich sagen will.

Der Weg mich schmerzlich wieder lenket
Hin, wo Liebchen sah herab,
Daß sie ja noch mein gedenket,
Drück ich zwei Pistolen ab.

Bald jagt vor dir in diesen Gassen,
Manches Windlein dürren Staub,
Meine Seufzer sinds, sie lassen
Vor dir nieder trocknes Laub.

So steh ich wirklich nun im Schiffe,
Meinen Koffer seh ich drauf,
Wie der Schiffer herzhaft pfiffe,
Zogen wir wohl Anker auf.

Ich seh den Sturmwind rauschend gehen,
O mein Schiff hat schnellen Lauf,
Wird es wohl zu Grunde gehen,
Wanket nicht Gedanken drauf.[20]

As "Abschied von Bremen" illustrates, the most fundamental state of reception is that of the immediate environment provided by the body itself and its surroundings, including weather. The traveler who is depicted here leaving his sweetheart changes his tone in each stanza as he thinks of moonlit nights, bleak streets, clouds of dust, and dry leaves. The little song moves from the steadiness of the ground of Bremen to the instability of the ship on the sea. It is a poem that quite literally draws its feeling up through its contact with earth and water—this is emphasized by the strange scene of shooting a pistol into the ground as a mnemonic for the sweetheart, a "dry" gesture that counters the fluid erasure that a death at sea threatens by the poem's end.

Our moods are shaped by the ultradian rhythms of ninety minutes or so duration that affect our senses of vigilance, sleepiness, and capacity to daydream and also by the infradian rhythms of more than twenty-four hours that are associated with menstruation and other bodily cycles, including our responses to changing seasons of the year.[21] We are thus bound as natural beings to natural rhythms, including those of our own bodies.[22] Solar pulses and the ebb and flow of tides are part of this larger set of forces. Rhythm indeed may be a necessary, if not sufficient, condition of human life, for the embryonic heart begins to beat eighteen to twenty-one days after conception; at that point there is no blood to pump and no function for the heart to serve, but if the beat stops, the embryo dies.[23] Circadian rhythms, which rule our sleeping and waking as heliotropic creatures, the waxing and waning responses of biological processes of many kinds to the twenty-four-hour cycle of light and darkness, are not only responsive to environmental cues but also persist for many organisms, from fruit flies to human beings, in the absence of such cues, indicating that the organism either has incorporated the pattern or already was embedded within it.

Our "on and off" reception of the world, the dynamic between mark and interval, or positive and negative space, is also fundamental to the creation of signifying forms. If we return to the Hebrew psalms, we find a recurring exposition of the emotions we associate with the circadian cycle. "Thine is the day, thine also the night; thou has established the luminaries and the sun. / Thou hast fixed all the bounds of the earth; thou hast made summer and winter" (Psalm 74:16–17). In the tides of sleeping and waking, night and day, that circle so prominently through the Psalms, the day brings vindication (Psalm 37) or chastening (Psalm 73) or steadfast love (Psalm 92), and the night and day bring different emotions to the speaker and different responses from the deity. In the day "he led them with a cloud," and "all the night with a fiery light" (Psalm 78); "weeping may tarry for the night, / but joy comes with the morning" (Psalm 30); out of the landscape of the heavens and firmament, "day to day pours forth speech, and night to night declares knowledge" (Psalm 19). The psalmist declares, "I call for help by day; I cry out in the night before thee" (Psalm 88). Like any number of later poems, the psalms thereby instantiate the moods that marked their initial occasion, moods that respond to the light and to the darkness, to the changing circumstances of the most fundamental aspects of their contexts.

Recent studies show that our moods are responsive as well to positive and negative ions in the atmosphere. The warm, dry conditions that facilitate air pollution and result in positive ions produce negative moods, whereas the negative ionic concentrations characterizing the period after rain, or the atmosphere that surrounds circulating water like waterfalls and seashores, or even running shower water, inversely result in good moods.[24] The relation between good moods and the environment, and what happens when the poet brings the wrong mood to the weather, is a topic for poetry, especially love poetry of one kind or another, as early as Raimbaut de Vaqueiras's twelfth-century "Kalenda maya," which begins:

Kalenda maya
Ni fuelhs de faya
Ni chanz d'auzelh ni flors de glaya
Non es que-m playa,
Pros domna guaya

This translation is offered by W. D. Snodgrass: "This May Day bringing / new lilies springing / with songs of birds through beechwoods ringing / can scarce delight me / unless you'd write me."[25] The atmosphere is unsuited to the actual mood of the speaker and vice versa, thereby emphasizing how deeply embedded the speaker is in some prior state—the narrative will provide a self-reflexive account of how the poet comes to develop it. We might call such poems works of "unsympathetic nature," even as they emphasize our expectation that some coherence should bond the artist to his or her surroundings.

Opening lines are the place to make the point, as Keats does in the first stanza of his 1820 "Ode to a Nightingale."

My heart aches, and a drowsy numbness pains
My sense, as though of hemlock I had drunk.
Or emptied some dull opiate to the drains
One minute past, and Lethe-wards had sunk:
'Tis not through envy of thy happy lot,
But being too happy in thine happiness—
That thou, light-wingéd Dryad of the trees,

In some melodious plot
Of beechen green, and shadows numberless,
Singest of summer in full-throated ease.[26]

The contrast here is not merely one of moods, but one of a receptive, reciprocating mood between the bird's song and its environment and the dull insensibility of the poet, who is somehow beginning to be stirred by that song. Shelley similarly plays on this contrast between mood and surrounding by emphasizing feeling in the opening lines to his carefully dated and contextualized poem "Stanzas Written in Dejection—December 1818, Near Naples." He highlights the features of the atmosphere that should, but do not, cheer him:

The sun is warm, the sky is clear,
The waves are dancing fast and bright,
Blue isles and snowy mountains wear
The purple noon's transparent might,
The breath of the moist earth is light
Around its unexpanded buds; . . . [27]

In the end, however, he suggests his suffering is made milder by the atmosphere around him. The speaker of this poem of loneliness, which commences in the feeling of "for I am one / Whom men love not," is constantly distracted by the initial warm touch of the sun that characterizes the poem's opening lines: his "cold cheek" feels the "warm air," and the poem ends with the lingering warm touch of the sun "enjoyed, like joy in Memory yet."

Although poets do not usually, as Shelley does here, register the weather along with the date in their manuscripts and published work, we sometimes get a glimpse of the circumstances of composing and their effects on the poet's emotions. Thomas Carew, for example, in his 1640 poem "Mediocritie in Love Rejected," has his speaker look to some force, torrid or frozen, that might push him away from the stasis of his "calm estate." He cries:

Give me more love, or more disdaine;
    The Torrid, or the frozen Zone,
Bring equall ease unto my paine;

The temperate affords me none:
Either extreme, of love, or hate,
Is sweeter than a calme estate.

Give me a storm; if it be love,
Like *Danae* in that golden showre,
I swimme in pleasure; if it prove
Disdaine, that torrent will devoure
My Vulture-hopes; and he's possest
Of Heaven, that's but from Hell releast;
Then crowne my joyes or cure my paine:
Give me more love, or more disdaine.[28]

If we made a small anthology of poems of sympathetic and unsympathetic nature, we would also have to include Henry Vaughan's poem of the same period "The Storm," as a narrative of yearning and release wherein a storm and a body are in perfect concert:

The Storm

1
I see the use: and know my blood
Is not a sea,
But a shallow, bounded flood
Though red as he;
Yet have I flows, as strong as his,
And boiling streams that rave
With the same curling force, and hiss,
As doth the mountained wave.

2
But when his waters billow thus,
Dark storms, and wind
Incite them to that fierce discuss,
Else not inclined,
Thus the enlarged, enraged air
Uncalms these to a flood,

But still the weather that's most fair
Breeds tempests in my blood;

3
Lord, then round me with weeping clouds,
And let my mind
In quick blasts sigh beneath those shrouds
A spirit-wind,
So shall that storm plunge this *recluse*
Which sinful ease made foul,
And *wind*, and *water* to thy use
Both *wash*, and *wing* my soul.[29]

Vaughan's closing use of chiasmus, whereby "wing" wings back to "wind" and "wash" to "water" underlines the poem's theology as it also pins it to its circumstances: X indeed marks the spot.

In a similar manner, Vaughan's ecstatic poem of 1655 "The Waterfall" captures much of the feeling of sympathy between liquid motion and human emotion. Here are the opening lines describing his plunge into thought:

With what deep murmurs through time's silent stealth
Doth thy transparent, cool and watery wealth,
Here flowing fall,
And chide, and call,
As if his liquid, loose retinue stayed
Ling'ring, and were of this steep place afraid,
The common pass,
Where, clear as glass,
All must descend
Not to an end:
But quickened by this deep and rocky grave,
Rise to a longer course more bright and brave.

He juxtaposes the even measure of pentameter couplets against the uneven dimeter passages: first a couplet, then, doubling, a pair of couplets in succession. Thus although the entire poem shares a common rhyme scheme, the meter is used to plunge and prolong the motion of the syntax—one sentence running through a dozen lines. A sense of change and motion is also created by the initial juxtaposition of murmurs and silence; by the striking rendition of water's cold transparency; by the tension between flowing and being turned aside by chiding, calling, and lingering; by the anthropomorphization of the water as something that holds back at the edge of "this steep place afraid," which is a visual rhyme, as the syntax cascades into the "common pass" of the second dimeter passage; and finally here by the faux closure of a deep grave that then "rise[s] to a longer course." As we saw earlier in passages in Pindar, the listener/reader's sense of immediacy and immersion is all the more emphasized by the use of deictic gestures of presence—in Vaughan's case, "here," "this steep place," "this deep and rocky grave."

In the succeeding tetrameter stanza Vaughan turns to praise the waterfall, with its "quick store" of drops rotating between the sky and the earth, observing:

O useful element and clear!
My sacred wash and cleanser here,
My first consigner unto those
Fountains of life, where the Lamb goes.
What sublime truths, and wholesome themes,
Lodge in thy mystical, deep streams!
Such as dull man can never find
Unless that Spirit lead his mind,
Which first upon thy face did move
And hatched all with his quickening love.

The waterfall twice "quickens" the poet—the language is that of the unborn child quickening in the womb. Yet for Vaughan what is quickened by this elemental force is "the Spirit" that truly is leading his mind. The transparent waterfall, "useful element and clear," produces in the poet the theological paradox that such literal water, passing into a brook, "restagnates," whereas the human agent, made of water himself, strives for the invisible world of eternity. The poem ends thereby with a celebration of the "liberty" afforded by the promise of an afterlife, the "channel" the "soul seeks," and turns away from the literal channel of "cataracts and creeks."

As this loud brook's incessant fall
In streaming rings restagnates all,
Which reach by course the bank, and then
Are no more seen, just so pass men.
O my invisible estate,
My glorious liberty, still late!
Thou art the channel my soul seeks,
Not this with cataracts and creeks.[30]

For a divine in 1655, transport alone does not suffice, and the poem's energy is diminished and withdrawn in this pious desire. In Vaughan's lines we can sense a great deal of the transfer of force from the natural phenomenon to the brooding poet himself, and indeed something of the moment of inspiration seems to drive the reader from the opening to the close of the work with a commensurate energy.

Nevertheless here we also find a more basic drive toward symbolization that releases rhythm from contextual limits and has free rein within the domain of possible meanings. As Susanne Langer explored the nondiscursive properties of human rhythms, she became particularly interested in how such rhythms were epitomized in the patterns, crises, and cadences of sexual action and passion. Noting humanity's relation to animal existence in particular ways, she further suggests, "The pure sense of life springs from that basic rhythm [of passional desires], and varies from the composed well-being of sleep to the intensity of spasm, rage, or ecstasy. But the process of living is incomparably more complex for human beings than for even the highest animals. . . . The powers of language and imagination have set it utterly apart from that of other creatures. In human society an individual is not, like a member of a herd or a hive, exposed only to others that visibly and tangibly surround him, but is consciously bound to people who are absent, perhaps far away, at the moment. Even the dead may still play into his life."[31] If now we know far more about the continuity of our species with other species—with the capacity, more like ours than not, of other animals to communicate, grieve, remember, and even imagine in response to certain contextual markers—a drive toward abstraction in human experience frees us from those contextual determinations that embed us in pattern and rhythm, a freedom that enables us to reform and restructure movement in such patterns within finite fields of our own determination.

Beyond Shelley's comments on the nature of poetic composition—and myriad anecdotal remarks by fellow poets about composing in the shower or, among male poets particularly, while shaving—I know of only two accounts, one from life and one from fiction, that describe from a poet's perspective the creative state of mind the twentieth-century sculptor David Smith recorded in the passage that serves as this chapter's epigraph. In a 1946 essay, "The Making of a Poem," Stephen Spender summarized some of the ways that a mental concentration with what he called "a special focus" characterized the beginning of the process of writing a poem. He wrote, "Schiller liked to have a smell of rotten apples, concealed beneath the lid of his desk, under his nose when he was composing poetry. Walter de la Mare has told me he must smoke while writing. Auden drinks endless cups of tea. Coffee is my own addiction, besides smoking a great deal, which I hardly ever do except when I am writing. I notice also that as I attain a greater concentration, this tends to make me forget the taste of the cigarette in my mouth, and then I have a desire to smoke two or even three cigarettes at a time, in order that the sensation from the outside may penetrate through the wall of concentration which I have built around myself." He goes on to describe how all these sensual cravings and practices result somehow in forgetting one has a body,[32] and adds that concentration can be immediate in some instances and plodding in others.

How do we reconcile this description of embodiment with the idea that poetic composition involves an immersion in contextual feeling? As makers set to work, one action compels the next—immediacy somehow leads to anticipation. Perhaps this is an instance of what psychologists call selective attention, which is the first step between being in an environment and responding to it; this kind of attention seems to be independent of the work of the senses per se, and our responses in language especially seem to be tied to the emotions.[33] The snapshots of Auden automatically drinking tea, of Spender with two or three cigarettes in his mouth at once, suggest the necessity of stopping up or blocking whatever needs—primitive and oral as they are—would call the poet away from making. To this extent I would disagree with Levinas's claim that rhythm is an impediment to intention, for by removing inhibitions and prior needs and instantiating the artwork the poet experiences a simple mode of cognitive freedom, one that keeps thought open to rhythm, motion, and anticipation, releasing the poet into the sphere of the form itself.[34]

The second account of how a poet begins a poem appears more recently in a passage in *Snow*, the 2004 novel by the Turkish writer Orhan Pamuk. In this passage, the hero of the novel, Ka, is watching snow fall with some young Islamic fundamentalists, who have just asked him, "Who makes the snow fall from the sky? What is the snow's secret?" They continue to watch silently as the snow falls, and Ka falls, too—into a poetic mood:

> What am I doing in this world? Ka asked himself. How miserable these snowflakes look from this perspective, how miserable my life is. A man lives his life, and then he falls apart and soon there is nothing left. Ka felt as if half his soul had abandoned him but still the other half remained; he still had love in him. Like a snowflake, he would fall as he was meant to fall; he would devote himself heart and soul to the melancholy course on which his life was set. His father had a certain smell after shaving, and now this smell came back to him. He thought of his mother making breakfast, her feet aching inside her slippers on the cold kitchen floor; he had a vision of a hairbrush; he remembered his mother giving him sugary pink syrup when he woke up coughing in the night, he felt the spoon in his mouth, and as he gave his mind over to all the other little things that make up a life and realized how they all added up to a unified whole, he saw a snowflake. . . . So it was that Ka heard the call from deep inside him: the call he heard only at moments of inspiration, the only sound that could ever make him happy, the sound of his muse. For the first time in four years, a poem was coming to him; although he had yet to hear the words, he knew it was already written; even as it waited in its hiding place, it radiated the power and beauty of destiny.[35]

This remarkable and rich passage, circling from one snowflake simile to another, the memory shifting from "fall" to "call," reveals a certain sensory sequence—the smell of the father after shaving, the imaginative identification with the mother's aching feet, the hairbrush vision, the taste of the syrup, the feeling of the spoon in the mouth, and then the inchoate inarticulate sound that indicates that a poem, as yet unknown, is on its way to its final form. Here the process of making the poem is even less willed than Spender suggests, for Ka does not begin by smoking or drinking tea, or closing himself up with his desk, but rather is out in the world. The mesmerizing spectacle of the falling snow—a striking example of what we could consider to be a silent rhythm, one patterned object following another at intervals—leads the poet to a process of association that in turn leads to the beginning of a poem's form.

"[Pure consciousness] is only a movement *towards* thinking, and so is devotion. Its thinking as such is no more than the chaotic jingling of bells, or a mist of warm incense, a musical thinking that does not get as far as the Notion, which would be the sole, imminent, objective mode of thought. This infinite, pure inner feeling does indeed come into possession of its object; but this does not make its appearance in conceptual form, not as something [speculatively] comprehended, and appears therefore as something alien," wrote Hegel in his *Phenomenology of Spirit*.[36] What consciousness is doing in this preconceptual state is not exactly clear; it is indeed not clear by definition and hence eludes any analysis.

We sometimes describe consciousness as playing or racing. Describing good moods, the psychologist William Morris notes that flights of ideas or the subjective experience that one's thoughts are racing not only come to mind but produce more associations between words. In turn, when we find relations between things, we feel happy. Morris and his colleagues have discovered that good moods "prime positive material in memory." Hence racing minds do not merely spin their wheels; they enable subjects to create unusual associations among words and groups of words. When this happens, the subjects of such experiments do very well on standard tests of creativity, and Morris explains, somewhat tautologically, that "the likelihood of perceiving relatedness among stimuli [is] a tendency that has been asserted to be the essence of creativity." In sum, a good mood evokes more, and more diverse and extended, associations and may lead to fresh insights and an urge to make art. Yet too much and too little resemblance, a wandering concentration anxious about fixity—in this we can discern another dimension of the environment of falling snow—the mind is drawn to comparisons between not only individual but also unique phenomena that are at the same time the consequence of crystallization. Motions are incorporated into the shape of ends.

More soberly, Morris notes that "creative artists and manic depressives perform similarly on tests of thought processes . . . and such artists, especially writers and poets, show a much heightened degree of susceptibility to affective disorder. . . . Good moods seem to increase the availability of remote and unusual associations." At the same time, Morris concludes that artists must keep a balance between focusing and wandering, between noting and ignoring, with the relative simplicity or complexity of the task affecting the kind of attention needed.[37]

For a closer consideration of the mutual relation between intensity and numbness brought about by the feelings of composing, we might turn to Keats's lyric poem of late 1817 "In Drear-Nighted December." Here he speaks of "the feel of not to feel it":

I.
In drear-nighted December,
Too happy, happy tree,
Thy branches ne'er remember
Their green felicity:
The north cannot undo them,
With a sleety whistle through them;
Nor frozen thawings glue them
From budding at the prime.

II.
In drear-nighted December,
Too happy, happy brook,
Thy bubblings ne'er remember
Apollo's summer look;
But with a sweet forgetting,

They stay their crystal fretting,
Never, never petting
About the frozen time.

III.
Ah! would 'twere so with many
A gentle girl and boy!
But were there ever any
Writh'd not of passed joy?
The feel of not to feel it,
When there is none to heal it,
Nor numbed sense to steel it,
Was never said in rhyme.[38]

"The feel of not to feel it . . . was never said in rhyme." What is this feeling of not being able to feel, a feeling that rhyme has never said? In the worst of winter, the tree doesn't remember its greenness, but it buds in the spring nevertheless; the bubbles of the brook endure their frozen time without a thought to the flow of summer, yet the flow of summer will return.

The poem is fired by a strange rubbing together of words, each of which has its source in a metaphor of contact: *fretting* indicates a decaying or wasting, a chemical change arising from the contact between two surfaces, or an irritation or chafing caused by such rubbing, as when "crystal" branches, here encased in ice, fret against once another; *petting* is cosseting, stroking, or caressing in a sexually stimulating way. The freezing and thawing of Renaissance love poetry appear in this poem as a continuous process: "frozen thawings [cannot] glue" the first buds that will come in the spring. Even so, according to Keats, human beings, represented by the poem's young lovers, are acutely aware of the passing of their happiness and suffer that knowledge—they have no capacity for this numbness that fortifies and no promise of a natural renewal that heals. These undoings/doings happen even at the level of transposed sounds and letters: *sleet* evokes *steel*; *writh'd* evokes *write*; *brook* evokes *book*; *feel* evokes *leaf*. What this little poem and its later descendants can tell us is something about the feeling of making itself—a feeling of intensification and diminishment—like the difference between feeling pain and being numb, between feeling hot and feeling cold, between being near and being far, between moving and writhing, or, as Keats puts it at the end of his ode to a nightingale, the difference between being awake and being asleep.

II Metaphor and Music

After several thousand years of speculation on poetics, we still seem to know very little about what it does feel like to make a poem. "Nature in the subject (and by means of the disposition of its faculties) must give the rule to art, i.e., beautiful art is possible only as a product of genius," Kant writes in by now familiar language in his third critique. And he goes on to claim, with regard to aesthetic value, that "the art of poetry (which owes its origin almost entirely to genius, and will be guided least by precept or example) claims the highest rank of all."[39] But how the poet does this and what the experience is like, not only before composition proceeds but also during its process and once it is finished, is something of a mystery. Nevertheless, for a poet like Keats, making poems is not just compensatory for suffering in a thematic way—it is compensatory in an actual experiential sense. As the first generation of British Romantic poets reminded us, the rhythm, meter, and rhyme of poems have a physical impact, drawing us away from pain and the bleakest necessity.

Even so, as soon as we ask what the experience of making a poem "feels like," we draw on the psychologist's explanation of "more unnatural associations to words"—the realm of metaphor. It almost goes without saying that all feeling, from intense pain to the disequilibrium that any sense impression brings about, must be conveyed through the likenesses offered by metaphors or similes. This transport or translation of phenomena into other phenomena involves the creation of sensory equivalents that themselves rely on a mixing of categories (simile) or a creation of new categories (metaphor). If the particulars of praise end in an ascensional dynamic that both maintains and spiritualizes the form, the work of metaphor is to draw on the material qualities of the phenomenon to reshape and reform it, to hypothesize about what had formerly been fixed.

Indeed, the first way we might think about the emergence of poetic thought is to note that it is metaphorical. That is, something strikes us as being like something else, and we draw a connection through a simile or, more strongly, through a metaphor proper, and in consequence, by this gesture alone, we have made something new part of the world. This is the kind of *poiesis* the early eighteenth-century Neapolitan philosopher Giambattista Vico writes about—it often involves figuration or other visual images, and for Vico it is the origin of all other forms of thought, including those philosophical, religious, and social thoughts that serve as the foundation for the institutions of human culture.[40]

But such transformations are not exactly what I am trying to get at in thinking about the feel of thought at the inception of a poem, for such a shaped kind of metaphorical linking and framing comes further along in the process of making a poem and may be mostly a mode of ordering or even creating categories of things. And rather than leading to poems, establishing fixed figures of metaphor may be just as well suited to rhetoric or to the construction of aphorisms if doing so builds up terms, or to the making of riddles if it breaks them down. I am not suggesting that metaphor and image making are not vital to poetry, for of course they are, and of course poems can and often do have rhetorical ends. But a metaphor or simile is not all you need to start a poem, and metaphors in speech lose their vitality even if poems made of metaphors do not. As Percy Shelley wrote in his "Defence," noting that "their [poets'] language is vitally metaphorical . . . it marks the unapprehended relations of things and perpetuates their apprehension, until words, which represent them, become, through time, signs for portions or classes of thought instead of pictures of integral thoughts."[41]

In *The Philosophy of Rhetoric* I. A. Richards quotes this passage from Shelley, leaving off the possessive pronoun to claim that all language is "vitally metaphorical." Richards invented the terms *tenor* and *vehicle* to describe the transformative power of metaphorical interaction. He points out that if metaphor involves a comparison, then it might be a matter of "putting two things together to let them work together," or a way of seeing "how they are like and how unlike one another," or a process that calls attention to how they are alike or draws out "certain aspects of one through the co-presence of another."[42] For Richards, the function of any particular metaphor is context specific, and yet metaphor is a universal aspect of language—there cannot be any improvement in its use. Nevertheless, he writes that "in all interpretation we are filling in connections, and for poetry, of course, our freedom to fill in—the absence of explicitly stated intermediate steps—is a main source of its powers."[43]

As early as Quintilian's first-century rhetoric, theorists of metaphor realized that metaphor involves a permutation between terms that are animate and those that are inanimate.[44] Language quickens and alters the phenomenon, and the natural world sparks language into a process of continual growth and change. Monroe Beardsley similarly notes that metaphor is "intensional," a product of mind and the relation between words and things, for metaphorical qualities are found in language, not in the qualities of those objects to which they refer.[45] Drawing on the insight offered by our everyday distinction between "dead" and creative metaphors, Beardsley discusses the virtues of complex metaphors over simple ones—the former opening up more powers of language and hence leading to change and "live" metaphoricity. He provides a reading of Wallace Stevens's "The Motive for Metaphor" as a poem showing how "metaphor enables us to describe, to fix and preserve, the subtleties of experience and change ('the half colors of quarter things' in springtime), while words in their standard dictionary designations can only cope with 'The ABC of being / The ruddy temper, the hammer / Of red and blue.' "[46] This example nicely shows how the nuances of meaning pointed up by metaphor are a kind of painting or shading of words. Much as Schopenhauer wrote of subjects and their environments exchanging "hues" and of the "colors" of surroundings, we speak of phenomena "coloring our mood" or of moods themselves as being of a certain color—black or blue, or Andrew Marvell's "green thought in a green shade."

In all these ways, we find the persistence of metaphor's etymology as the notion of carrying over or movement—something is transferred or transported. We are used to thinking of transport as an effect of poems and music, but perhaps transport begins at the beginning as a kind of dislodging of or, more passively, a drifting away from terms and orders and the transfer of motion from thought to language. Via this process, we are coming closer to an activity that metaphorizes metaphor itself, one that keeps turning one thing into another, as St. Ambrose's poetry was said to rest upon the subtle transformation of one picture into another, as in a transparency,[47] or as Coleridge described the incessant associations of fancy, or as Kant described aesthetical ideas or symbols in their unresolved fecundity. Such forms are redundant and even catachrestic, but in each case—the metaphor of metaphor, the transparency, the fancy, and the aesthetical idea—centripetal force is at work, spinning into new surroundings.

In *The Birth of Tragedy out of the Spirit of Music*, Friedrich Nietzsche turns, as Spender did, to Schiller's practices of composing. Nietzsche, however, does not recount the legend of Schiller's work above the odd ambience of rotten apples; instead he draws from a letter Schiller wrote to Goethe—a letter that bears a rather uncanny resemblance to Pamuk's description of the onset of Ka's poetic mood. "Schiller," Nietzsche writes, "has thrown some light on the poetic process by a psychological observation, inexplicable but unproblematic to his own mind. He confessed before the act of creation he did not have before him or within him any series of images in a causal arrangement, but rather a *musical mood*." (Schiller actually wrote, "With me the perception has at first no clear and definite object; this is formed later. A certain musical mood comes first, and the poetical idea only follows later.")[48] Nietzsche is quick to conclude from this quote that the lyric poet and the musician have a great deal in common.

For Nietzsche a musical mood, too vague to take form as music itself, is almost always a necessary, if not sufficient, condition for composing a poem. Why a musical mood? Perhaps the answer lies in a description Schopenhauer has left of the ways that music is not only nonmimetic but also an expression of will itself. He writes: "I recognize in the deepest tones of harmony, in the bass, the lowest grades of the objectification of will, unorganized nature, the mass of the planet. It is well known that all the high notes which are easily sounded, and die away more quickly, are produced by the vibration in their vicinity of the deep bass-notes. When, also, the low notes sound, the high notes always sound faintly, and it is a law of harmony that only those high notes may accompany a bass-note which actually already sound along with it of themselves . . .

on account of its vibration."[49] He deduces, however, "that music . . . never expresses the phenomenon, but only the inner nature, the in-itself of all phenomena, the will itself. . . . Hence it arises that our imagination is so easily excited by music, and now seeks to give form to that invisible yet actively moved spirit-world which speaks to us directly, and clothe it with flesh and blood, i.e., to embody it in an analogous example. This is the origin of the song with words."[50]

The musical tone poem and the poetry of an intentionally "musical" poet like the symbolist Arthur Symons, beautiful as they might be, still suffer from a kind of heavy-handed illustrativeness. For it may not be that the poet and musician share a common set of tasks. Instead, a musical mood, bound up with, and perhaps the consequence of, a series of sensual impressions, seems to jump-start a movement into the time necessary for a poetic composition. As a metaphor makes us skip tracks and creates its own space of appearance, so does music let us drift into a radical reorientation of time. Any child who plays a wrong note at a recital and wails "Wait!" knows, as he or she plunges back into the merely real time of the quotidian world, that a spell has been broken; a musical mood is a metaphorical equivalent of such a spell.

In Schopenhauer's description, too, regardless of its mysticism, the transposition of form from earth to music to words is one of successive analogies. The proximal relation is established and then temporally explored, just as a melody has an actuality and transcendence from its circumstances but is revealed only in the actual conditions of listening and attending to its unfolding. Yet the analogy between the abstracted and immanent form is, to continue in the vein of Verlaine, one of penetration—the listener's experience of time is formed concretely by the abstracted form, and that form is realized in being "played" in its own "measure." One of Verlaine's own lyrics, "Art poétique," begins, "De la musique avant toute chose, / Et pour cela préfère l'Impair / Plus vague et plus soluble dans l'air, / Sans rien en lui qui pèse ou qui pose" (Music before anything else, and for that choose uneven meters—the more vague and the more melting in air, with nothing heavy or fixed).

As Nietzsche follows in the footsteps of the poet about to make poems, the inchoate and nonappearing, nonfigural and so nonspecific sense of such a musical mood is paramount. It is an idea with which we are familiar from other poems. For example, Lorenzo's lines (83–88) of act 5, scene 1 of *The Merchant of Venice*:

> The man that hath no music in himself,
> Nor is not mov'd with concord of sweet sounds,
> Is fit for treasons, stratagems, and spoils;
> The motions of his spirit are dull as night,
> And his affections dark as Erebus:
> Let no such man be trusted. . . .

The poet's suggestibility is precisely what opens him or her to emotion and the motions of spirit, making a world harmony potential. Yet here, too, what is internalized shapes the spirit and comes from a relation of sympathy. Music arrives in fact already shaped by its moods or modes. As Plato outlined in book 3 (398–99) of the *Republic*, the different emotional states produced by each mode—the melancholy Lydian, the soporific Ionian, the fortifying Dorian, the prudence-inspiring Phrygian—are attached to cities and characterize their spaces, much as Heidegger claimed that particular ages are characterized by particular moods.

(Pamuk's Ka, meanwhile, rushes back to his hotel room and writes out his poem as it comes to him, word by word, in a flash of inspiration. When, like Coleridge writing "Kubla Khan," he is interrupted before he finishes by a knock at the door, he has two lines to go and never again can recover them by deliberative means.)

Before we decide that poetic thought is different from other thoughts, let's remember, however, that all thoughts arise or come to us. We cannot will a thought; in this sense, we are not the authors of our thoughts, and when we say a thought belongs to us, we'd be hard put to make that claim independently of having uttered or spoken the thought. And thought itself can be felt; we feel the activity of thought in something of the way—to choose a metaphor encountered frequently—a quickening is felt in the womb. Indeed, even Antoine Arnauld's Port Royal Logic of 1662, *The Art of Thinking*, so hostile on theological grounds to the argument that ideas originate in the senses, talks about the nature and origin of ideas as a treatise on "conception." There he concedes that "we say an idea originates in the senses . . . when some sense-induced excitation in the brain stimulates the mind to form an idea the mind would not otherwise have formed."[51]

All thought may arrive by the quickening of such an impulse, but as we have seen, some thought is directed toward particular ends. As Aristotle distinguished between contemplative and deliberative thought, the thinking that Arnauld and Kant are describing is bound up with such concerns as cause, quality, quantity, and modality that drive the impulse to think through and arrive at another perspective. A musical mood has no content. It thinks within and around rather than through; time and melody unfold in sequence but without attributable cause, and the subordination of content to sound and rhythm moves content closer to the sounds and rhythms of the living world.

Every poem moves by the propulsion and rhythm of a speaker's intake and outtake of breath. We are the organs that make the music here, and when we play musical instruments or use our pens to write poems on paper, we extend by prosthesis the capacities of voice and breath that are ours by birth. Lyric poetry has in its very etymology the presence of musical accompaniment, and even when such accompaniment is no longer used, lyric necessarily internalizes music. Still, though musical conventions proper have been applied to our sense of poetry's "musicality," they don't necessarily overlap with poetry's meter. It is not that some speech is organized rhythmically and other speech is not. Victor Zuckerkandl has suggested that "melody and harmony are essentially musical phenomena, native to the world of tone and not to be found elsewhere—the adjectives derived from these terms can be applied only metaphorically outside the realm of music. But rhythm is a truly universal phenomenon. . . . Rhythm is one manifestation," he says, of "the reign of law throughout the universe."[52] We find ourselves again swept up by rhythm, derived not only from wind and water and moving forces of all kinds but also from the beating of our hearts and the pulsing race of our blood, from the back-and-forth movement of our eyes and the regular blinking of our eyelids, from the patterned jittering of our nerves and other dimensions of what Walt Whitman called "the body electric." Things hum and we hum with them.

Making particular rhythms, in contrast to being swept up by them, involves volition, yet because those very rhythms come to inhabit us as soon as we transitively engage them, it also involves a compromise between what the poet wills and what the meter needs. And the experience of making rhythms and the experience of hearing are at odds in the sense that—unlike listening or making patterns of sound—hearing does not necessarily involve the will. We can close our eyes and withhold ourselves from touch, but our ears remain open to the world. We might remember that when the Sirens sang, Odysseus, whose name *outis* can mean not only "no one" but also "big ears," had to be tied to the mast for this very reason.

In the same passages regarding music that we considered above, Schopenhauer has suggested that "rhythm and rhyme are partly a means of holding our attention, because we willingly follow the poem read, and partly they produce in us a blind consent to what is read prior to any judgment, and this gives the poem a certain emphatic power of convincing independent of all reasons."[53] Such a relation between the involuntary and voluntary in hearing is comically expressed in the beginning of one of Nietzsche's own "rhymes," as he called them: "Dichters Berufung," or "The Poet's Call." It comes from his series with the ambiguous title "Songs of Prince Vogelfrei"—the songs of a prince who is free as a bird but also a renegade or outlaw, and so determined by the law in his unfreedom. This is the opening of "The Poet's Call":

Als ich jüngst, mich zu erquicken,
Unter dunklen Bäumen saß,
Hört' ich ticken, leise ticken,
Zierlich, wie nach Takt und Maß.
Böse wurd' ich, zog Gesichter,—
Endlich aber gab ich nach,
Bis ich gar, gleich einem Dichter,
Selber mit im Tiktak sprach.

and here is Walter Kaufmann's witty translation of these lines:

In the woods upon the ground,
I was sitting at my leisure
When a distant ticking sound
Seemed to beat an endless measure.

I got mad, began to show it,
There was nothing I could do,
Until I, just like a poet,
Spoke in that strange ticktock, too.[54]

As Keats responded to the nightingale, here Nietzsche tells how he came to internalize and reproduce the distant tick-tocking of a woodpecker. Invocation leads to repetition, repetition leads to rhythm, and rhythm leads to an order of words—the repetition of the woodpecker's ticktock becomes the speaking of a "strange ticktock"—a ticktock that *means*. If we sound like insects when we hum and like birds when we sing, we can also imagine that insects and birds sound like us, but it is to other responding beings that we send the sounds we make.

Poetic rhythm is made of sounds, but sounds in poems tend to take on color and light and tactile qualities of brittleness and smoothness—a wide range of sensual associations can come to mind with particular sounds and sound clusters. Alertness and absorption and transport are conditions or states of mind that do not necessarily require attention to the outlines or limits of any objects. The concern of eighteenth-century aestheticians such as Baumgarten with the dynamic between clear and confused ideas and Kant's interest in moments when the imagination and understanding are suspended or blocked make for convincing descriptions of what is happening at the onset of poetry's musical mood. States of poetic intensity also suspend the separation of the transitive and intransitive—they are liminal or threshold experiences where agency and receptivity, will and compulsion, are inseparable.

Rests and silences in music and poetry, like negative space in visual art, are also form giving. When we say poetry is organized in lines, we are thinking of units of time and space that are both finite and capable of being broken, through caesuras, or of being carried over, through enjambment. So a line can be opened or extended, but it also lends itself to turning and turning back. Given the subjective basis of all orientation in thought, we are turning ourselves as we turn the line, and one way to think about what happens within the frame of a stanza or the frame of a poem as a whole is to consider the sequence of turns that take place there. As Augustine, in meditating on what it was like to read one of

St. Ambrose's hymns aloud, famously described those unfolding poetic turns as central to our concept of the unfolding of the past, present, and future,[55] we could in fact read the history of poetry as the dialectical history of sets of emotional turns that turn out to be, or turn into, cognitive turns as well—from the simplest movement between narrative and song in cante-fable to the two- and three-part turns of sonnet forms, to the multiple turns and twists of baroque and metaphysical poetry. And then we would find poets looking again to song and refrain structures, for it seems poets can build their work to a certain amount of complexity and then must move back to the clarity of simple forms in order to renew their practice.

Musical moods, whether we hold to a Dionysian poetics or not, characterize moments of nonalienation between the physical experience of the world and the mind's reaching after what it cannot grasp. What is perhaps even more remarkable is that such moods lead to the creation of poems that themselves can produce musical moods.[56]

4 / FREEDOM FROM IMAGINATION

I se that makaris amang the laif
Playis heir ther pageant, syne gois to graif;
Sparit is nocht ther faculte;
Timor mortis conturbat me.

—WILLIAM DUNBAR, "Lament for the Makaris"

I see them all so excellently fair,
I see, not feel, how beautiful they are.

—SAMUEL TAYLOR COLERIDGE, "Dejection: An Ode"

I Composing Anxiety

The unobligated expression of praise—that is, praise untied to any exterior motivation or reward—is, as we have seen, one of the most fundamentally free of all the poet's free acts. Yet praise arises as a response to a preexisting phenomenon and so, for better or worse, is always bound to an object. In more secular contexts, and composing out of and against the inchoate feelings of moods, makers no longer have the thing before them but proceed, as experiences of emotional states proceed, by either releasing or clarifying in time what begins as feeling, outline, or touch. The poets of British Romanticism were intensely preoccupied with the possibilities of composing by mood and its problematic relation to originary phenomena. For example, from childhood forward, William Wordsworth needed to touch things in order to be sure of their reality, lighting down on walls and trees as players light on "base" in their games. In a note dictated to Isabella Fenwick in 1843, he testified to this early feeling:

> I was often unable to think of external things as having external existence, and I communed with all that I saw as something not apart from, but inherent in, my own immaterial nature. Many times while going to school

> have I grasped at a wall or tree to recall myself from this abyss of idealism to the reality. . . . In later periods of life I have deplored, as we have all reason to do, a subjugation of an opposite character, and have rejoiced over the remembrances, as is expressed in the lines [142–44 of his "Ode: Intimations of Immortality from Recollections of Early Childhood"]—
>
> "Obstinate questionings
> Of sense and outward things,
> Fallings from us, vanishings;" etc.[1]

Throughout much of his writing, the further Wordsworth might be from the reality of things, the vaguer his images—a problem he himself explained in *The Prelude* of 1850 (at line 160):

> —Of that external scene which round me lay,
> Little, in this abstraction, did I see.

Beginning with the division of labor he and Coleridge decided upon in their joint composition of the 1798 *Lyrical Ballads*, where Coleridge took responsibility for the supernatural lyrics and Wordsworth for those rooted in reality yet "viewed through an imaginative medium," Wordsworth's tactile empiricism stands in stark contrast to Coleridge's otherworldly symbolism.[2] Wordsworth explicitly critiques Coleridge in this regard in book 6 of *The Prelude* II, lines 305–16 of the 1805 text and lines 294–305 of the 1850 text, as he writes:

> I have thought
> Of thee, thy learning, gorgeous eloquence,
> And all the strength and plumage of thy youth,
> Thy subtle speculations, toils abstruse
> Among the schoolmen, and Platonic forms
> Of wild ideal pageantry, shaped out
> From things well-matched or ill, and words for things,
> The self-created sustenance of a mind
> Debarred from Nature's living images,
> Compelled to be a life unto herself,
> And unrelentingly possessed by thirst
> Of greatness, love, and beauty.[3]

These are high thirsts, but the criticism is clear: "the self-created sustenance of a mind" that is "a life unto herself," despite its independent powers of form making, is bound to suffer a certain stasis and distance from nature. These thoughts were hardly news to Coleridge, and yet in one of the great Romantic odes on emotion, the poem we now call the "Dejection Ode," Coleridge turns this Wordsworthian dilemma back on itself, narrating how he suffers in the face of a nature he can apprehend only objectively and not by means of his imagination. In this poem we find ample testimony as to how the imagination can be both a source and an impediment to artistic freedom.

In much of his work, Coleridge was driven to ask the question "How can I know I am alive?" This is not, perhaps, a very interesting question for those of us who don't have to bother to ask it. But out of his acute physical and mental suffering, Coleridge obsessively returned to the problem of the inspiriting of his body and the possible sources for such animation. In 1802, the year of the composition of the Dejection Ode, he wrote to William Godwin: "My ideas, wishes, and feelings are to a diseased degree disconnected from *motion* and *action*."[4] In October 1803, he wrote in his Notebooks, "I write melancholy, always melancholy: You will suspect that it is the fault of my natural Temper. Alas! no.—This is the great Occasion that my Nature is made for Joy—impelling me to Joyance—& I never, never can yield to it.—I am a genuine *Tantalus*."[5] And in 1810 in his journal *The Friend*, he wrote about his baffled relation to being itself: "The very words,—There is nothing!, or,—There was a time, when there was nothing! are self-contradictory. . . . Not TO BE, then, is impossible: TO BE, incomprehensible. The power, which evolved this idea of BEING, BEING in its essence, BEING limitless, comprehending its own limits in its dilatation, and condensing itself into its own apparent mounds—how shall we name it?"[6]

Here is Coleridge's long-standing concern with a notion he often referred to as "the abyss of being." This abyss was the "depthless depth" out of which creation was made of nothing and perhaps borrows from the abyss of freedom described, as we saw earlier, in Schelling's 1809 essay on the essence of human freedom. Coleridge, like the Jena circle before him, also drew directly on the concept from the writings of the mystic Jakob Boehme, who wrote of "the Darkness that is the Bearer of all Light. But it is peculiar to God that he hath the ground of *his* Existence within himself."[7] The evidence of being is its very incomprehensibility; the impossibility of nonbeing is evidenced by the ever-present activity of a being that knows itself through its exercise of itself and its capacity for withdrawal and self-formation. Analogously, the physical effort of composing poetry conveys knowledge of the maker as a living being among other living beings and provides relief, in Coleridge's case, from the feeling of disembodiment that gives rise to such a question in the first place. In the Dejection Ode, instability and restlessness, interrupted by a leaden immobility—the results of Coleridge's ill health and the pattern of stimulation and withdrawal consequent to his opium taking—find their expression in a dynamic and divagating form.

It may be helpful to remember how the argument of the Dejection Ode develops and especially how, although the poem does not closely follow a Pindaric three-part progression of turn, counterturn, and stand, Coleridge makes extensive use of the Greek form's openness and irregularity. In overall structure, the speaker charts a path from dejection to joy, and along the way he narrates the progress of a raging storm that eventually produces a sense of calm in the speaker himself.[8] In the initial strophe the speaker waits for such a night storm, hoping it might "startle [his] dull pain and make it move and live." In II he sees the beauty of the phenomena of the night sky, but, as our epigraph records, he can only see, not *feel*, how beautiful they are. In III, what would conventionally be the first epode, he concludes that his dejected state is what impedes his feeling and that he "may not hope from outward forms to win / The passion and the life, whose fountains are within." In the next strophe, IV, he turns to an interlocutor, saying, "We receive but what we give." He names the soul as the source of several goods: a light, a glory, and a luminous cloud enveloping the earth; he awaits as well the birth of "a sweet and potent voice." In the antistrophe to this, V, he explains that the light, glory, and cloud are forms of joy and that such joy enables us to rejoice "in ourselves." But in the next section, VI, which could be viewed as a second epode, he draws back from happiness, explaining that in the past he had been able to feel joy even in the face of distress, for he was able to maintain hope as a resource. But now he is troubled by afflictions, and his "abstruser research" of philosophy has become merely habitual. In consequence, he finds he can no longer feel. In VII he turns toward the external world again and announces that the storm he has been anticipating has by now long raved "unnoticed." He addresses an apostrophe to the wind. In the wind, he hears both the loud sounds of those suffering in war and the alternating moans and screams of a lost child. In the last stanza, VIII, spoken at midnight, he presents an apostrophe to Sleep and asks that a number of blessings be extended: that healing sleep visit his friend, that the storm be a "mountain birth," that the friend awaken with joy, and that all the life of all living things becomes the "eddying" of her "living soul." Then the speaker addresses an apostrophe to the friend herself: "thus" may she "ever, evermore rejoice." There is no concluding epode, adding to the sense that the speaker will not, as he did in the second epode, draw back from joy yet again.[9]

Coleridge is a poet who often depicts himself or his speakers/protagonists as awake while others are asleep or dead, as if to emphasize that his thoughts and imagination are at work while the rest of humanity is dreaming or lacks consciousness—such scenes can be found, for example, in "Inside the Coach," "To a Friend," "The Rime of the Ancient Mariner," "Christabel," "Parliamentary Oscillators," "Lewti," "Frost at Midnight," "An Ode to the Rain," and "The Pains of Sleep." In these situations, however, the poet/speaker faces the problem of the absence of intersubjective recognition: the mind feeds on itself and has no external interlocutor. And so in the Dejection Ode, in addition to the poem's apostrophes to the wind and Sleep, the speaker constantly changes the identity of his phantom listener. Consider the five versions that exist of the following single line—line 295 in "A Letter to ____" and line 48 of the Dejection Ode:

O Sara! we receive but what we give (manuscripts, April 1802)
O Wordsworth! we receive but what we give (letter to Sotheby, July 1802)
O Edmund! we receive but what we give (*Morning Post* version, October 1802)
O William! we *receive* but what we give (letter to Beaumont, August 1803)
O Lady! we receive but what we give (*Sibylline Leaves* edition, 1817)[10]

Although critics and biographers have attended to the resourceful ambiguity of Coleridge's writing of a love letter to one Sara (Hutchinson) while he was unhappily married to another Sara (Fricker Coleridge), transpositions of many kinds can be found in all the various editions and fragments of the poem. Wordsworth is apostrophized by first and last names when Coleridge is writing to another William, William Sotheby. And when the poem was published in a public newspaper, the unattributed name Edmund is added to mask the identities of both Sara Hutchinson, who was the recipient of a love letter that served as the prototype for the poem, and Wordsworth, her brother-in-law. This publication was on October 4, 1802, the day Wordsworth married Mary Hutchinson and the seventh anniversary of Coleridge's own wedding. By 1817, once Wordsworth and Coleridge grew estranged, the addressee became the generalized "O Lady." The poem's publication history thereby traces its path from private feeling to an abstracted public audience. Details from the original "A Letter to ___" make their way into "The Day Dream," which then is given the subtitle "From an Emigrant to His Absent Wife" when it, too, is published in the *Morning Post* fifteen days later.[11]

We can also see that the economy of borrowings and loans, not only between Coleridge's earlier and later versions but also between Wordsworth and Coleridge, comes into relief against a vast process of commensurable and incommensurable substitutions.[12] Although Coleridge signed some variants STC, the *Morning Post* version, which appeared under the journal's title *ORIGINAL POETRY*, was signed with the Greek pseudonym he sometimes used: ΕΣΤΗΣΕ. The effect after so much flux and substitution is to underline the effort and the establishment of a printed text with this transitive (aorist) term—"he decreed (it)" or "thus (it) stands or was established"—in the place of the signature. Strophe, antistrophe, epode, or turn, counterturn, and stand—here a set of versions and a speaking subject turn and counterturn until the "signature" declaims the final stand as an expression of will.[13]

Coleridge begins his poem by suffering from a lack of feeling, and the completed Dejection Ode can be said to address this initial problem by means of its outpouring of mutations, transpositions, and turns of many kinds. Yet agitation is not inspiration, and it is only by means of stand or finality that the work of the ode can be accomplished. Here we find a deep analogy between composing artworks and composing the emotions. In the *Biographia Literaria*'s discussion of Pindar,[14] in "Devonshire Roads," where Coleridge writes, "The indignant Bard compos'd this furious ode," in "my spirit I to love compose" from "The Pains of Sleep," in Dorothy Wordsworth's journals,[15] and in other discursive records of Romanticism such as William Hazlitt's famous account of Coleridge saying "he himself liked to compose in walking over uneven ground, or breaking through the struggling branches of a copse-wood,"[16] *to compose* is the verb applied to the making of poems.[17]

Consider the many meanings of *compose*—a bringing together of disparate parts to produce calm and tranquillity, as in composing one's thoughts or feelings; a making up or combining of elements to produce an integrated form; an arranging or setting down, as in composing type in printing or composing music on paper.[18] Yet Coleridge plaintively states that the aim of his ode is "to startle this dull pain, to make it move and live!" He is *composing* an ode on and to *dejection*—and dejection as a throwing or casting down is the very counterforce to the activity of making that composition involves.

In these withdrawing and extending gestures of composition, the birth imagery of the traditional English ode that we explored earlier is specifically linked to the qualities of the dilating and contracting moon. Coleridge's Dejection Ode is under the moon's feminine transformations and not the sun's fixed radiance. And Pindaric rhythmic postures of extending and retreating groups of lines are the aural equivalent of such visual waxing and waning. Remember that for Coleridge this was the account of being itself: "comprehending its own limits in its dilatation, and condensing itself into its own apparent mounds—how shall we name it?" Resolved at the hinge of midnight, the poem is lit by a moon that bears the past in its new crescent arm—the infant is holding the parent and the forecast is doom. Yet this visual image is countered by the poem's reigning aural image—the terrible screams of the wind that has within it the sound of past wars and the lay of the child. Like many other Pindarics, including Wordsworth's Intimations Ode, the Dejection Ode juxtaposes a spoken pentameter line with interjected trimeter and tetrameter lines that evoke singing and shouting. If a poet hopes to create the effects of distant sounds within a circling wind, this is the form to use.

The title "Dejection: An Ode" implies a causal and temporal relation where the feeling precedes the form. And Coleridge's refusal to specify which of the ode's traditional prepositions is dominant—is the poem "on" or "to" its object?—also serves his need to make composition transitive, carrying it over into psychological experience.[19] As touch is transitive and intransitive at once, feeling can be both "on" and "to." We could say that Coleridge is further demonstrating that the passivity of inspiration will not suffice to enable what must *transpire* as living motion so that the mountain birth can create the re-joicing self. The struggle to feel when only seeing is possible becomes, in the apostrophe, the struggle to see when only feeling is possible.

In addition to his erotic and filial substitutions of interlocutors, consider some of the other changes Coleridge made in his various versions: *grand* as *dear*; *cloud* as *clouds*; *moans* as *drones*; *upon* as *amid*; *were* as *was*; *by* as *with*; *raised* as *roused*; *dark* as *dull*; *peculiar* as *celestial*; *cloudless, starless* as *starless, cloudless*; *craig* as *crag*; *bitter* as *utter*; *yule* as *yell*; *Devils'* as *devils*; *impulse* as *influence*; *her* as *him*; *her* as *his*; *she* as *he*; *her her* as *his his*; *it doth* as *doth it*; *exist* as *subsist*; *flows* as *comes*.[20] His permutations include singulars into plurals, discrete sounds becoming homonyms, female possessives turned to male possessives, orders reversed, and alterations of propinquity and scale. And he also effects a number of circular, reversing repetitions in the poem, signaled by the initial chiasmus as he describes the moon: "and overspread with phantom light, / (With swimming phantom light o'erspread) / But rimmed and circled by a silver thread." What matters is not the final choice but, as in much of Wordsworth's work, the obsessive process of revision and alteration in itself and for itself as evidence of motion and vitality—evidence of the living mind producing, as Kant called them, aesthetical ideas or symbols.[21]

In the *Critique of the Power of Judgment*, Kant describes "aesthetical ideas" as contents that have a richness exceeding any rules—such ideas are representations "of the imagination associated with a given concept, which is connected with such a manifold of partial representations in the free use of that faculty that no expression designating a determinate concept can be found, which therefore adds much that cannot be named to a concept, [and] the feeling of which quickens the cognitive faculty."[22] At this point the operative concept of the imagination, and particularly the one relied upon by Kant, is that of a visual presentation alone and one that is a precondition for the constitution of space. The consequence of this emphasis on the imagination as quite literally an image-making faculty is that seeing is separated from other senses, such as feeling. And it is difficult as well to move from the production of visual images in space—a device—to cognition. As I have noted, in reflective judgments of the kind we use in creating new scientific knowledge or in apprehending aesthetic experiences, the visual presentation cannot be brought under the understanding's existing categories. In consequence, a new category must be created, as in scientific judgments, or a free play between the imagination and the understanding will follow, with neither dominating the other, as in the judgment of beauty, or the imagination will be halted at the threshold of the understanding and hence blocked from any relation, as in the judgment of sublimity.

In accounting for works of genius, which in Kant's system do not come under the work of aesthetic judgments, Kant solves this dilemma by assuming that the central concepts of aesthetical ideas will be concepts of the reason—intellectual ideas such as virtues, vices, and heaven and hell. Thus works of art offer a general experience of freedom of the imagination, one that can envision the moral freedom of the will. And such works as well illustrate ideas of the reason, bypassing the already existing concepts of the understanding and so protecting the imagination's freedom. Further, in the presence of a work of genius, the receiver of an artwork has an insight into the cooperation between nature and human will that results in what we know as artistry.[23]

The schematizing function of the Kantian imagination is reproductive, organizing and giving sequence to sense intuition, helping us to form wholes. In contrast, the productive imagination has a role in that transcendental synthesis that gives us an impression of continuity in experience, forming the pure understanding. Without the a priori productive imagination, we would be bombarded by sense particulars and lack understanding in general. Without the reproductive imagination, we would have no means of forming objects and would lack understanding in particular.

Relying heavily on these Kantian frames, Coleridge developed his own theory of the imagination—distinguishing first between the fancy and the imagination, then, later, between the primary and secondary imagination as he struggled to explain the difference between mere sensual associations and transformations and what he called the "esemplastic" or synthetic power of imaginative freedom.[24] As he continued, relying on his reading of German thinkers, to build these concepts into a theory of the symbol, he envisioned the play of imaginative associations and substitutions as a means of penetrating to abstract truths. He wrote in 1816 in *The Statesman's Manual*, "A symbol . . . is characterized by a translucence of the special in the individual, or of the general in the special, or of the universal in the general; above all by the translucence of the eternal in and through the temporal. It always partakes of the reality which it renders intelligible; and while it enunciates the whole, abides itself as a living part in that unity of which it is the representative."[25] For Coleridge, one function of the symbol is to synthesize perceptions into ideas and simultaneously make ideas flesh. This realized synthesis could produce the kind of incarnation promised in the Dejection Ode by Coleridge's hope for a *mountain birth*—a term particularly linked to the idea of a "glory" or reflection of the self projected back in the light of a mountain mist as a shadow rimmed with light.

In the "Aids to Reflection" Coleridge explains that a "glory" is "a Phænomenon not very uncommon in Mountainous Countries, when the Air is filled with subtle particles of frozen Snow, and the person is walking with the sun at his back, his Shadow is projected on the invisible Snow-mist, at a moderate distance before him, and leads the way with a Painter's Glory round its head."[26] The image appears as well in Wordsworth's *Prelude* and in Coleridge's poem "Constancy to an Ideal Object." The "glory" of the Dejection Ode thereby is a visual echo in human form of the silver-rimmed spreading shape of the new moon. Yet more broadly, for the Romantics, such a "glory," partaking of reality and indicating the eternal, was scientific or physical evidence of our dwelling in the "light and life" of being. In his explanation of the glory in his notes for "Constancy to an Ideal Object," Coleridge states that "Pindar's fine remark respecting the different effects of music on different characters holds equally true of Genius, as many as are not delighted by it are disturbed, perplexed, irritated. The beholder either recognizes it *as a projected form of his own being, that moves before him with a glory round its head*, or recoils from it as a spectre."[27] The nimbus or *perigraphé* of this figure dominates its content, as form creates the possibility of iteration under other terms and natural cycles regulate the leaps and gaps of historical time. Coleridge here has conflated a set of remarkable metaphors—the mountain glory around the head of the poetic genius; the Pindaric celebration of the "crown-bearing" contest where the athlete's only official prize is a wreath, regardless of other honors and later premiums that are offered;[28] and the "crowning" of second-stage childbirth where the child's head appears and the cries of labor are about to turn to expressions of joy at the subsequent cries of the child.[29] Written throughout the course of Sara Fricker Coleridge's pregnancy, the Dejection Ode would appear a few months before the birth of another Sara, his daughter, in Christmas 1802. In this poem, the generation of symbols annuls any division between subject and object. The mountain glory comes to life literally as the projecting of a perceiving subject "crowned" by his dynamic and thought relation to what he apprehends.

Under any mandate of "emotion recollected in tranquility" as a means of reconstructing the knowledge of emotion, Romantic poetry is almost always in a belated relation to emotion itself and involves a dynamic tension between presence and absence, suppression and recollection. The Dejection Ode especially pursues the Coleridgean task of merging opposites and joining reason with emotions. The central problem of the poem, the problem of the protagonist who can only see, not feel, and realizes that "outward forms" cannot create the liveliness that must come from "within," is resolved via the "shaping spirit of the imagination." What was stalled in the speaker is animated by composing itself. In a Kantian formula he often repeated in the *Biographia Literaria*, Coleridge wrote that the artist must "out of his own mind create forms according to the severe laws of the intellect, in order to generate in himself that co-ordination of freedom and law, that involution of obedience in the prescript, and of the prescript in the impulse to obey, which assimilates him to nature, and enables him to understand her. He merely absents himself for a season from her, that his own spirit, which has the same ground with nature, may learn her unspoken language in its main radicals, before he approaches to her endless compositions of them."[30] It was through such composition that body could become mind, and it was via symbols that Coleridge hoped to limn the universal out of the particulars of his experience.

II The Free Work of Symbols

The Enlightenment dream that freedom and imagination are productively yoked to one another and the consequent Romantic theory of the symbol as a synthesis of the particular and the universal have an obvious appeal to the poet who is their magus. Yet the history of the Western concept of the imagination is more ambivalent than triumphant. Visual imaginative powers especially are seen as positive and aural powers far more neutral or negative. Remembering music without a sensual stimulus is surely one of the greatest of human gifts. But a claim to hear purely imaginary voices and sounds is not of quite the same status as a claim to see visions, and the persistent legends of poetic inspiration by ear still link the poet's fantasies to madness.

Plato's view of imaginative art as producing imitations of imitations led to a claim that the imagination leads to deceptions of many kinds.[31] Epicurus and Lucretius saw their primary task as purging the fear of death by taming overheated imaginative powers. And in the oddly secular, that is, only implicitly Christian, *Consolation* of Boethius we find a similar claim that the fear of death can be assuaged by reason alone.[32] As Philip Sidney's *Defence of Poetry* contends that the imagination allows us to create another nature,[33] modern rationalists of all kinds have continued to view imagination and its corollary, memory, as threats to reason; Descartes, in particular, is suspicious of both.

Joseph Addison's pathbreaking survey, *The Pleasures of the Imagination*, appeared in eleven essays in June and July 1712 issues of *The Spectator*. As he completed his studies of the imagination's benefits, Addison realized some uncomfortable truths: first, that the imagination has limits—it is not capacious enough for some objects of "extraordinary grandeur or minuteness";[34] and, second, that the imagination has no particular obligation to produce pleasure. He explains: "The imagination is as liable to pain as pleasure. When the brain is hurt by any accident, or the mind disordered by dreams or sickness, the fancy is overrun with wild dismal ideas and terrified with a thousand hideous monsters of its own framing." Addison makes no distinction between fanciful flights of the imagination and its synthesizing powers, and he concludes: "There is not a sight in nature so mortifying as that of a distracted person when his imagination is troubled and his whole soul disordered and confused. Babylon in ruins is not so melancholy a spectacle."[35] In the end, Addison attributes to God the power to excite images in the mind—whether "beautiful and glorious visions" or "ghastly specters and apparitions." Turning to Milton's claim that "the mind is its own place," he explains that "God can so exquisitely ravish or torture the soul through this single faculty as might suffice to make up the whole heaven or hell of any finite being."[36]

Empiricists, however, have proved to be more predisposed to imagination, for otherwise they have no way of explaining how experience can be continuous. David Hume worried, after Addison, about the effects of the imagination. He wrote in 1739, "The memory, senses, and understandings are . . . all of them founded on the imagination, or the vivacy of our ideas. No wonder a principle so inconstant and fallacious should lead us into errors," and concluded that "nothing is more dangerous to reason than flights of the imagination and nothing has been the occasion of more mistakes among philosophers."[37] Yet in the writings published as *Philosophical Essays concerning Human Understanding* of 1748, he also wrote in a more positive frame, concluding that "nothing is more free than the faculty of the imagination."[38]

In the extant student notes from Kant's 1784 lectures on moral philosophy, we find a similar caveat about association: "If [a man] does not have himself under control, his imagination has free play; he cannot discipline himself, but is carried away by it, according to the laws of association, since he willingly yields to the senses; if he cannot restrain them, he becomes their plaything, and his judgment is determined by the senses."[39] As Coleridge was eventually to turn away from the associative powers of the fancy, Kant here discerns that the purely substitutive powers of the imagination's free play can disperse significance rather than, like the symbol, concentrate it. The expanding forces of similes and the fancy and the concentrating forces of the symbol are not merely contrasting powers of mind; they also are posed in a dynamic and sequential relation that repeats the diffuse, associative work of mood prior to the focus of composition. Conversely, once symbols break down or dissolve into mere parts, they lose their aura and must be replaced by new symbols.

Yet Kant's "lost soul," plaything of the imagination's flights, has more at stake than the symbolic. As Epicurus, Lucretius, and Boethius all warned, we find here the recurring maxim that the imagination turns painful when it turns to death, for if imaginative powers give sequential form to sense particulars, including our experience of the continuity of our own existence, such powers can, too, pose the dissolution of finitude, along the way stocking otherworlds, afterlifes, and other supersensible domains with objects of dread and fear.

Coleridge's Dejection Ode narrates the mind's rebirth by means of the feeling and thinking involved in processes of composing; Percy Shelley's 1816 "Hymn to Intellectual Beauty," published by his friend Leigh Hunt in 1817, is a retrospective poem that traces the subordination of an out-of-control imaginative faculty to a respect for nature and persons. In structure, it can be seen to follow the order of the classical hymns we considered earlier: the Homeric hymns (which Shelley would himself take up as a translation project in 1820) and the Hellenistic hymns of Callimachus and Cleanthes. In Shelley's poem, the first four strophes constitute an exordium; strophe 5, the exposition; and the last two strophes, the peroration.

Shelley uses a twelve-line form, rhyming *abbaaccbddee*, that, though somewhat indebted to Horace's homostanzaic odes, seems to be his own invention. His poem begins, appropriately enough for a hymn, with a set of apostrophes to the divinity. We can see the first two strophe/stanzas as an initiating "call" to Intellectual Beauty, which, although "unseen," makes its presence known:[40]

1

The awful shadow of some unseen Power
        Floats though unseen amongst us,—visiting

> This various world with as inconstant wing
> As summer winds that creep from flower to flower.—
> Like moonbeams that behind some piny mountain shower,
> It visits with inconstant glance
> Each human heart and countenance;
> Like hues and harmonies of evening,—
> Like clouds in starlight widely spread,—
> Like memory of music fled,—
> Like aught that for its grace may be
> Dear, and yet dearer for its mystery.

At this opening moment, we might wonder where we are in time and space. We are in the present tense, but the visual field is unstable. When we view the first lines—"The awful shadow of some unseen Power / Floats though unseen amongst us"—we are compelled to puzzle over whether the shadow is full of awe or fills those who see it with awe. What are we seeing when we see a shadow, and, to move things into an even more difficult register, what is the (presumably) seen shadow of an unseen Power? And how can the qualities of this Power turn out to be floating amongst us, though unseen? Twice we learn the Power is unseen; indeed, being unseen is the Power's defining quality, and despite its absence from the visual field, its floating amongst us is somehow revealed.

At this point we could express a complaint opposite to that of the Dejection Ode—we feel, but do not see, how beautiful the phenomena are. Many readers at this point might think of the most familiar, yet potentially awful, unseen power floating among us—that is, the wind. But we learn that the awful shadow not only floats but visits, and the wing of its visiting is as inconstant as summer winds that creep—*creep*, an oddly earthbound word to use for the wind and in this case indicating a stealthy motion from flower to flower.

To continue following the syntax, we must disentangle the noun *shower* from the verb *shower*—it is not that *it* visits with inconstant glance just as moonbeams behind a piny mountain shower do, but rather that the moonbeams *shower* behind the piny mountain in the same way that the awful shadow visits each human heart and countenance with inconstant glances. If we have a grasp of the likeness between floating wings and creeping winds, we will also be able to follow how this visiting is like hues and harmonies, that is, muted colors and concordant sounds, of evening and like clouds in starlight. The almost struggling pure stress tetrameter of the first three lines gives way to the more or less regular iambic pentameter of lines 4 and 5, followed by the fast-unfolding regular iambic tetrameter of lines 6 through 11 before the pentameter of line 12: *Dear* and yet *dear- er*. We must say the two syllables as spondees, and the sound echoes so that we hear the *mist* and *missed* in mystery.

If this first stanza describes Intellectual Beauty as a fleeting phenomenon that resembles other transient features of nature even as it seems to have some particular intention toward humankind, the second stanza opens with an apostrophe to that form of beauty:

> Spirit of BEAUTY, that dost consecrate
> With thine own hues all thou dost shine upon
> Of human thought or form,—where art thou gone?
> Why dost thou pass away and leave our state,
> This dim vast vale of tears, vacant and desolate?
> Ask why the sunlight not for ever
> Weaves rainbows o'er yon mountain-river,
> Why aught should fail and fade that once is shown,
> Why fear and dream and death and birth
> Cast on the daylight of this earth
> Such gloom,—why man has such a scope
> For love and hate, despondency and hope?

Although two years after his composition of the hymn, in 1818, Shelley used the term "Intellectual Beauty" in his own translation of Plato's *Symposium*, here his use of the phrase evidently came from the influence of Plotinus's *Enneads* upon his summer 1816 reading.

Specifically, Shelley would have found in the eighth tractate of the fifth ennead, "On Intellectual Beauty," a discussion of the artist looking to mental forms already present within himself as indications of the higher nature of his own soul as he travels from matter to the spiritual realm of the One. Plotinus further suggests that it is our habit of separation that falsely sets one order before another. He writes that such a separating intellect is contrary to the true intellect, which is both inseparable and unseparating—the true order is the order of being and the "universe of things"[41]—a phrase integral to Shelley's companion poem of the same period of summer 1816, "Mont Blanc." When Shelley indicates that we cannot by means of any cognitive let alone sensual apprehension know Intellectual Beauty, saying this unseen Power is "unknown," he also claims, by the very progress of the poem, that we can grasp such beauty's effects and move toward its source—beginning with its awe-inducing shadow. As the poem proceeds, this shadow falls several times on the speaker even as, by the poem's final and seventh section, the moment of shadowlessness—high noon—is past.

Edmund Spenser's 1596 *Four Hymnes*, classical adaptations that include his "Hymne of Heavenly Beauty," are models here,[42] and we would expect that a classical hymn would mention the gifts that are being brought to the god. But in Shelley's hymn, consonant to his final vow, a list of the deity's manifold gifts to humankind is given: the deity's colors; grace-giving and truth-giving light; its sublime voice; its potential for inspiring human immortality and omnipotence; and its sustaining nourishment. Shelley endows Intellectual Beauty with only two proper names: in the apostrophe of section 2, "Spirit of BEAUTY"; and in section 6, "O awful LOVELINESS." The poem thereby braces itself by means of two kinds of loveliness—the loveliness of beauty's free comparisons and the loveliness of human bonds and obligations—those forms of "Love, Hope, and Self-esteem" that are like clouds. First we saw clouds in section 1—"clouds in starlight widely spread," a phrase that makes it impossible to tell whether what is widely spread is the clouds or the starlight or both. The third stanza steps back to comment on the problem of names and responses before dissolving into further plays of comparisons. The appearance of a logical argument via "Therefore" is as fleeting as the appearances of the deity:

3
No voice from some sublimer world hath ever
　　To sage or poet these responses given—
　　Therefore the name of God & ghosts; and Heaven,

Remain the records of their vain endeavour:
Frail spells—whose utter'd charm might not avail to sever,
    From all we hear and all we see,
    Doubt, chance and mutability.
Thy light alone—like mist o'er mountains driven,
    Or music by the night-wind sent
    Through strings of some still instrument,
    Or moonlight on a midnight stream,
Gives grace and truth to life's unquiet dream.

In this critical section, Shelley explores the paradox that whereas human systems can confuse us, our encounters with mutability can compose us. Because sages and poets, including, we assume, the speaker, have never heard any voices from a sublimer world than this one, where Intellectual Beauty makes its occasional and fleeting appearance, they turn to God, ghosts, and heaven as modes of signifying these unheard realms. Such terms evoke only frail spells and doubt; chance and mutability remain features of our hearing and seeing. Only the light of Intellectual Beauty can give grace and truth to the troubled surface of reality.

What is that light like? Shelley returns to this question and now says that it is like mists driven over mountains, or like music sent through the "strings of some still instrument," such as an aeolian harp, without human agency, by only the night wind, or like moonlight on the surface of a stream at midnight. He multiplies the phenomena by analogy to other phenomena and at the same time collapses hearing into seeing and the silent into the invisible—the effect is a displacement of any empirical use of the senses, hence an effort toward the purely intellectual. We do not remain at the level of the similes' associative movement but must ask what these similes themselves are like. According to Shelley, if God, ghosts, and heaven represent the imagination's weakest powers, these transposed features of nature, which in the end appear as products of the poetic mind, represent its strongest powers.

4

Love, Hope, and Self-esteem, like clouds depart
    And come, for some uncertain moments lent.
    Man were immortal and omnipotent,

Didst thou, unknown and awful as thou art,
Keep with thy glorious train firm state within his heart.
    Thou messenger of sympathies,
    That wax and wane in lovers' eyes;
Thou—that to human thought art nourishment,
    Like darkness to a dying flame!
    Depart not as thy shadow came,
    Depart not—lest the grave should be,
Like life and fear, a dark reality.

Shelley ingeniously reverses the motion of clouds in this section by making them go and then come. With this simple transposition, "Love, Hope, and Self-esteem" retain their relation to uncertainty. Although it is always arriving, and both "unknown" and awe-evoking, Intellectual Beauty can keep a firm state in the human heart. Its relation to "human thought," however, is depicted in far more mutable and dynamic terms. As darkness feeds a dying flame, making it visible when it otherwise would disappear, so does Intellectual Beauty provide nourishment for thought. Shelley reaches a literal dead end at this point, as he imagines the flame of human thought going out at life's end. He implores the deity to remain so that the grave will not be, like "life and fear," a "dark reality."

The grave is metonymic to the word that is not here—the dark reality of death—and indeed it is not "like" death but *is* death. And the reality of death can only be *like* life and fear; the strange pairing of all of life with a particular emotion, the suggestion that fear follows life and is an outcome of it, adds to the inverted metaphor of darkness nourishing a dying flame. Shelley underlines the vast asymmetry between our endless substitution of metaphors for death and the literal irredeemable fact of death itself.

Shelley's hymn reaches its epitome as section 5's ending noise—the shrieking and clapping conversion—then leads, in section 6, to the poet's allusions to the dream and hope his own words cannot express: that Intellectual Beauty will free the world from its "dark slavery."

5
While yet a boy I sought for ghosts, and sped
    Through many a listening chamber, cave and ruin,

And starlight wood, with fearful steps pursuing
Hopes of high talk with the departed dead.
I called on poisonous names with which our youth is fed;
I was not heard; I saw them not;
When musing deeply on the lot
Of life, at that sweet time when winds are wooing
All vital things that wake to bring
News of buds and blossoming,
Sudden, thy shadow fell on me;
I shriek'd, and clasp'd my hands in ecstasy!

Here the twenty-four-year-old Shelley is describing his boyhood fascination with ghoulish notions and lifelong enjoyment of horror stories. When he was a child, he especially liked to scare his sisters with invented legends like "The Great Snake." And his biographer Richard Holmes records how just two years before, when Shelley, his wife Mary, and her sister Jane (Claire) Clairmont were together in London, Jane and Percy would stay up late frightening each other out of their wits. Narrating these "horror sessions," Holmes concludes that at this time the poet turned away from political sources of inspiration and yielded to psychological imagery and concerns. The poems describe heightened mental states, and an "aesthetic of terror" began to reign.[43] Two years later, however, with the shriek of fear transposed, Shelley awakened to the more "vital" powers of Intellectual Beauty.

6
I vow'd that I would dedicate my powers
To thee and thine: have I not kept the vow?
With beating heart and streaming eyes, even now
I call the phantoms of a thousand hours
Each from his voiceless grave: they have in vision'd bowers
Of studious zeal or love's delight
Outwatch'd with me the envious night—
They know that never joy illum'd my brow
Unlink'd with hope that thou wouldst free
This world from its dark slavery,

That thou, O awful LOVELINESS,
Wouldst give whate'er these words cannot express.

How will such a dream of Intellectual Beauty be sustained, if not realized? Not by claiming any material permanence but by traveling along the forms of matter to another state. These passages speak of Shelley's conversion to atheism, away from his boyhood beliefs in the poisoned names of conventional religion mentioned in the third strophe.[44] But Shelley also summons and redirects the "phantoms of a thousand hours"—the dead who have accompanied him in his nightly vigils before he turns again to his more recent belief in, and worship of, all manifestations of the fair spirit of Intellectual Beauty. If God, ghosts, and heavens are entities, Intellectual Beauty, or awful loveliness, is only fleetingly manifested in a range of phenomena and only fleetingly intuited by the prepared acolyte.

7
The day becomes more solemn and serene
When noon is past—there is a harmony
In autumn, and a lustre in its sky,
Which through the summer is not heard or seen,
As if it could not be, as if it had not been!
Thus let thy power, which like the truth
Of nature on my passive youth
Descended, to my onward life supply
Its calm, to one who worships thee,
And every form containing thee,
Whom, SPIRIT fair, thy spells did bind
To fear himself, and love all human kind.

Shelley's ingenious stanza form is one demonstration of such fleetingness—too brief for a sonnet, and so too early; he allows the *a* and *b* rhymes to linger into the ensuing couplets, breaking open the initial envelope structure, allowing the middle rhymes to lack any balance as they tip in and out of couplets; meanwhile the opening and ending quatrains juxtapose envelope structure to couplet structures. But the most remarkable device for representing mutability here is Shelley's anaphoric use of similes and substitutions. Let's look at these similes in the order in which they appear:

As summer winds that creep from flower to flower
Like moonbeams that behind some piny mountain shower
Like hues and harmonies of evening
Like clouds in starlight widely spread
Like memory of music fled
Like aught that for its grace may be
like mist o'er mountains driven
Or music by the night wind sent
Or moonlight on a midnight stream
like clouds depart
Like darkness to a dying flame

These are visual and, less often, aural images, for the most part taken from transient features of nature. Yet the transience is also a feature of perception—whether intermittently seen and heard or intermittently felt and thought—as strings of abstract emotions and concepts come and go, go and come, at once parts of nature and reflections on nature.

The poem echoes the issue of *natura naturans*—not nature as received, already created, but the active production of nature in nature that we can follow in the writings of Aristotle, Sidney, and Spinoza. In Kant's thought, too, as he writes in his discussion of aesthetical ideas, the productive imagination has the power to create, "as it were, another nature, out of the material which the real one gives it."[45] Such mutability, and ringing down of successive changes, extends as well to the various names and attributes of the deity: "awful shadow of some unseen Power"; "Spirit of BEAUTY"; "messenger of sympathies"; "nourishment" to "human thought"; "O awful LOVELINESS"; "SPIRIT fair."

It is not surprising that a hymn to a god would fear to name the god—the presentation of substitutions is a euphemistic practice that spares the acolyte the full power of the god's presence. In the presence of power, such as Mont Blanc's horrifying amoral magnitude, the imagination exercises its gentle force. The imagination can lend significance and comprehension to the vacancy of such sublime natural forms and hence overpower them. When Hume suggested that nothing is more free than the imagination, he was emphasizing that it need not admit impediment. To this extent, the imagination offers us a fantasy of making without violence. Making is imagining, imagining is making—a godlike power where wishes are indeed horses and beggars can ride.

But what is striking is the way Shelley indicates this origin of imaginative substitution in fear of the gods. He takes on not only the problem of origins but also the correlative problem of ends, the truth that looms over all sense certainty: we cannot have empirical knowledge of death, and so the powers of imagination with regard to death are potentially sources of poison—Shelley's God, ghosts, and heaven. This radical dismissal of Christian eschatology is not shaped by the poet's well-known and early adherence to atheism alone; it also acknowledges the imagination's confrontation with the ineluctable.

Meanwhile, the poem itself must necessarily come to a close, and Shelley decides upon an asymmetrical number of strophes as he draws back to a retrospective view and then ends with a promise that necessarily binds him to the future. This image of binding spells, so familiar from the final lines of Coleridge's "Kubla Khan," brings forward the powers of speech and books to contain the imagination and carry intentions into the future. Shelley, with his lifelong hope that the poetic imagination would prove a force of liberation in human history, is in this poem at the near point of the more general and enduring Enlightenment dream of the inherent freedom of the imagination and the imaginative potential of the free mind. Yet with its implicit acknowledgment that the poisoned names of the fear of death are at the root of imaginative energy, Shelley also taps the equally strong tradition of the imagination's perils.

How, then, can the imagination be the source of so many goods—the basis of our continuous sense of the self and the world, and of our ability to think and make plans, to form opinions and judge, to go beyond the limits of the senses and circumstance—and at the same time be the source of so many evils: obsession, for example, or delusion, or anxiety, or paranoia? Obsession demonstrates that the free play of imaginative substitution can readily become mere repetition; delusion gives evidence that the imagination has no interior faculty of judgment; anxiety realizes the prolific, unanchored emptiness of projection; and paranoia speaks inversely to the indeterminate aspects of causality—an endlessly associative form of retrospection. We might remember therefore that Kant's insights into how sublimity can ensue from a terror that does not pose a threat to our persons, and hence be a kind of pleasurable terror, are based on the assumption that in such situations the imagination is blocked.[46] When the imagination is not blocked in the company of fear, it feeds upon it—like, well, darkness to a flame.

Given all these ways in which the imagination's free play seems to be at our expense, what, then, do we mean when we say the imagination is a vehicle of freedom? We usually, but not always, mean that the imagination frees us from the limits of the senses, or, on a different scale, that the imagination frees us from the bonds of necessity. The immateriality of the imagination's powers is the quality most treasured when we are seeking such freedom, perhaps as a residue of those Neoplatonic notions that so influenced Shelley.

Here, too, then, we might return to the distinction between negative freedoms (freedoms from certain constraints or limits) and positive freedoms (freedoms that involve the creation or formation of as yet unanticipated states), for we can make a corresponding distinction between positive and negative forms of the imagination. But this distinction would seem truly to lack imagination, since the aims of imagination would be set from the start. Even secular moralists and censors may believe that there are good and bad imaginative powers and that our individual reason is capable not only of knowing the differences between them but also of regulating them. Failing that, such moralists might go on to assert that there are social powers, from education to law to force, that can be marshaled to set the imagination right. But the imagination is by definition an unregulated power—it makes freely of things, and indeed makes freely without things.

Further, if the basis of negative freedom is mere, and particular, reversal—that is, the overturning or canceling of boundaries—the limit of positive freedom, in contrast, is unintelligibility and all the lack of grounding unintelligibility might bring. Negative freedoms thereby have less potential than they may seem to have. And positive freedoms are inevitably restricted by their very lack of restrictions. Yet positive freedoms are wrested from the curse of incoherence at the point where they take shape, becoming forms. Ethics and aesthetics, though separated by their quite different consequences, here share in an open, sequential way of proceeding. We find, then, that beyond the imagination's contribution to our sense of continuity mentioned earlier, the imagination, as a device of the hypothetical, contributes as well to ethical judgments—as when, for example, we create and engage fictions and sharpen our abilities to picture, to people scenes, to forecast and reframe.

When we speak of forming freedom, we also indicate some of the differences between passive and active uses of the imagination. Perhaps the vexing way, in English, that we speak of "the imagination" more often than of acts of imagining reflects the passive dimension of our relation to imagining. Yet as we have seen, it is possible to surrender oneself to associations on the way toward unifying them into symbolic form—a power to entertain conditions of "as if" and "otherwise" retrospectively and proleptically—as the poem we have followed says, "as if it could not be," "as if it had not been!"[47]

In making, we exercise a free power of forging and judging, unencumbered by external constraints, on the one hand, and by any demand to establish finality of form prematurely, on the other. Forging and judging defend us against being completely carried or swept away by the force of mood and the open infinity of imagination. The central feature of form's boundedness is its reliance on repetition. To repeat is to bind, for the integrity of the phenomenon is assured by the promise of its repeatability. Form is an action considered by an action, a unity asserted in our ability to be conscious of it. Mood and the motion of the imagination cannot be controlled by the will, but their repetition can be.

Shelley's "as if it could not be," "as if it had not been," is a reminder that the liberating powers of Intellectual Beauty are all the more evident in climates where they are invisible. His exclamation bears a poignant resemblance to Kant's political utopianism, with its assertion that the end of wild freedom is the beginning of an order of perpetual peace. And as Jean-Marie Schaeffer has suggested, we can find an inherent utopian dimension to Kant's aesthetics as well: "The experience of finality without representation of any end shows us that the ultimate identity of the phenomenal world and the noumenal world, while it is inaccessible to the phenomenal world, is not a mere chimera. In other words, through the experience of finality without representation of an end we experience the unity of the sensuous and the supersensuous, even if it is in the simple mode of the 'as if.'"[48] The hypothetical, the promise, the metaphor all yoke reality to dream and project it into the future as an emerging form.

Even with a sketchy knowledge of Kant, Shelley seems to have grasped deeply the complementary and necessary relationship between the imagination and the will. His final promise to be bound, that is, obligated, to fear himself and love others is a claim that the products of his mind are inalienable and that a loving reverence for all of humankind, a respect without exception, is the ground of human freedom. Liberated from time and space, the imagination is nowhere and we are thrown back on the task of forming our freedom. That freedom can never be guaranteed or sustained independently of activities of making—activities we can only undertake, at the outset, by exercising our imaginations.

5 / FORMING

He has filled him with the Spirit of God, with ability, with intelligence, with knowledge, and with all craftsmanship, to devise artistic designs, to work in gold and silver and bronze, in cutting stones for setting, and in carving wood, for work in every skilled craft. . . . He has filled them with ability to do every sort of work done by a craftsman or by a designer or by an embroiderer in blue and purple and scarlet stuff and fine twined linen, or by a weaver—by any sort of workman or skilled designer.

—EXODUS 35:31–35

I Ovid's Contests of Making

In English, we speak of someone being the "poet of" a theme or subject—poet of mountains, poet of the city—but we speak of being the "master of" the sonnet, the nocturne, the long poem. Praising, we are servants of phenomena; making, we are masters of our forms. Yet the metaphor of domination or mastery is in many ways a tragic one; the maker who masters a work to the point where the material or the concept no longer poses any tension has made his or her way to a deadly stasis, leaving the receiver, including the maker, with nothing to do.[1] A work that is alive continues to pulsate with its initial spark; its interpretive possibilities have multiplied as the maker's choices come closer to its final realization.

The artist conceals the ordeal of labor in order to manifest the work. Created in time, and as well received in time, works of art have absolute beginnings in intention and absolute ends beyond their effects. They are open to appearances as a consequence of this great secret of effort in time, yet their finality of form, the all-at-once-ness of their appearance, belies the duration of their making. Even a form that exists in human memory alone—a universal tale, a deep-rooted song—is subject to the vicissitudes of materiality. Nevertheless, during its life as a work of art, such materiality comes under a regime of meaning and significance. This plenitude of meaning is a kind of mantle for the work, an aura, certainly, but also another opening to time: our absorption in a work of art goes on so long as we are willing to attach our attention to it, investing it with coherence. What remains outside of our efforts toward meaning is this residual, waiting, fact of materiality—that which cannot be brought into human terms and concepts. And despite all the care in the world, works of art are subject to the decay and destruction of all material things.

Form is thus bound up with duration in ways that may not at first be evident when we consider an art work primarily in spatial terms. All making involves temporal overreaching in that the work is projected into the future and beyond the actions of the maker, but the actual, lived reality of the process and the finitude of its product counter the sheer idealized and imaginative audacity of making and reception. In the West, we have a number of founding myths that keep human making in its place. Many of these stories of making and aspiration are gathered in the well-known compendium, dating to the beginning of the first century AD, provided by Ovid's *Metamorphoses*. In the opening pages of his work alone, Ovid offers several different accounts of the creation of humankind. Acknowledging these multiple versions, Ovid tentatively begins, here in A. D. Melville's translation:

> . . . perhaps from seed divine
> Formed by the great Creator, so to found
> A better world, perhaps the new-made earth,
> So lately parted from the ethereal heavens,
> Kept still some essence of the kindred sky—
> Earth that Prometheus moulded, mixed with water,
> In likeness of the gods that govern the world—
> And while the other creatures on all fours
> Look downwards, man was made to hold his head
> Erect in majesty and see the sky,
> And raise his eyes to the bright stars above.
> Thus earth, once crude and featureless, now changed
> Put on the unknown form of humankind.[2]

This labor of Prometheus is followed by an account of the ages of humankind: the golden, silver, bronze, and iron ages in succession. That last, evil and hard age, characterized by human know-nothingness, intransigence, and war-mongering, is a time when Giants, offspring of Earth, challenge the gods and are crushed. Earth in consequence gives life to their blood, fashioning it in the shape of another race of rebellious and brutish humans. As a result, Jove sends a great flood. All people are killed, with the exception of the devout Deucalion, son of Prometheus (meaning "forethought") and nephew of Epimetheus (meaning "afterthought"), and his wife and cousin Pyrrha, who is the daughter of Epimetheus and hence niece of Prometheus. By means of this marriage—a second-generation phenomenon of the relations between forethought and afterthought, intention and consequence—humankind will repopulate the world. This regeneration will not come about by the obvious means of biological generation but rather by offerings of praise to the gods and the reception of the goddess Themis's auspicious instructions. Themis enigmatically tells the cousin-couple: "Leave / My temple, veil your heads, loosen your robes / and cast beyond you your great mother's bones."[3]

Deucalion only gradually understands the prophecy—they are to throw stones (the bones of the earth) behind them in order to generate new beings. When the two follow the goddess's instructions, they find the stones transformed:

> Their rigidness grew slowly soft and, softened,
> Assumed a shape, and as they grew and felt
> A gentler nature's touch, a semblance seemed
> To appear, still indistinct, of human form,
> Like the first rough-hewn marble of a statue,
> Scarce modeled, or old uncouth images.
> The earthy part, damp with some trace of moisture,
> Was turned to flesh; what was inflexible
> And solid changed to bone; what in the stones
> Had been the veins retained the name of veins.
> In a brief while, by Heaven's mysterious power,
> The stones the man had thrown were formed as men,

Those from the woman's hand reshaped as women.
Hence we are hard, we children of the earth,
And in our lives of toil we prove our birth.[4]

As if to emphasize the turn away from biological reproduction and toward mimesis, the stones from Deucalion's hand create men and those from Pyrrha's hand create women.

Why are these two figures given the extraordinary godlike task of regenerating life by means of their ritualized actions? They see themselves as "patterns of mankind" (*hominumque exempla manemus*), and, approaching the goddess, Deucalion laments that he does not have his "father's art" (*paternis artibus*) to restore the human race, and further asks "by what art [*arte*]" he might do so. It is the couple's piety that moves Themis to help them: their emergency is not hers, until we remember that their finitude invites the same problem that we encountered in the Homeric "Hymn to Demeter"—without humans to make sacrifices, the gods will suffer.

At the same time, Ovid records a range of myths that tell of the gods' punishment of human pride in making. The daughters of Minyas decide, in book 4, to continue weaving at their looms instead of leaving their work to join the festival of Bacchus. As they go about their tasks, ignoring the god and his festival, the scent of myrrh and saffron fills the air, their looms begin to turn green, and the fabric they are weaving breaks into leaves like ivy, growing vines and tendrils; then, an uncanny gift: bunches of grapes protrude through the tapestry's purple surface. As evening comes, the house is shaken by a tremor, and the daughters, fleeing to the corners of the building, are turned into bats.

This punishment re-forms their bodies by means of a power of making they cannot begin to fathom. And it returns their art to a nature they did not intend—one signifying the power of the wine god. Even if, like all transformed mortals in the *Metamorphoses*, they retain their human consciousness, their haplessness is all the more emphasized as they lose their human hands and voices. Yet when we remember the transformation of stones to flesh in the creation story, we also can see that Ovid's insistence on the continuity of human consciousness in animal, vegetable, and inanimate forms variously humanizes the nonhuman world. If the inner life of the nonhuman is something that cannot speak to us across the noumenal-phenomenal divide, it is in Ovid something that can be imagined as more than animate.

In book 5, the nine daughters of Pierus challenge the muses on Helicon to a singing contest. This is an affront in itself, but the lay singer who begins starts with the story of the wars of the heavens and makes her heroes the rebelling giants, hence belittling the reputations of the gods. When Calliope, representing the Muses, sings her story of the rape of Proserpina with a coda spoken by the nymph Arethusa, the nine daughters vow to attack the Muses but find they have been turned into magpies. Their talk continues on as the mere chatter of those birds who can imitate any sound. Here, too, the mortals' "art" is ruined by the gods—their music has gone from their voices, their originality is reduced to imitation, and their sounds are stripped of significance.

Subsequently, in book 6, Arachne, whose spinning and embroidery are admired by the nymphs themselves and characterized by especially graceful movements, boldly claims that her skill is sui generis. Although in truth she had learned her art from Pallas, she insists not only that she has had no teacher but also, upping the stakes, suggests that Pallas herself should come to participate in a weaving contest with her. Pallas does come, disguised, and counsels Arachne to ask pardon of the goddess. Even when the goddess reveals herself to the recalcitrant girl, Arachne persists in her plan for a competition, contending she can win. Pallas responds by weaving a masterpiece on the theme of combat and contest: a panorama of the gods competing to name the city of Cecrops, the location that will become her namesake, Athens. In the course of her work, and around this central image of her victory, Pallas adds four miniature scenes that reveal the punishment of humans who dare to compete with the gods. Arachne in turn weaves a tapestry revealing Jupiter's various tricks: his deception of Europa, the rapes of Asterie and Leda, the seductions of Antiope, Alcmena, Danae, Aegina, Mnemosyne, and Proserpina. She shows the guises of Neptune, Phoebus, Bacchus, and Saturn as well. This record of the gods' crimes is flawless and Pallas tears it to pieces, striking Arachne with her shuttle. The girl tries to hang herself, but Pallas stops her and says she will live on by hanging in a different mode: suspended as a spider, she will be the consummate weaver.

Arachne is punished for daring to compete with a goddess in a context of cultural production; her story is immediately followed by that of her friend Niobe, who, in an even more audacious boast than Arachne's, claims her fertility is greater than that of an immortal woman. Like the daughters of Minyas, Niobe gets into trouble initially by failing to show respect for the gods—she refuses to worship Latona. Bragging about her own birth, Niobe goes on to point out that Latona has borne only two children to Niobe's fourteen. Latona's womb, she claims, is therefore worth only a "seventh part" of hers. The shocked Latona complains to Phoebus and Phoebe, and they assassinate all fourteen of Niobe's children; the mortal mother sees her children as rigid corpses, and she joins their state as she, in turn, becomes a marble figure fastened to a mountain.

The satyr Marsyas is another Ovidian protagonist who dares to compete with the gods—in his case as well, in a context of art making. Challenging Apollo to a piping contest, he is subsequently stripped of his skin. Thus in these final two examples we find echoes, once more, of the story of human creation brought about by the softening of stones: Niobe too hard, her very veins turned to "veins" of marble; Marsyas too soft, bereft of surface and so bereft of form. The fragility of the fleshly state is the locus of mortal vulnerability.

Certain features characterize these stories of divine and human making overall. First, the dynamic between planning and judging is drawn forward, but as we can see with the preparations of Deucalion and Pyrrha, of the two, forethought is of greater significance. The gods possess their talents as natural attributes, but humans who have learned and then act impulsively will be punished; those who follow instructions and express the reverence and humility of *pietas* are rewarded. Second, the stories do not show any inherent differences in the means and modes of art making as practiced by mortals and immortals—the contests themselves are strangely fair: the same materials are used, the same instruments. The gods administer their punishment by divine means, but they make their art as we do; indeed, in the case of the independent blacksmith Hephaestus, the only figure to be expelled from and then returned to Olympus, human skill is even perhaps superior to the gods' talents.[5] And certainly the moral force of Arachne's weaving brings a greater response from Pallas than Pallas's rather narcissistic history draws from Arachne.

Humans are made of earth, the most fundamental of materials, and thereby they have a particular affinity to those materials they will take up in their art. When they are punished, they are literally demoted—to a spider's weaving, to a magpie's singing. The nonhuman world is, as we have seen, given an unintelligible consciousness—at least unintelligible to us—by these punishments. But in turn human making is justly framed as a superior kind of animal making, not merely as an imitation of godly creation; hence perhaps the pride of Arachne in claiming that she has had no teacher.

Nevertheless, if there is no essential difference between the ways gods and mortals make things, no recourse to magic in these ostensibly "fair" contests, there is one fundamental difference between humans and gods that is emphasized by such transforming punishments: The gods complete their making without suffering its labor; regardless of their efforts, work brings them no closer to death. Humans, however, are changed by their work; the being who begins the task is not the one who completes it. Each act of making wears down the maker, returning him or her all the more to the condition of clay from which he or she arose. It is striking that the genius of making, Hephaestus, is the only one of the gods noted for his deformities; he is ugly and lame, halting in his motions. His lived diminishment is all the more emphasized by the endlessly supplemental forms of reality that he is able to create by means of his forging art. In a masterpiece like the shield of Achilles, each part opens up to a world of reference, and yet the boundary of the work is so fixed that it can be lifted and held up in the sunlight. The great shield is a functional object of supernatural power—a power rooted in the potential force of its user, who stands behind it with its makers; its significations are held up to those who stand before it for all time.

The stakes of making remain intense in a quite different way for the human makers Ovid describes: humans are making and unmaking themselves at once in those artifacts they produce and upon which they reflect. When we consider the temporal dimension of the process of making art, we could say that there is only the decision to begin the work, intervening in nature, and the decision to end it, releasing the work back into the world, where it now maintains not only a place in nature but also a social relation to those who receive it. What is middle or process is available only through retrospection, and the end comes to dominate as all of the possible "otherwises" in the artist's choices fall away and the work emerges as what it is, as being as well as happening—the outcome of a series of decisions that are dense with the possibilities of what was not chosen, what was not actualized.

Forming, as we have seen, thus resolves the flux posed by mood and the infinity posed by the imagination. Genesis reveals that the dynamic between hand and eye in the story of creation is vital; alone the eye cannot make, alone the hand cannot shape; only vision and action in concert result in intelligible forms: "neben der Hand und im Blick" (near our hand and within our gaze), as Rilke wrote in the ninth Duino Elegy's exhortation to praise. His choice of prepositions underlines both the specificity of the onset of making—the hand about to take up the material, the gaze already framing—and the moment's afterlife, as the "thing" continues to offer itself uniquely to the reach of hand and eye. Human arts are arts of combination that bring ontological status to objects that otherwise would not exist and that cannot be repeated, no matter how often they might be replicated.

II Forming as Knowing

What, then, is a form? Our understanding of this word, both noun and verb, has a complicated and often confusing history. Derived from the Latin *forma* and used in all the Romance and Teutonic languages, the word may have its origins in the verb *ferire*, to strike, or a Sanskrit term meaning to position or hold—exactly contrary senses that indicate the simultaneous specificity and mutability of forms themselves.[6] As I have by now often emphasized, any mimetic theory of art, such as Plato's, considers works of art as merely imitations of imitations that themselves conceal the reality of underlying forms—often written "Forms" with an initial capital. For Plato, the particular materiality of such works is of no importance. The universal forms, hidden from human cognition and intuited by the mind as ideas of the true, good, and just, and as the perfections of geometry, all exist in realms beyond human experience. They cannot be reached through the senses; here on earth we encounter only their shadows, but because as presouls we knew them in a previous life, Plato suggests we might take on the disciplined and reasoned mental work of bringing their memory back to consciousness. In Plato's account, artists and artisans may follow archetypes of these forms in their creation, but they themselves create nothing that can be an inherent object of knowledge.

Thus, no matter how many accounts of the history of aesthetics begin with Plato, "aesthetics" as such cannot be posed in Platonic philosophies. The very term *aesthesis* emphasizes the sense impressions that Platonic philosophies claim from the outset are misleading. In contrast, our prevailing contemporary view that artworks are new forms, with an ontological reality of their own, is one we derive in part from Aristotle's claim that making brings into being what otherwise would not exist, from Scholastic discussions of form and matter, from Baconian ideas about the generative possibilities of knowledge of forms—and, in the main, from the expressive theories of eighteenth- and nineteenth-century discourses on art.[7] The Aristotelian distinction between form (μορφή or εἶδος) and matter (ὕλη) indicates that materials become things by acquiring particular dimensions and shapes discernible by the senses and, analogously, by thought. We are able to know things by their forms, and our concepts themselves take form or shape, in turn enabling us to create new forms based on those we have come to know.

To make art is to bring being out of nonbeing and nonbeing out of being and thereby manifest the potential for change inherent in all of nature; at the center of the human project, art making is also our primary means of self-transformation. We can know materials in the world, but we know the limits of our knowledge only as we encounter them; in art making, we reflect all other forms of production and understanding. The speculative writings of Novalis, the Schlegel brothers, and, as we have seen, Schelling and Hegel turn to a philosophy of art that becomes more and more concerned with universal, generic, and abstract frames for such making. In the end, Hegel elevates philosophical speculation above the arts, which he ranks according to their abstraction—placing, as Kant did, poetry above all other art practices. For Hegel, poetry goes beyond music and music beyond painting and painting beyond the materiality of sculpture and architecture—all measured by the degree of spiritual freedom the practice offers.

Although judgments of taste, and the discourses about them, create a descriptive account of artworks, emphasizing the features they lend to appearance and necessarily giving some special attention to visual forms, the ensuing focus on generality and abstraction in the work of philosophers of art has left something of a vacuum in the discussion of form making. Works of art are either presented in their entirety for analysis or enlisted in a philosophical program of universal purposes.

Nevertheless, artists can find something of use in each of these earlier approaches. The Platonic emphasis on archetypes underlines a point we have followed in several contexts: that artists commence their work within a natural world that presents itself not as an array of "raw" materials but as a summons to making. Artists do not create under this model so much as shape what already exists; they unify multiple parts to make a one out of many. Indeed, this is how we often describe what it is "to form." Such a summons to making, taken up by other animal species as well, is one we answer with our physical selves—subject to the tones, rhythms, colors, and light of experience. We make in accordance with necessity, out of our fundamental needs; but we also make in accordance with our desires, out of choices we cannot fathom or anticipate beyond the internal purposes of the process itself. As Aristotle described the construction of the unities out of successions of events in tragedies, as Leon Battista Alberti described the subordination of figures to the narrative and spatial needs of paintings, as Michelangelo contended he was releasing the form from the imprisoning stone, and as Friedrich Schiller described the artist's command over materials in all the arts—the history of thought about art making in the West has emphasized the freedom the artist exercises over his or her material far more than the impositions and limits that the materials pose to the artist.[8]

We ourselves are wholes made up of unlike parts—parts that have different functions that are nevertheless brought into coherence by the continuity of our individual lives even if, so long as we are alive, that coherence is emergent rather than given a finite form. Hence, although individual artworks bring diverse parts and functions into finite wholes, the history of art is, like the history of the individual, a continuous and open transformation in time. If philosophers of art tend to emphasize mastery and the knowledge of tools and techniques necessary to acquire it, they reflect upon the nature not of individual works but of the maker who makes them. Thus we might attend to what is missing from this process—missing from the Platonic denigration of the material form, missing from the late start of a descriptive aesthetics or poetics, and missing from the philosophical allegories of Hegel and others: the process of coming into form.

The relation of art making to freedom is not simply the negative freedom of a "license" granted to the artist; nor is it only the positive freedom from use and prior purpose that the artist might enjoy. As Henri Bergson explained in his 1889 treatise on time and free will, *Essai sur les données immédiates de la conscience*, and in his 1907 *L'évolution créatrice*, the aesthetic or felt dimension of existence is not coterminous in either quality or quantity with the physical determinism that rules the universe; human beings experience time and act in accordance with feelings of intensity in their lived experience of duration. In his pursuit of a notion of "creative," rather than mechanistic, evolution, Bergson described a process that borrows in many ways from the temporal experience of art making: a practice of breaking from habit, of carving out and reframing perceptual experiences into discrete objects, of making choices and acting in accordance with an ever-becoming sense of the self, of moving, in our apprehension of phenomena, between intuitions and concepts.

Finite as they are, when viewed as intended projects whose purposes are ever-emergent, our human lives have a dynamic relation to the finitude of those forms we make. Even if Hegel's concern is not particularly with artworks proper until he writes his *Lectures on Aesthetics* intermittently between 1818 and 1829, his account in his 1807 *Phenomenology* of the slave who acquires self-consciousness through concerted acts of making is one of the most revealing here. In this argument, Hegel emphasizes how the activity of making initially overcomes the fear of death. Let's consider the full passage:

> The formative activity has not only [the] positive significance that in it the pure being-for-itself of the servile consciousness acquires an existence; it also has, in contrast with its first moment, the negative significance of *fear*. For, in fashioning the thing, the bondsman's own negativity, his being-for-itself, becomes an object for him only through his setting at nought the existing *shape* confronting him. But this objective *negative* moment is none other than the alien being before which it has trembled. Now, however, he destroys this alien negative moment, posits *himself* as a negative in the permanent order of things, and thereby becomes *for himself* someone existing on his own account. In the lord, the being-for-itself is an "other" for the bondsman, or is only *for* him [i.e., is not his own]; in fear, the being-for-self is present in the bondsman himself; in fashioning the thing, he becomes aware that being-of-self belongs to *him*, that he himself exists essentially and actually in his own right. The shape does not become something other than himself through being made external to him; for it is precisely this shape that is his pure being-for-self, which in this externality is seen by him to be the truth. Through this rediscovery of himself by himself, the bondsman realizes that it is precisely in his work wherein he seemed to have only an alienated existence that he acquires a mind of his own. For this reflection, the two moments of fear and service as such, as always that of formative activity, are necessary, both being at the same time in a universal mode. Without the discipline of service and obedience, fear remains at the formal stage, and does not extend to the known real world of existence. Without the formative activity, fear remains inward and mute, and consciousness does not become explicitly *for itself*.[9]

Hegel's story of making and self-making is only at its initial phase in this passage—the slave's work has revealed that he or she is a thinking being whose thinking self-consciousness is a free self-consciousness, whose "I" has an external facticity and is in and for itself. This moment is the beginning of the notion of the person—as it has come down to us from Stoic philosophy, from Roman law, and from much of the philosophy of the Enlightenment—and for Hegel, the bondsman's initial turn to work remains a Stoic project that sets aside the reality of necessity and contingency as it constructs the paradise of a purely formal and free thought.[10] The abstract "freedom" of Stoicism, in Hegel's argument, is both the inverse and correlative of the absolutely negating, purely destructive, activity of skepticism. In these moments in the development of the slave's self-consciousness, the struggle of master and slave becomes internalized to consciousness; the slave must suffer the unhappiness of knowing that an absolute freedom is empty and an absolute negation deluded. Life and its facticity remain before us; we are thrown into them and into our own mortality; we have no choice but to acknowledge that our consciousness is in and of life.

Hegel calls this situation one of "unhappy consciousness." The bondsman finds himself caught between transcendence and changeability and realizes that to be in and for one's self is to be an unthought essence. Hegel suggests that to think this essence is to externalize and form it, to make it thinglike, and such consciousness of self-consciousness is what begins to absorb the singular subject into the universality of reason and spirit. In Hegel's aesthetics, in turn, art making will free itself from material constraints and lead to the freedom of play with pure concepts; poetry is itself merely a stage on the way to philosophy.

Hegel thus follows Kant in arguing that art making involves us in the experience of freedom. Idealizing the powers of imagination and association, Hegel writes early in his aesthetics: "It is precisely the *freedom* of production and configurations that we enjoy in the beauty of art. In the production as well as in the perception of works of art, it seems as if we escape from every fetter of rule and regularity. In place of the strictness of conformity to law, and the dark inwardness of thought, we seek peace and enlivenment in the forms of art; we exchange the shadow realm of the Idea for a bright and vigorous reality. Finally, the source of works of art is the free activity of fancy which in its imagination is itself more free than nature is." He further argues that producing art meets both our theoretical need to understand what moves us and recognize ourselves in such forces and our practical need to manifest ourselves and, by means of such manifestations, similarly to recognize ourselves: "This aim [man] achieves by altering existing things whereon he impresses the seal of his inner being and in which he now finds again his own characteristics. Man does this in order, as a free subject, to strip the external world of its inflexible foreignness and to enjoy in the shape of things only an external realization of himself."[11] The Hegelian account of the emergence of Spirit is thus one of an ever-self-overcoming-forming—the meaning of human being is this unfinished project.

Hegel's story of our self-conscious development thereby in several ways continues the paradigm we observed in Ovid's contests of making, wherein individual mortals counter their finitude with the creation of artifacts that might survive them. In doing so, human beings take on at least the skills of the gods, and supernatural beings here have need of a talent that otherwise seems particularly human. The lord requires the recognition of the slave, and therefore some threshold of intelligibility must make the products of the slave, like the sacrificial offerings of humans to the gods, of value. Hegel's system in turn is an important precursor to later phenomenologies of mind and matter, including Bergson's. If in the late eighteenth and the nineteenth centuries such narratives were tied up with concepts of development, progress, and a self-congratulating mastery over the physical world that no longer seem completely convincing, it is also the case that the value of art making remains bound to the provisional and speculative dimension of its practices.

Human culture takes part simultaneously and globally in every phase of its history; we have only to look around us, in this age when the world conceals few secrets, to see the juxtaposition of the Stone Age to what we conceive of as First World advancements, and in situations of emergency the atavistic takes no time at all to arrive on the scene. Analogously, despite the direction of Hegel's narrative of the self-overcoming of spirit, and despite the continual demand for new art and "new songs" that we have explored, art makers neglect to, or decide not to, or simply are unable to, throw off "earlier" practices.

We could say that this is because our desire for novelty cannot allow anything to remain beyond its purview—least of all the quintessential nonnovelty of the past. Somewhere between the deadening certainty of pure repetition and the chaos of pure variation, human beings proceed to make the forms of art. At the moment of instantiation, the new becomes an actual quality of the work. But unlike intrinsic qualities such as color or texture or scale, novelty is destined to disappear in time. When a work loses its significance as "the new," its effects nevertheless survive first in the imperative to go beyond it, and later in its status as a precursor of what has followed.

Concern with the originality of art was especially intense in the eighteenth century, when judgments of taste were put into crisis by expanding culture contacts and by new distributions of works of art and literature, a crisis that coincided with the emergence of the discourse of aesthetics itself. Edward Young's 1759 treatise *Conjectures on Original Composition*, written in a letter to his friend Samuel Richardson, puts forward one of the first critiques of the mechanical dimension of imitation in favor of an organic model of composition. Young writes: "An imitator shares his crown, if he has one, with the chosen object of his imitation; an original enjoys an undivided applause. An original may be said to be of a vegetable nature; it rises spontaneously from the vital root of genius, it grows, it is not made: imitations are often a sort of manufacture wrought up by those mechanics, art and labor, out of preexistent materials not their own."[12] With a kind of Rousseauvian plaintiveness, in a late edition of his treatise Young asks, "Born originals, how comes it to pass that we die copies?"[13]

Although for the ancient Greeks *technê* was a notion that could extend from boat making to statecraft, this spectrum of possibility for technique also lies beneath our own distinctions between what we view as the practice of craft and the inventions of art. Within a craft tradition, tools, designs, and procedures are all intelligible to each practitioner. Indeed, nothing exemplifies a Platonic model for artistic making more than a craftsman's practice of the reproduction of perfected forms, even if such forms are perfected in human time rather than in an ideal and transcendent realm. In the practice of craft, purpose is established as a prior condition, and modifications in the practice need be made only in light of that purpose. There is only one function for a water jug, to hold water, and only one function for a kayak, to move through water. How successful is the jug's insulating power, how smooth its lip, how well balanced its tilt; how light the kayak, how steadily balanced in the water—these are the factors that will put pressure on materials and design. So long as the use remains constant, the individual examples are mere instantiations on the way to a continually deferred perfection.[14]

But once the maker intends to create an object without any view to purpose, the object is necessarily, if solipsistically, "aestheticized"—made into an object of art as surely as the antique tool hung against the white wall of a gallery is no longer to hand for its prior uses. The "ready-mades" of early modernist sculpture—the bicycle wheel, urinal, and bottle holder of Marcel Duchamp, for example—serve to reframe useful objects in just this way and to invite the receiver to attend to them as works of art. For Duchamp, this reframing was a triumph of intention, and the consequence was a heightened attention to the formal qualities arising in such objects once they were endowed with the formal integrity of artworks. If, as some controversial recent scholarship has indicated, Duchamp in fact made these "ready-mades" himself, thus presenting original and singular works of art as if they were products of mass-manufacture, the "reframing" is not yet over and Duchamp, as he had the first laugh, has also had the last.[15]

In contrast to those craft traditions that speak to fellow practitioners, art practices informed by invention and singular originality lead to conditions of reception that are at once both more idiosyncratic and more open; such art practices will have an impact beyond their particular modes or means of production, affecting practitioners in other fields. In conceptual art, which is not merely a matter of mixing media but also, despite the use of language, a matter of foregoing actualization, such transparency is most evident. To rely on and depart from Hegel at once, we could say that the conceptual, like all Stoical forms of self-consciousness, is nevertheless its own dead end if it does not reenter into an engagement with what it excludes—the sensuous.

In another domain of relatively recent formal innovation, the practices of the Arte Povera group—artists practicing mostly in Italy in the late 1960s who sought a minimal, but deep, acquisition of means in the pursuit of maximal sensuous and conceptual ends—emphasized the freedom inherent in the widest possible use of materials. As the sculptor Giovanni Anselmo, seeking to replace a notion of form with one of force, wrote in a paradigmatic Arte Povera manifesto: "It is necessary, for example, that the energy of a torsion lives within its free force; it certainly wouldn't live just by its form. I think that to operate in this direction, since the energy exists under the most various appearances and situations, there must be the most absolute liberty of choice in the use of materials." Anselmo's sculptures were thus designed and executed to capture the physical force of actions used to make the form in the form itself. In contrast to the maker of a "ready-made" who draws attention to the intrinsic form and textural qualities of an existing object, Anselmo is suggesting that the artwork might remain "open and alive" by means of the expression of an energy that is never reified or transposed, as he writes, to "style, form, or antiform."[16]

Anselmo's comments illuminate the radical liberty in choice of materials and technique that many late twentieth-century sculptors claimed. David Smith's work with the steel abandoned in an welding plant in Voltri in 1962, for example, similarly captured the energy of attaching a piece of metal to another until, at a point that seemed determined by whimsy more than by intention, a form was placed and given over to the perambulations of a viewer. Or we might think of Richard Serra's early pieces from the late 1960s made of molten lead thrown onto walls and his "Torqued Ellipses" of the late '90s. The latter are made of corroding steel plates that can be apprehended in endlessly divergent ways, both on the level of their macrostructures, which allude to the geometrical forms they embody and project architecturally into space, and on the level of their microtextures, as the observer moves above, around, and through them. The self-sealing rust that accumulates on the surfaces of the weatherproof steel may be technically the "exterior" of the work, but it is experienced as an interior by the viewer who touches and sees it on the scale of individual perception.[17]

Snowflakes and crystals, the patterns of a seed cone and the petals of a daisy—all natural forms proper—are created by rules that it is the task of science, including mathematics, to uncover. Kant made the argument that the existence of such patterns gives evidence that nature is constantly offering forms of beauty for our aesthetic apprehension. In the discussion of genius in the *Third Critique*, he elaborates on the aesthetic purposiveness of nature, which works through humankind and yet in its mechanical and determinate ends is not a match for the aesthetical ideas of human beings with their idealism of purpose. He writes:

> The flowers, the blossoms, indeed the shapes of whole plants: the delicacy of animal formations of all sorts of species, which is unnecessary for their own use but as if selected for our own taste; above all the manifold and harmonious composition of colors (in the pheasant, in crustaceans, insects, right down to the commonest flowers), which are so pleasant and charming to our eyes, which seem to have been aimed entirely at outer contemplation, since they concern merely the surface, and even in this do not concern the figure of the creature, which could still be requisite for its inner ends: all of these give great weight to the kind of explanation that involves the assumption of real ends of nature for our power of aesthetic judgment.[18]

As much as nature works through us, for Kant our judgments of taste cannot be based in empirical experiences of nature but must rely on a priori faculties and proceed as reflective, rather than determinate, judgments.

Yet artists often have been inspired by such natural forms, and aestheticians have at times sought to bring the historical forms of art under them. For example, in *The Shape of Time*, George Kubler attempts rather platonically to classify the visual arts by geometrical form. He writes, "Architecture and packaging tend in the modern schools of design to gravitate together under the rubric of envelopes; sculpture absorbs the design of all sorts of small solids and containers; painting extends to include flat shapes and planes of all sorts, like those of weaving and printing. By this geometric system, all visible art can be classed as envelopes, solids, and planes, regardless of any relation to use, in a classing which ignores the traditional distinction by 'fine' and 'minor,' or 'useless' and 'useful' arts."[19] But such a geometric classification has little to do with the diverse array of forms and functions at play in the parts of a work of art, and even less to do with artistic intention. The sculptor and painter, whether inspired by an ideal geometry or the dynamic manifold of lived experience, do not set out to reproduce an envelope, a solid, or a plane per se, any more than they set out to reproduce the phenomenal world. Rather, they create a completed and unique object that will be *this* work, having *this* effect and import.

Even in the Cartesian "all-at-onceness" of visual art organized by single-point perspective, such an effect is created by means of duration and intensity. The sensuous dimension of a work is not derived from a single impression but is rather emergent in a sequence of relations—to the boundary of the work and to the patterns arising in its apprehension. The form is a total relation of parts, unfolding on both an overall scale and a microscale of texture and local effects: such aesthetic values as variety and unity, tension and release, problem and resolution all speak to this dynamic connection between the elements of a work. Edges and outlines are features of perception and the moving gaze—as any student of Manet's blacks can testify. The "inside" of a patch of color in a Cézanne landscape changes its function if the viewer stands back at two feet rather than two inches, the rear view of a Bernini marble depends upon the tactile apprehension of a circling viewer—or the latter's expulsion when the maestro has decided, in the case of a terracotta *bozzetto*, that only the front and sides will "count." These formal outcomes of the experience of apprehending the work in time are extensions of the wanderings of boredom and the intensities of anxiety: the very words we use to describe such values are symptomatic of the states of the maker and receiver as they flow to and from the work.

Our dependence on an internalized image of the maker's intention as we receive a work of art is evident in such a simple clue as the museum wall label. Any museum will specify the "ingredients" of a work of art: oil on canvas or oil on wood; bronze, clay, and steel; watercolor on paper; feathers, glue, and glitter. Unless such labels are written by the ghost of Lucretius, they will not say "subatomic particles." They are concerned with the field of materials as perceived by the maker—with forms given to hand and intention, and not with matter itself. Diamonds and lamp black, as the saying goes, are both carbons, but our sense of form in art is derived from and depends upon the intelligibility of forms in nature—an intelligibility that is the product of our form-making and form-discerning predilections as we grasp the world offered to our senses and reshape it into meaning.

Kubler's geometrical analysis rather quickly shifts from artifacts to technique. Given the bounty of the material world, the fundamental gestures of art involve extracting and augmenting—a pair of gestures we have encountered before in narratives of the creation of human beings themselves. Sculpture consists of two kinds: that which models and hence supplements and that which hollows or carves, dispensing with its residue and drawing forward significant shape. Some arts give weight to what is transient, including dust; others, like dance, lighten the burden of gravity. The arts thus provide prostheses to the human body—we have only to look at an assembled orchestra to see the resources music lends to our physical capacity for making meaningful patterns of sound. Other arts, such as weaving, have at their core techniques of binding that enact the role of form making itself.

The unity of form is given in appearance and grasped in synthetic acts of perception. The two-dimensional arts of modeling and projection, painting, and stamping are on a continuum with the arts of low relief, such as embroidery, ornamentation, appliqué, and collage, whose dimensionality has both facade and depth. Even so, supplementing a spatial geometry of the arts with a classification of gestures does not suffice to account for the range and complexities of art forms. Forming is an organic process that envelops the maker in its path. Consider that from the picture making of the Lascaux caves, to the Roman development of perspective views, to the long modern dialogue between abstraction and figuration, painting includes more than one plane of reality—an animal image accompanied by nondiscursive symbols, such as the fingers of the hand expressed or withheld as an indication of number; sacred or mythological scenes brought up against the vignettes of genre painting, and vice versa. Perhaps, like the tension between empiricism and metaphysics in the history of philosophy, the continual effort to yoke or otherwise combine experienced and imagined phenomena within the artwork is one way that we overcome our lived separation from other realms—from nature, but also from the unborn and the dead.

III Gathering toward Abstraction

Some practices, such as still life painting, bring forward an especially vivid sense of the continuity between natural forms and made forms, exemplifying the fossilization of organic life into mineral layers and the processes of decay and transformation that characterize all created things. The petals, leaves, and flowers of plants, the varied shapes and textures of fruits, vegetables, slabs of meat, and cheese, might become patches of negative and positive space. Patterns of color and light can be brought up against representations of human artifacts—porcelain, glass, cloth, wooden implements, and surfaces—that lend themselves to hand. All this is accomplished by means of mineral pigments, oils, and other substances applied by touch to the surface of more cloth or wood. Speaking of a trompe l'oeil work by the late nineteenth-century American illusionist painter J. F. Peto, Alfred Gell has written:

> The painting's power to fascinate stems entirely from the fact that people have great difficulty in working out how coloured pigments (substances with which everybody is broadly familiar) can be applied to a surface so as to become an apparently different set of substances, namely, the ones which enter into the composition of letters, ribbons, drawing-pins, stamps, bits of string, and so on. The magic exerted over the beholder by this picture is a reflection of the magic which is exerted inside the picture, the technical miracle which achieves the transubstantiation of oily pigments into cloth, metal, paper, and feathers.[20]

Whether a painter of still life is in pursuit of religious allegory, the evocation of silence, a sublime self-consciousness of the dynamic between planes and textures, or other meanings, the act of abstraction—literally from *abs-tractus*, to draw off, remove, or transpose—is his or her task, which takes its force from the manifested materiality both within and on the surface of the painting.

Wallace Stevens, who was interested, as the title of one of his late poems claims, in "not ideas about the thing but the thing itself," was nevertheless also one of the most pathbreaking poets of abstraction. For Stevens, this relation between the perceived world and ideas was not an antinomy but a lived relation: in his thought and practice, the idea maintained its etymological root in the *eidolon* or image, and he constantly reminds us, in a kind of homegrown Platonic mode, of the source of all images in the sun's light. Many of his poems of still life—for example, "A Dish of Peaches in Russia," "Floral Decorations for Bananas," and "Study of Two Pears"—underline the temporal process of observing spatial forms, emphasizing what a poem can do. They testify to the sensual apprehension of the thing: "With my whole body I taste these peaches, / I touch them and smell them . . . they have peach fuzz, ah!"; claim a moral importance for it: "I did not know / That such ferocities could tear / One self from another, as these peaches do." Or, in the case of bananas, juxtapose the existing thing—"these insolent, linear peels / And sullen, hurricane shapes / Won't do with your eglantine. / They require something serpentine. / Blunt yellow in such a room!"—to the ideal thing: "You should have had plums tonight, / In an eighteenth-century dish, / And pettifogging buds." Or, in the case of pears, yoke the reality of the object—"The pears are not viols, / Nudes or bottles. / They resemble nothing else"—to the reality of perception: "The shadows of the pears / Are blobs on the green cloth. / The pears are not seen / As the observer wills." In each of these poems the sun is the first cause of all meaning; the sunlight that falls at the moment of apprehension is what makes the pears' shadows and touches them with red; the sunlight makes the peaches red, too, and fills the nearby curtains; and its "precious light" is what should accompany the plums in their "eighteenth-century dish."

These are only a few of Stevens's still life poems; the representation of natural forms brought into a relation with human nature runs throughout his life's work. In a trio of meditations on the notion of bouquet—"The Bouquet," "Bouquet of Belle Scavoir," and "Bouquet of Roses in Sunlight"—Stevens similarly emphasizes the role of human nature in shaping natural forms at various removes from their "found" state. Bouquets are made from nature, but there are no bouquets in nature: the bouquet is thus constructed of found things and endowed with form and meaning by the mind of the beholder.[21] Bouquets become an analogue for the work of the poet who chooses words from the stream of speech and assembles them into new forms that have their own qualities of composition, their own edges and interiors, and their own resulting freshness and significance. But just as a real bouquet is destined to die and decay, so are the poet's metaphors, no matter how lively at the moment of their creation, fated to become dead metaphors; the poet looks to feeling, and the persistence of feeling in memory, as a counterforce to this inevitable natural closure.

"Bouquet of Belle Scavoir," from Stevens's wartime book of 1942, *Parts of a World*, is the first of these poems, and it plays with quatrains, for the most part written in tetrameter, that often waver on their fourth line, giving an uneven quality to what would otherwise be one of the most traditional stanzas. In this poem, Stevens invents an imaginary character who has made the bouquet and "everything in it is herself"—the speaker of the poem describes the longing of "he" who only glimpses the shadows of Belle Scavoir. The name of the bouquet maker is an elaborate and anachronistic pun: "scavoir" is the pre-nineteenth-century spelling of *savoir*. And so the title and name indicate the poem's central crux: how to know beauty and hence to know what beauty knows. "The thought of her takes her away. / The form of her in something else / Is not enough." The "he" wants to see "her" directly, but whether the "this she has made" is the referent of the poem—the bouquet—or, by means of a final deictic gesture, the poem itself, beauty remains the hidden invisible cause of all her visible manifestations.

Stevens's postwar collection of 1950, *The Auroras of Autumn*, includes two poems on the theme of the bouquet—both in the same regular pentameter triplet form. In the first of these, "Bouquet of Roses in Sunlight," Stevens lays out his argument with an unflinching clarity, beginning with these lines:

> Say that it is a crude effect, black reds,
> Pink yellows, orange whites, too much as they are
> To be anything else in the sunlight of the room,
>
> Too much as they are to be changed by metaphor,
> Too actual, things that in being real
> Make any imaginings of them lesser things.
>
> And yet this effect is a consequence of the way
> We feel and, therefore, is not real, except
> In our sense of it, our sense of the fertilest red,
>
> Of yellow as first color and of white,
> In which the sense lies still, as a man lies,
> Enormous, in a completing of his truth.

Stevens's knowledge of roses was an intimate one; he grew them as a gardener, and he was as well a near-daily visitor to Hartford's Elizabeth

Park with its enormous rose gardens. He begins with images of the exact, but new-fangled and artificial, mixed colors of hybrid tea roses—secondary hues under which he glimpses the underlying primary colors (each a "first color"), just as the rose varieties themselves have been developed by grafting onto older forms. The poem begins with "black red," the hue that has the most specific capacity to absorb the light and so the most specific color, and moves to white, the hue that reflects all colors infinitely. This never-ending plenitude of white is, for Stevens, like the never-ending plenitude of human meanings, refracted through each individual consciousness, including that of the speaker and his listener.

In the remaining three stanzas of the poem, he draws out the differences between sense impression and metaphor, the ineffable and the overdetermined. The poem ends by emphasizing the instability of meaning in its last line break: "This is what makes them seem" springs back to seeming as a consequence of seeing. But the completion of the syntax, "This is what makes them seem / So far beyond the rhetorician's touch," raises the wry self-consciousness of a speaker landing on a fixed closing point—seeing is contrasted to touch; the sensual viewer, standing in the light, is contrasted to the mere rhetorician, maker of finite metaphors. Yet it is the rhetorician who has touched the poem into closure—the viewers of the bouquet stand in the light of its infinite opening to meaning.

The third bouquet poem, and second one to be found in *The Auroras of Autumn*, is a complex narrative, titled simply "The Bouquet," and it is also concerned with the relation between bouquets and metaphors. It begins, in fact, with what seems to be a commentary on Giambattista Vico's theory of the origin of metaphor in the primitive experience of being terrified by lightning and inventing the name of a god to explain it:[22]

> Of medium nature, this farouche extreme
> Is a drop of lightning in an inner world,
> Suspended in temporary jauntiness.
>
> The bouquet stands in a jar, as metaphor,
> As lightning itself is, likewise, metaphor
> Crowded with apparitions suddenly gone

And no less suddenly here again, a growth
Of the reality of the eye, an artifice,
Nothing much, a flitter that reflects itself.

The flash of the bouquet, like the flash of lightning described in Vico's *New Science*, calls for the construction of terms and mythologies that grow into purely human significance—as artifice reflects itself and is "nothing much," except that it becomes everything by being more than material and more than its moment of instantiation: the bouquet becomes "a symbol . . . a sovereign, a souvenir, a sign . . . the infinite of the actual perceived, / A freedom revealed, a realization touched, / The real made more acute by an unreal." In the end, the reality of a soldier's arrival—bringing into the empty house an announcement of perhaps a homecoming, perhaps a death, we never know—somehow results in the bouquet's falling over the edge of the table and lying on the floor. It is literally gone once its unity is dispersed, but that unity now is maintained on another scale by the poem itself, just as the makers of metaphor no longer need, or even have access to, the instantiating experience of lightning.

In other poems that also participate in this mode of ekphrasis, wherein the poem is made by reference to made forms and as well to the natural forms from which they are derived, Stevens relies upon the ancient kinship between weaving and texts: *tek*, to make, *texere*, to weave, *textus*, a woven thing. His mysterious lyric "Tattoo," from his first book, *Harmonium* (1923), earlier expressed not only the patterned lines of a tattoo but also, in its quietly resonant repetitions and slant rhymes, the tattoo that is a heartbeat.

The poem brilliantly plays on a series of comparisons: the light is like a spider in the way it crawls over water and the edges of the snow (which are also water); the light crawls like a spider under your eyes and spreads its webs; these webs of light are fastened to flesh and bones; the way they are fastened is the way light (like spiderwebs) is fastened to rafters or grass; the filaments (from *filare*, to spin; *filum*, thread) of your eyes are on the surface of the water and in the edges of the snow like light, and hence like spiders. The thing seen sees the one who sees, and the way one sees becomes bound up with the thing seen—filaments of our eyes and spiderwebs are literally woven together on the poem's loom. Similes via *like* and *as* and the unfolding set of prepositions indicating position—*over*, *over*, *under*, then *to*, *on*, and *in*—weave together the concrete images of spider, water, snow, eyelids, webs, flesh, bones, rafter, grass, and then, once again, water and snow—the water's own architecture is revealed in snow, as the eyes have, too, their filaments that weave a surface. By calling the poem "Tattoo," Stevens is able to unify these lines and involve their aural form with their visual form.

"The Dwarf," also from *Parts of a World* (1942), continues his exploration of weaving as a reciprocity of textures and accumulating insights. He describes how "it is the mind that is woven, the mind that was jerked / And tufted in straggling thunder and shattered sun." These lines are only an excerpt from this semisonnet of fourteen couplet lines that describes the fabrication of a cloth out of thoughts of summer as the speaker heads for winter seclusion. Stevens's ending—"It is all that you are, the final dwarf of you, / That is woven and woven and waiting to be worn / Neither as mask nor as garment but as a being"—has a beautiful symmetry that is revealed by the double entendre of "worn": a weaving might be worn as a whole cloth, placed over the face or the body, concealing as a mask or revealing a shape as a garment, or it might be worn as in worn away or worn down, used up by life just as a being is. These high modernist poems thereby draw on ancient traditions of weaving and designing, but they also participate in contemporary practices of collage and fragmentation. By means of such practices, Stevens and other artists might break down the synthesis that all form making promises and reveal the persistence of nonform and nonmeaning that lies beyond the closure and lifetime of the work itself. [23]

An obvious analogue for the *technê* of making in general, weaving, along with sculpture and singing, is one of the arts the Ovidian myths emphasize. Why these arts? What do they share as processes? As the philosopher Étienne Gilson has noted, no major arts have been invented since the Greeks,[24] and in this trilogy of arts we see the spectrum of an abstract relation to materials through music and singing, the two-dimensional relation of weaving and picture making, and the three-dimensional domain of sculpture. Furthermore, if we consider these practices not only in the frame of their resulting forms but also in terms of techniques, like all making, they require processes of augmentation and reduction, adding to and taking away, that derive from the release and shaping of materials prior to their emergence into their own finitude. The *Metamorphoses* itself, with its tumbling, accumulating narratives, turns every story of loss into a story of connection, as if relation were the compensation for loss of form and voice.

Yet the one human art that Ovid reminds us cannot be subdued by the will of the gods here is poetry itself, which endures as the form binding and surviving the stories it recounts. Indeed, as we have often glimpsed, poetic form has had an especially privileged status in Western aesthetics. In Kant's system, the fine arts hold second place to the powers of natural beauty, but within the hierarchy of the arts, Kant argues, as I have indicated earlier, for poetry's precedence:

> The art of poetry (which owes its origin almost entirely to genius, and will be guided least by precept or example) claims the highest rank of all. It expands the mind by setting the imagination free and presenting, within the limits of a given concept and among the unbounded manifold of forms possibly agreeing with it, the one that connects its presentation with a fullness of thought to which no linguistic expression is fully adequate, and thus elaborates itself to the level of ideas.[25]

This is a compressed and somewhat confusing statement, for Kant emphasizes first of all that poetic language, although itself language, can present a wealth of thought to which no verbal expression corresponds. What does this mean?

Poetic language is in and for itself and cannot be paraphrased or transposed to other language; its integrity of form depends on the facticity of what it is. And this "wealth of thought" is not so much conceptual as indeterminate. Unlike the plastic arts such as painting, which remain tied to sensuous appearance, poetry does not lend itself to sense knowledge or to the categories of the understanding. Poetry opens thought to the intuitions alone of sense impression and indicates the supersensuous realm of Ideas. The phrasing of a "sort of schema for the supersensuous" seems to refer to the imagination presenting a schema for something that can't be understood, hence echoing the thwarted schematizing of the imagination in the experience of beauty despite

Kant's concerted efforts to separate aesthetic judgments from the qualities of aesthetic objects. Kant's own poetic examples rely upon metaphorical descriptions of the setting sun that indicate the power of the aging Frederick the Great in one instance and peace shining forth from virtue in another.[26]

Kant's emphasis on aesthetical ideas, which we have been considering in relation to processes of metaphor, is derived from his sense that beauty is experienced as a free, unresolved play between the understanding and the imagination—the former almost, but not quite, offering up a concept or category for the phenomenon; the latter almost, but not quite, offering a visual schema for it. As we saw in the writing of Coleridge and Shelley, the "aesthetical idea," like the changing configuration of the setting sun or the multiple possibilities of symbols that are not resolved into signs, comes from the domain of the simile—of the provisional unstable comparison radiant with change and play. In post-Kantian thought, as art becomes the optimal means of philosophical reflection, Friedrich von Schiller especially will distinguish tensions between this kind of play drive and the drive to finite form in all works of art. Yet we can also see that simile is revealed as quite a different kind of trope from metaphor—the latter fuses and creates a new entity. That entity will inevitably become reified, passing into the history of the language, as Stevens emphasized, as a "dead metaphor," while new metaphors are generated.

Poetry, as an art of metaphor, made of thoughts via the materiality of the human artifact of language, thus helps to keep the language alive; the more the language is used, the more it is renewed. Similes and metaphors constantly open up the signifying power of language to abstraction and multiplicity and veer away from its functional uses. Above all, language is free of its dependence on finite meaning, or what we might call indexicality. All art resists such resolution into determined meaning in favor of a meaning effect, a capacity for meaning, and openness to it. Yet language is our primary vehicle of significance, a made accomplishment of the history of all speakers of the language, existing before we do and maintaining a place for us within it. Hence, when we take up language in forms of art, we intervene subjectively in the very substance of the cause of our own subjectivity. In this the import of Hegel's description of the maker's self-reflection comes into its own, for as earth is the source of all forms of natural beauty, language is the source of all forms of artifactual beauty; to reshape the language is to reshape the human world and to make a permanent change in the bounds of intelligibility. It is not surprising that, as we have seen, for Hegel, poetry is "the universal art of the mind, which has become essentially free."[27]

Even so, as German idealism has left us with a hierarchy of the arts that places freedom from material constraints high on the list of artistic values, with poetry—that art of felt thought—given pride of place, Kant, Hegel, and other philosophers in truth had little or no practical knowledge of art making itself and perhaps could not grasp that any art form involves the transformation of materials and the manifestation of an immanence drawn forward by imaginative thinking. For example, consider some rudimentary differences between making poems and making lithographs. Lithography, "writing on stone," is a form of printmaking invented only six years after the appearance of the *Critique of the Power of Judgment* by Kant's fellow Bavarian Alois Senefelder. It is an intensely process-oriented art form: the stones must be cut and then grained precisely; an image is drawn onto the stone with crayons, pencils, pens, and brushes that employ grease of various densities; rosin and talc are used to prepare the image for etching; the etching proceeds by the application of precisely determined solutions of acid, gum arabic, and other chemicals. The stone is then buffed; the lithographic ink is softened and readied; the paper is chosen for each state; the press is set at the correct pressure; the image is successively inked and washed as the states are explored. And then a second etch is applied, with a repetition of each stage, until finally an edition can be produced. Even if the lithographer manufactures some of his or her own materials—the ink, or the paper, for example—he or she is well aware that the stone, the ink, the rosin, the talc and chemicals, and the press itself all depend upon the labor and manufacturing activities of others. A poet may be able to begin with a closing couplet and construct the remainder of the work. Or a poet might easily start over or produce a fragment, but the lithographer has little or no flexibility in following through this process—and given the great expense of lithography stones, his or her debt to the past is often exaggerated by the fact that the first step in preparing a stone is often the erasure of a specific prior image.

Yet it would be a mistake not to recognize that the lithographer is, with each step, truly writing on and with stone. Something inside the stone is revealed, and the qualities of stone are placed in concert with the qualities of grease, water, acids, and solvents. Something beyond spoken language becomes a visual language of marks that designates significant spaces. Myriad possibilities, beyond the scale of any single lifetime, are at hand for making the mark, combining the materials, preparing the etch, printing the paper.

The poet as poet, in contrast, cannot draw forward the qualities of the surfaces upon which he or she writes. Nor can the poet alter the natural world, yielding it to speech. It therefore would be difficult to claim, as the idealist does, that the materiality of marks in stone is less free than the materiality of speech on the page. The poet's medium of language is dense with prior sounds and meanings; the poet cannot, like Lewis Carroll's Humpty Dumpty, control the meanings of words, establishing their significance "no more and no less." The poet trades in the living dynamic potential of ambiguity and metaphorical transposition; poets have a quicksilver material, and with every reading, whether silent or voiced, their work will be newly inflected. Their use of words changes all consequent uses of words, entering into the stream that is the always unfinished history of language.

In the end, any artist will exercise particular skills upon the material world and yield particular consequences; the artist feels pressure not only to pursue new directions and ingredients for any existing media but also to combine media and to create new media, including those that grow out of earlier techniques. The gestures of earth drawn from earth in sculpture, ceramics, and jewelry making, fibers isolated and woven in weaving and basket making, the press of a mark on an existing surface, the building up of new surfaces in printmaking and painting—all continue through time, with artists revising their objects, dimensions, and outcomes. The accumulating, never-ending history of art is the history of the development of the human senses. Each new material and technique is an opportunity or opening that further clarifies our relation to nature.

Those human artifacts drawn from the earth are transformed into worldly, speaking forms that continue to resist, in their *thing*ness, our human frames. Yet language is the material of self-actualization in both a passive and an active sense; there is no question of the "ready-made" in poetry; every resource of the poem is already in the language. Poems made of "received language" merely underscore their own unworked qualities; they are interventions in the figure of the artist and not in poetic form itself. This problem was addressed as early as Schiller's 1795 discourse "Naïve and Sentimental Poetry," where he concludes that the naive artist, with an unmediated relation to his material, is overly indebted to tradition, while the sentimental artist—the artist of reproductions, revivals, and innovations—is so taken by his own free spontaneity that his work lacks gravity. Schiller writes, "If one therefore sometimes misses the spirit in the creations of naïve genius, one will frequently seek in vain in the products of the sentimental for the matter. Both, therefore, albeit in entirely opposed ways, fall into the error of *emptiness*; for matter without spirit, and a play of spirit without matter, are both a cipher in the aesthetic judgment." Schiller's tension between play and form is here rehearsed as a conflict between thought and feeling, and he concludes that thought that is not anchored in "sensuous truth" is "overstrained."[28]

As aesthetic experience brings forward the dynamic between a natural beauty arising as display, most often for reproductive ends, and a nature that loves to hide, in arts made of language we see the hidden beauty behind all "functional" language; wrought into forms of the same substance, all functional dimensions of language disappear, all metaphors die, returning not to dust but to pure potential. Let us next take a closer look at two particular powers of poetic form—rhyming, which, by the utterly material means of sound, creates patterns abstracted from the unfolding meanings of experience; and encountering, which creates free associations and speculations independent of the limits of space and time.

6 / RHYMING

orange, chimney, breadth, circle, desert, monarch, month, virtue, wisdom

—English words that "cannot be rhymed at all"
listed in the *Princeton Encyclopedia of Poetry and Poetics*

De rithimorum quoque habitudine, prout sunt in fronte, vel in cauda, videtur omnis optata licentia concedenda . . .

— DANTE, *De vulgari eloquentia* 2.13.7[1]

I Rhyme's Opening

Two lines of poetry came to me one day in the form of a paradox: "There is a kind of leaving when you arrive / even though it's the place you've come from." And as I continued to write, *arrive* became *alive*, and *from* grew into *none*, and I found myself composing in terza rima, as each new stanza followed with increasing insistence and increasing ease. What drove this insistence and ease? It was, it seems, a sense of living voice—to arrive "alive" in a poem that, in fact, turned out to be an elegy. The dangling preposition in the second line already seemed to have framed the poem as spoken rather than written. Perhaps every elegy cannot help being concerned with aliveness, and its own living speech, in the face of a death, but to begin by writing and then to find yourself in speech can be the difference between death and life in any poem, and rhyme, along with other intelligible repetitions of sounds, is often the symptom or indication that the poem is quickening. If a poem remains predominantly writing, however, never coming alive to voice and to sounds as voiced, it will remain only a sketch for a work.

In the case of this poem that emerged to be concerned with the shedding succession of generations, inherited memories, and the differences between closed and open kinds of knowledge, it wasn't difficult to see how terza rima seemed to "fit" the theme. Or was it the other way around? Was—is—terza rima there waiting, an opening to a certain means of shaping inchoate feelings and experiences into form? Later, as I looked at that first line, I realized that "a kind of leaving when you arrive" is exactly what terza rima does. As the second rhyme of a stanza "arrives," the middle line-end word "leaves" to form its own new pair in the ensuing stanza.

Rhyming is at once both intended and compulsive, an art practice that makes full use of sound's potential for resonance and saturation. As Hegel noted, "What belongs peculiarly to lyric is the ramified figuration of rhyme which, with the return of the same sounds of letters, syllables, and words, or the alternation of different ones, is developed and completed in variously articulated and interlaced rhyme-strophes."[2] In other words, it is not only that stanzas can demand rhymes but also that rhymes can create stanza structures; lyric process is propelled by the sounded repetition of sameness and difference, of rhymes thrown forward as both moving line and anchor.

How is it, then, that as early as Aristotle's denigration of mere verse in the *Poetics*,[3] in Milton's arguments against the "troublesome and modern bondage of rhyming" in his preface to *Paradise Lost*, and on to modernist theories of free verse, rhyming has been viewed by many as both a purely formal device and a kind of restraint? Our English word *rhyme* does come from Latin and Greek *rhythmus* or *rhythmos*, and our speech rhythms are only a small instance of rhythm as a force in nature, indeed a force in the cosmos. Solar pulses, the ebb and flow of tides—as we have seen, those circadian rhythms that affect our sleeping and waking as heliotropic beings—are all part of this larger set of forces. And as we saw in my discussion of mood, the heartbeat is a feature of life before its function in the circulation of the blood has emerged.[4] What does this rhythm have to do with syntax? The rhythm of prose inevitably must grow out of the human experience of rhythms of all kinds, but nothing about syntax makes it the basis of natural rhythm. To hope to free rhythm from meter, as early proponents of free verse including Richard Aldington and Ezra Pound did, is to return to a real, rather than ideal, relation to nature. Yet it is hardly to create a condition of freedom, for natural rhythms are a contingent force everywhere in our existence, bearing down upon and transporting us as surely as we have breathing lungs and beating hearts.[5]

The Old English word *rim* signifies number and reminds us that meter is a determinative and ideal pattern placed over rhythm. Pure repetition of course is never possible—even within the logical realms of mathematics and physics, the temporal situation of the beholder fragments the possibility of such perfect isomorphism. Yet meter admits the possibility of organizing the language in ways that may include, and may also go beyond, the spoken language, and meter can function as an abstract grid even as it is never totally realized. Syllables have a life in meter that they cannot have in the actual ordinary practice of spoken phonemes—a fact exploited beautifully, for example, in the sprung rhythms of Gerard Manley Hopkins. Consider the opening lines of his 1885 sonnet "(The Soldier)." If they were written as a prose argument, they would look like this:

> Yes. Why do we all, seeing of a soldier, bless him? Bless our redcoats, our tars? Both these being, the greater part, but frail clay, nay but foul clay. Here it is: the heart, since, proud, it calls the calling manly, gives a guess that, hopes that, makes believe, the men must be no less. It fancies, feigns, deems, dears the artist after his art.

Hopkins writes them, however, like this:

> Yes. Whý do we áll, séeing of a / soldier, bless him? bléss
> Our redcoats, our tars? Both / thése being, the greater part,
> But frail clay, nay but foul clay. / Hére it is: the heart,
> Since, proud, it calls the calling / manly, gives a guess
> That, hopes that, mákesbelieve, / the men must be no less;
> It fancies, feigns, deems, déars / the artist after his art;

Hopkins had written in his journals that hexameter lines, such as these, would not work in English without splitting down the middle. In this poem, written while he served as confessor to the Cowley Barracks at Oxford, Hopkins uses that very effect, emphasized by his placing of a virgule in each line and by laying out a set of fissures: the see in seeing, the red in redcoats, the be in being, the call in calling, the less in bless, the man in manly, the makes in makesbelieve, the art in artist. Reading down his diacritical marks—*why all see/ bless// these// here// makes// dears*—the emphasized monosyllables are like an x-ray of the opening syntax whereby soldiers are blessed and endowed with certain attributes. This syntax is in tension with the dense language that remains unmarked in the poem: the frail and foul clay out of which this art is made; the sacrifice that "dears," exemplified at the volta between the octave and sestet by "Mark Christ our King." The simple exact rhyming: *abbaabbacdcdcd* (bless/art/heart/guess/less/art/smart/express/through/bliss/do/kiss/too/this) contrasts the enveloping, protective, structure of the octave's blessing to the marchlike duality of the sestet's two rhyme-words, designed to emphasize the soldiers' own point of view.

To ask what is obviously a rhetorical question: which admits of more freedom of expression, the regular prose syntax here or the poetic line, with its complex interplay of end rhyme, internal alliteration and consonance, split phrasing, and re-marked syllables? Even if a rhyme scheme is anticipated, the unfolding consequences of its manifestation can be full of surprises, particularly surprises of content and perspective.

Nevertheless, we still might wonder if rhyme is, as we assume rhythm is, a feature of nature, for the degree of mastery we have in using rhymes depends, in the largest sense, on the answer to this question. Whereas no poetry appears without rhythm and few poems appear without meter, ancient poetry, especially Greek poetry, in the West rarely used rhyme, and when it did, rhyme was often a feature of ridicule or comedy, as in the rhyming speech of the drunk Hercules in Euripides's *Alcestis* at lines 782–89, where the lines sound like hiccupping:

brotois hapasi katthanein ophéiletai,
kouk esti thnêtôn hostis exepístatai
tên aurion méllousan ei biôsetai:
to tês túkhês gar aphanes hoi probêsetai,
kast' ou didakton oud' halísketai tékhnêi.

Here is the free verse advocate Richard Aldington's 1930 translation of these lines, which, perhaps not surprisingly, do not rhyme:

> Know the nature of human life? Don't think you do. You couldn't. Listen to me. All mortals must die. Isn't one who knows if he'll be alive tomorrow morning. Who knows where Fortune will lead? Nobody can teach it. Nobody learn it by rules.[6]

The slightly tipsy veering quality of the Greek lines is lost in this prose version.

Rhyme appears as a dominant feature of poetry in the West only with the gradual substitution of accent for quantity in poetic measures. *Homeoteleuton*, the repetition of words that end alike, regardless of stress or quantity, was frowned upon by most classical and medieval rhetoricians, especially with regard to unstressed syllables, and the fact that most words of more than one syllable adhered to the Latin rule of penultimate stress meant that few words could be rhymed.[7] The hymns of Hilary of Poitiers and Saints Ambrose and Augustine in the third and fourth centuries begin a syncretic tradition of using both assonance and end rhyme. Following the rhyming couplets of the "Dies irae" ("The Day of Wrath") of St. Columba (521–97), we can see in this sixth-century Latin hymn the influence of Irish rhyming practices, which themselves date to a tradition of pre-Christian oral poetry surviving from the Celtic invasions of the fourth century BCE to fifth-century monastic transcriptions and beyond:

> Regis regum rectissimi
> prope est dies domini,
> dies irae et vindictae,
> tenebrarum et nebulae,
> diesque mirabilium
> tonitruorum fortium,
> dies quoque angustiae,
> maeroris ac tristitiae,
> in quo cessabit mulierum
> amor et desiderium,
> hominumque contentio
> mundi huius et cupido.[8]

The end-rhymed couplets play on a cumulative and receding pattern of sound like a wave, with the most variation at either end: *aabbccbbccdd*. They are offset by initial assonance and much internal rhyme.

It is surely one of the ironies of literary history that a powerfully refined ancient Irish system of rhyming converged in medieval Latin with an earlier classical tradition of discounting rhyme. Book 5, chapter 13, of Caesar's *Gallic Wars* is the first Western record of the social context of such Irish rhyming practices, and includes an account of the professorial duties of the Druids. The young men sent to Druid schools studied verses for as long as twenty years to acquire the sacred and juridical knowledge encoded in their complex systems of meter and rhyme. This poetics, practiced as well by Goidelic, Brittonic, and Welsh poets, established, in addition to rules of line length and syllabic patterns, what are known as generic rhymes—rhymes based on identical vowel sounds, certain nasal clusters, and clusters of consonants, particularly *g-d-b*; *dd-l-r*; *gh-f*-w.[9] Just as the incantatory power of rhyme remains evident on any playground, we still see throughout the West vestiges of the shamanic power of rhyme in rhyming choruses and refrains of folk songs and folk stories.

The Germanic languages, including Old English, because of their emphasis on fore-stressed words, developed alliteration as the primary structural feature of their poetry. In the Romance languages, where word stress is not generally as strong as phrase stress, rhyme as we know it came to prominence, particularly in the period from 1100 to 1300 by means of troubadour verse and the evolution of an emphasis on sound in the *dolce stil novo*. At this moment the erotic and cognitive powers of art seem intensified as poets develop techniques that require inhabiting multiple perspectives and anticipated patterns. Ezra Pound notes, for example, that a canzon of Arnaut Daniel beginning "L'aura amara" praised by Dante depended upon holding seventeen rhymes in mind at once.[10] Gestures of withholding and release, calculation and surprise, typify a poetics eroticized by its courtly love context, where the metaphorical and imaginative had as much power as the literally realized, and the deferred pleasures of the aesthetic held sway.[11]

Consider this little poem, heir to the troubadour tradition and addressed to rhyming poets ("A diversi rimatori"), by a poet friend of Dante Alighieri, Dante da Maiano:

Provedi, saggio, ad esta visione,
e per mercé ne trai vera sentenza.
Dico: una donna di bella fazone,
di cu' el meo cor gradir molto s'agenza,

mi fé d'una ghirlanda donagione,
verde, fronzuta, con bella accoglienza:
appresso mi trovai per vestigione
camicia di suo dosso, a mia parvenza.
Allor di tanto, amico, mi francai,
che dolcemente presila abbracciare:
non sì contese, ma ridea la bella.
Così, ridendo, molto la baciai:
del più non dico, ché mi fé giurare.
E morta, ch'è mia madre, era con ella.[12]

Published in Dante Alighieri's *Rime* as number 39, this sonnet was written, like most of da Maiano's work, as a piece of coterie poetry.[13] It compresses a remarkable amount of action and thought into its brief compass. The shift between possessive pronouns (meo cor / mia parvenza / mia madre) and passive verbs (mi fé, mi trovai, mi francai, mi fé [giurare]) adds to the drama of possession and transformation. The rhyme scheme's transition at the volta from *abababab* to *cdecde* signals as well the change from the kissing couple to the presence of a third figure—the poet's dead mother.[14] A psychoanalytic treatise could be written about this development, but for now suffice it to say that it would be impossible to render the action of this poem in free verse without giving up a great deal: the braided garland, the twined lovers, the echoing *b* and "ci" sounds of kissing (baciare), the toll-like sounding of *bella*, *bella*, *bella*, into *ella*, and the ghostly triangulation of the third figure and third sound would be lost entirely.

Troubadour lyricists and poets of the *dolce stil novo* rely on rhyme patterns as much as accent. Nevertheless, poets can use rhyme as they compose in free verse and still remain independent of the relatively fixed meters of earlier poetry, as English poets have at least since John Skelton's work at the turn of the sixteenth century. Indeed, the Skeltonic two- to three-beat line, with patterns of increasing and subsiding density of rhyme, seems as close as one could come to a precision between the compulsions of rhythm and emotion. Here is Skelton's "Mistress Margaret Hussey," composed in 1495, revised, and first published in 1522–23 as one of a ten-lyric cycle, *The Garland of Laurel*, that the poet wrote for the women in attendance at the court of the countess of Surrey:

> Merry Margaret,
> As midsummer flower,
> Gentle as falcon
> Or hawk of the tower
> With solace and gladness,
> Much mirth and no madness,
> All good and no badness;
> So joyously,
> So maidenly,
> So womanly
> Her demeaning
> In every thing,
> Far, far passing
> That I can indite,
> Or suffice to write
> Of Merry Margaret
> As midsummer flower,
> Gentle as falcon
> Or hawk of the tower.
> As patient and still
> And as full of good will
> As fair Isaphill,
> Coriander,
> Sweet pomander,
> Good Cassander,
> Steadfast of thought,
> Well made, well wrought,
> Far may be sought
> Ere that ye can find
> So courteous, so kind
> Merry Margaret,

As midsummer flower,
Gentle as falcon
Or hawk of the tower.

At this moment of initial separation of English poetry from the alliterative verse that prevailed before it, we see certain changes wrought by rhyming. The alternating rhymes of the refrain seem to collapse into the insistent trochaic rhymes of the exposition. The poet inverts our usual expectation that refrains will rhyme or sing the closures of the more discursive lines of a poem. There is a compulsion to Skelton's use of falling meters, emphasized by the insistent rhymes, just as his rising meters seem to call up or slow the motion of his poems. In "Mistress Margaret Hussey" rhyme pairs separated by unrhymed lines turn into unseparated trios, then unseparated pairs again: Margaret/flower/falcon/tower; gladness/madness/badness; joyously/maidenly/womanly; demeaning/everything/passing; indite/write; Margaret/flower/falcon/tower; still/will/Isaphill; Coriander/pomander/Cassander; thought/wrought/sought; find/kind; Margaret/flower/falcon/tower. These moments of intense rhyming are matched by exact, epideictic details: the trio rhymes list adjectival nouns and adverbs that swirl around the person of Margaret Hussey as the poet barely is able to "indite" and "write" and "find" her "kind." Spinning proper names and metaphorical terms, the poet's naming practices effect the turns and metamorphoses of praise by something akin to uttering spells. Rhyme is in the end the main reason Skelton can make such bold observations about Margaret Hussey and other ladies-in-waiting.

A striking feature of the history of rhyme is that even when, as in our own era, rhyming does not dominate poetry, the use of rhyme, continuing or renewed, does not acquire an archaic cast. Milton's introductory remarks to the reader of *Paradise Lost* mentioned above argue that "Rime being no necessary Adjunct or true Ornament of Poem or good Verse, in longer works especially, but the Invention of a barbarous Age to set off wretched matter and lame Meter." He went on to say that "only in apt Numbers, fit quantity of Syllables, and the sense variously drawn out from one Verse into another, not in the jingling sound of like endings," was a "fault avoided by the learned Ancients."[15] Milton was well aware that classical poetry rarely rhymed. Nevertheless, in neoclassicism rhyming couplets return to become the dominant verse form.[16]

Analogously, despite the triumph of free verse in modernism, in contemporary works by poets as varied as the American L=A=N=G=U=A=G=E poet Charles Bernstein, the Northern Irish lyricists Paul Muldoon and Ciaran Carson, and the Milanese love poet Patrizia Valduga rhyme takes precedence over many other aspects of form. Rhyme returns as inevitably as, well, rhyme and the seasons that in many ways it emulates. If it disappears only to reappear in the practice of poetry, perhaps this is yet another level of the relation of rhyme to the aesthetics of interval. Rhyming is based in aural coincidences that themselves depend upon noncoincidence in time and space.

This natural cycle of rhyme and in rhyme was described by Emerson in his essay "The Poet": "A rhyme in one of our sonnets should not be less pleasing than the iterated nodes of a seashell, or the resembling difference of a group of flowers. The pairing of the birds is an idyl . . . a tempest is a rough ode without falsehood or rant; a summer, with its harvest sown, reaped and stored, is an epic song, subordinating how many admirably executed parts. Why should not the symmetry and truth that modulate these, glide into our spirits, and we participate in the invention of nature?"[17] Sound vibrations and color vibrations in fact do seem to have some correlation,[18] and rhyme can be a feature of visual experience as much as an auditory one. When Emerson speaks of the "resembling difference of a group of flowers," he could have in mind the abstractions of the color wheel or the way the yellows of daffodils, narcissus, and forsythia are followed each spring by the purples of crocuses and hyacinths, tulips and lilacs. This resembling difference is a feature of the numerical rhyme that underlies the appearance of the Fibonacci sequence in the seed heads of sunflowers and coneflowers, the fractal geometry of the chambered nautilus and pine cones, various twins and multiples in the living world, and the convergent evolution of similar species in different contexts. It is indeed possible to use the word *rhyme* to describe certain senses of rotation and repetition in time—as when we note coincidences or have a sense of déjà vu. Our temporal powers of retrospection and projection depend upon abilities to hold in mind and attend to resonances that are employed in the apprehension of rhyme.

Emerson's list of principles—resembling difference, iteration, pairing, sequence, symmetry, and ultimately invention under the pressure of truth—also indicates some of the relations rhyming holds to simile, and hence what Emanuel Swedenborg, Charles Baudelaire, and Emerson himself have thought of as correspondences in the most general sense. Swedenborg wrote that "order and the world are in an imperfect state when they do not harmonize; and in such degree imperfect, as they fall short of harmony."[19] And in his 1850 essay on Swedenborg in *Representative Men*, Emerson wrote of Swedenborg's theories of correspondence: "These grand rhymes or returns in nature,—the dear, best-known face startling us at every turn, under a mask so unexpected that we think it the face of a stranger, and carrying up the semblance into divine forms,—delighted the prophetic eye of Swedenborg; and he must be reckoned a leader in that revolution, which, by giving to science an idea, has given to an aimless accumulation of experiments, guidance and form and a beating heart."[20]

Emerson's idea that "we participate the invention of nature," however, surely stems as well from Aristotle's contention that *poiesis* as making is a means of discovery regarding our relation to nature.[21] What, then, does poetic rhyme—that is, rhyme that is both intended and received—draw on and complete? If rhyme is a feature of nature, or at least of our temporal perception of nature, rhyme also is an ever-present feature of language. Rhyme offers a particular kind of pattern—one that is only partly determinative. Unlike rhythm, which may exist as pure haptic or tactile feeling, rhyme comes with acoustical, if not always semantic, content; and unlike meter, which remains ideal, rhyme is always realized or manifested. In rhyming, poets explore a balance between the will and contingency, and such a balance is a recurring theme of poetic treatises on rhyme. As we follow, for example, the intermittent discussion of rhyme in the text that provides the epigraph on rhyme and freedom for this study, Dante's *De vulgari eloquentia*, we see a frequent play between describing rhyme as an active "weaving" (*texere*) and a passive "echo" (*eco*)—the dynamic between the intended production and involuntary reception of sounds could not be more clearly set forward.[22]

Nevertheless, in rhyming poets can produce sounds that "sound" involuntary, and their listeners can find their hearing gradually attuned to particular intervals. Wordsworth believed that our absorption in such patterns might help us endure painful feeling in poetry's content. He especially singles out the power of rhyme in this regard: "The end of Poetry is to produce excitement in co-existence with an overbalance of pleasure. . . . Now the co-presence of something regular, something to which the mind has been accustomed in various moods and in a less excited state, cannot but have great efficacy in tempering and restraining the passion by an intertexture of ordinary feeling. . . . There can be little doubt but that more pathetic situations and sentiments, that is, those which have a greater proportion of pain connected with them, may be endured in metrical composition, especially in rhyme, [more] than in prose."[23] In *The World as Will and Idea*, Schopenhauer also emphasized the mesmerizing power of rhyme when he described our "consent" to recurring sound. As he described it, such consent involves willingly following and blindly accepting what we read, withholding judgment, and surrendering to its "power of convincing."[24] Even as it is often an effect of conscious will, or, as we say, a "scheme," the urge to rhyme seems to come to us from somewhere else, from some outside that may be deeply inside, in the sense that it is unconscious, or perhaps simply compulsive.

The "I can't help myself" aspect to rhyming behavior can be found in babies' babbling and in the verbal dueling of many cultures, including contemporary hip-hop and rap music practices. Although rhyming is part of the language of the crib, most people are able to notice and use nonadjacent rhymes for the first time between the ages of five and seven—other phonological skills appear at this age, and this is of course also most often the age of the onset of reading, whether children are learning to read a language with a fairly transparent orthography, such as Italian, or a fairly opaque one, such as English.[25] One of the most suggestive aspects of the role of rhyming in language learning is that rhyming seems to precede, or help facilitate, phonological awareness per se.[26] When words are grouped by "phonological neighborhood," as in *brat, rot, at, rat*, adults have some difficulty recognizing individual words, but such density actually leads to better word recognition in infants and young children.[27] In attending to rhyme, we are deeply engaged in a poetry made of words. Our sense of individual words is renewed as we return to the childhood scene of distinguishing words from one another, hearing each word fully as both different from and similar to other words. As Schopenhauer indicates, to be on the receiving end of rhyme may involve a sensual surrender, but the conditions under which such surrender happens are the consequence of a deliberative and skillful intention, especially in those forms that have come down to us through oral tradition.

We could say that rhyming mediates the relation between the purely felt that is rhythm and the purely rational that is meter. Rhyme's relation to semantics remains both under- and overdetermined, for rhyming can endow meaning with greater depth or empty it of its syntactical or context-bound force. Using rhyme, poets introduce a relation between memory and anticipation that also is characterized by pattern and variation. As the perception of rhyme is both retrospective and proleptic, rhyming requires awareness in ways that the physical possession of rhythm does not. Rhythm is lulling; in contrast, rhyme, like meter, requires identification and attention; everything counts, including pauses and silences.[28] Rhyme is an effect at a distance; to this extent, rhyming can serve as an interruption of, counter to, or surprise amid rhythm and meter, both of which occur at a constant measure.

Because vowels are acoustically more alike than consonants, any vowel can be in slant rhyme with any other, and whereas the differentiation of phonemes that creates intelligible sounds is the task of everyday speech, the possibility of alliteration, consonance, assonance, and the vast array of other kinds of rhymes is always latent in speech and serves such functions as stabilizing the forms of irregular verbs.[29] Rhyming and punning bear a family resemblance in this sense, for as puns join multiple meanings within one morpheme and so make the integrity of a morpheme as a unit of meaning literally break apart, so does rhyming show that proximity in sound has little consequence for proximity of semantics.[30] Rhyme is in this sense always a showcase for the arbitrary nature of the sign and calls us short in our efforts to dominate meaning; rhyming draws us beyond ourselves with its potential for aural pleasure, which, when one is trying to concentrate on univocal meaning and syntactical sequence, can be something like aural pain.

Here is the basis of the tension between rhyme and syntax—a tension at the heart of the modernist rejection of rhyme. This disparity is also the reason that syntax motivated by the requirements of rhyme will seem unnatural. Rhyme punctuates and concentrates, it does not flow.[31]

II How Rhymes Rhyme

"Rhyme schmyme, I never use the stuff," a poet colleague said to me when I mentioned I was thinking about rhyme. His very reply echoes the everyday use of what we call in English "close rhyme" (in German *Schlagreim*, "hammer rhyme") as a mnemonic that somehow has a skepticism built in. When we hear *rhyme schmyme*, *helter-skelter*, *fender bender*, *double trouble*, *mishmash*, *hoity-toity*, *flimflam*, *ding-dong*, or such ancient examples as *hoi polloi* and *holy moly*, we are in the realm of instant parody. The reason for that, it seems, is the universal principle that the closer rhymes appear as adjacent pairs, the stronger the sound play and the lesser the stability of meaning in individual words. These mnemonics are models of equivocation; the second term modifies and weakens the force of the first as our attention is drawn to sound alone.[32] Poets use adjacency in a range of ways beyond rhyme, but it is memorable when rhyming words are stacked very close to one another in a poem, as they are, for example, in John Donne's "Song": "And swear / Nowhere / Lives a woman true, and fair."[33] Envelope stanzas, such as *abba*, foreground the possibilities of hearing the differences between consecutive and nonadjacent rhyme pairs and thereby require two kinds of suspension in the listener.[34]

Making rhymes involves separating marked and unmarked utterances, yet pausing does not affect it, and rhyme is neither universal nor precisely language specific. Poetic rhyme is a record of the living language, more particularly the poet's living language at a moment of relation between languages and poetic practices—it is thus both more local and more universal than any given language's storehouse of rhymes. Those third- and fourth-century Latin hymns mentioned above that work under both quantitative and qualitative systems of meter are a practice where diverging traditions meet.[35] The variable initial, internal, and terminal rhymes of Hebrew liturgical poetry in the fourth century and the free-floating rhymed strophes of early eleventh-century Iberian Arabic poetry are further examples of syncretic rhyming practices. Whereas Chaucer's rhymes tend, like those French rhymes on which they were modeled, to be full or "perfect" for the most part, from the time of Spenser forward similar, rather than identical, sounds are used. Sidney's *Defence of Poetry* suggests that rhyme is an ornament, adding a pleasing melody and harmony to a work.[36] Other writers, such as the prosodist George Saintsbury, have been concerned with rhyme as a punctuating device in rhythm.[37]

Moments of intense rhyming activity seem to coincide with the meeting of dialects and languages—the melting pot of troubadour culture, the macaronic verse of medieval scholasticism, Dante's turn between Latin and the Tuscan vernacular, Chaucer's encounter with Romance languages, Edmund Spenser's with Irish. We find other polyglot practices in Pushkin's use of Turkish rhyming words in his poems of 1829[38] and the Greek, French, German and English rhymes of Ezra Pound and T. S. Eliot. The freezing and melting that typify erotic poetry in the West also seem to characterize the social life of rhymes. Rhyming fixes sounds inflexibly at the ends of lines, or freezes a local pronunciation like a fossil. Yet rhyming forms a record of how pronunciation is constantly changing by means of living language.

The larger history of rhyme has yet to be written, but perhaps, as we saw in the earlier discussion of Druid poetics, that history will reveal close connections to a history of the ritual or magical manipulation of objects. As Aristotle noted, sensation continues even after an organ has ceased to sense it—he uses the analogy of the motion of any object that has been thrown even after the thrower ceases to touch it.[39] Rhyming and juggling, for example, are prominent in sixth-century Ireland, thirteenth-century Provence, and the street performances and hip-hop forms of our own era, and in all these practices we see a separation, or breaking up, of bodily purposiveness in the service of an external form or outline. That external form establishes a space with its own internal power—the power of the intrinsic artwork or a space of sacred attention, or both.[40]

Rhyming tends to overcome alliteration once words drop their unstressed endings. But as we have seen, rhyme does not have to show up at the ends of words or the ends of lines. And if it doesn't, the ends of lines are of course marked by measure, or ratio, or reason alone. Lines without rhyme or reason in this sense have to have some other means of ending—perhaps a dogma of "breath" or an adherence to prose syntax. Nevertheless, line-end rhyme seems linked broadly to the kinds of paralinguistic marking we find in clapping, stamping, and clicking speech play in many cultures, from the clicking markers that nursing mothers use in Chinese nursery rhymes to the recent fad for singing "Happy Birthday" in American restaurants with each phrase marked by a collective hand clap.[41]

Clapping, stamping, and clicking indeed emphasize the relation between our bodily symmetry and symmetrical sounds—like nonsense phonemes, they can be considered a secondary level of rhythmic punctuation. And once rhyme accrues around phonemes that are also morphemes, it becomes an indispensable and attached dimension of the poem's meaning. We could argue inversely that nonsemantic forms of punctuated sound become meaningful as they appear in poems. This is yet another way that *poiesis* keeps us ahead of the existing possibilities of a language, giving us the freedom to create meanings where there are none and deny them where they may seem to appear. When words are used at once linguistically and paralinguistically, separations between speech and sound do not hold, and the performative power of words is strengthened.

Line-end rhyme thus involves subduing or suppressing rhymes that occur elsewhere, as hearing rhymes in poetic forms involves subduing or suppressing rhymes in the spoken language in general. We could conclude that a rhyme is a rhyme only if it is heard as one, but we can also think of rhyme as a vector of arbitrariness and sound for its own sake that is always latent in any utterance. Perhaps a desire for emphasis or semantic reinforcement, or for a practice that makes perfect, underlies a dog's multiple barks, a bird's repertoire of more than one song, animal warning cries that continue even after a danger is gone. But the repetition of sound in human rhymes also is conducive to memory; as George Santayana wrote in his study of the cognitive claims of memory, a memory does not sink back into old experience but rather recovers knowledge by means of the awakening of affect or sentiment,[42] and the rhymes of any work create such an affective field.

We have only to think of rhyme's relation to the production of sound in music to have some clearer sense of this power to create effects across temporal distance. To hear external objects ring, chime, or otherwise produce sounds against one another, we must hold them next to each other, rub them against each other, or pluck or otherwise play them. But to create those sounding external objects that are rhymes, whether we are producing them or receiving them, we need only use our aural memory—the physical sound itself is not lost into space; it can be called back or summoned by the next instance of the complementary sound. And we need do this only three times to establish a pattern that makes it all the easier then to go on to play variations on that sound.

Remembering and anticipating the progress of a piece of music depends upon certain structural devices in the same way that remembering and anticipating rhymes does. For a rhyme to be held over so many lines, so great a distance, it also must resonate beyond its adjacent sounds. Rhyming practices, by varying between opening and closing consonant sounds and internal vowel sounds, give words interiors and exteriors; because there are many more similarities between vowels than between consonants, using rhyme also moderates and distinguishes those sounds. Similarly, the so-called unrhymed or unmarked end words of a poem can acquire a particular semantic cast simply because they do not rhyme: we are all familiar with the letdown effect of the World War I poets' use of such unrhymed words at closing. But consider how, for example, in the first two ballad stanzas of the "And Did Those Feet" passage of Blake's *Milton*, the lack of rhyme between *time* and *God* and *Divine* and *here* comes to outweigh the rhymes of *green* and *seen* and *hills* and *mills*:

And did those feet in ancient time,
Walk upon Englands mountains green:
And was the holy Lamb of God,
On Englands pleasant pastures seen!

And did the Countenance Divine,
Shine forth upon our clouded hills?

And was Jerusalem builded here,
Among these dark Satanic Mills?

Analogously, the slant rhymes of Emily Dickinson's "A Narrow Fellow in the Grass" (rides/is; seen/on; Corn/Noon Sun/gone) underline the intermittent exact rhymes of *Bone* and *alone*, as the latter pair also stand in stark contrast at the close of the poem to the easy meeting of the singular syllable *me* with the several syllables of *cordiality* in this version of 1865:

A narrow Fellow in the Grass
Occasionally rides—
You may have met him—did you not
His notice sudden is—

The Grass divides as with a Comb—
A spotted shaft is seen—
And then it closes at your feet
And opens further on—

He likes a Boggy Acre
A Floor too cool for Corn
Yet when a Boy, and Barefoot—
I more than once, at Noon
Have passed, I thought, a Whip lash
Unbraiding in the Sun—
When stooping to secure it
It wrinkled, and was gone—

Several of Nature's People
I know, and they know me—
I feel for them a transport
Of cordiality—

But never met this Fellow,
Attended, or alone
Without a tighter breathing
And Zero at the Bone—

The poem's geometry of meeting is made of lines and circles: lines that open into circles (like "Zero at the Bone") and circles that open the spaces between lines (like the path of a cylindrical snake through a patch of grass). In this poem Dickinson also uses a device that seems close to "close rhyme," and yet, so far as I know, we have no term for it: the pairing of identical letters. Our letters, after all, are made of circles, parts of circles, and lines. Here are the words of the poem that have one or more of such pairings: *narrow, Fellow, Grass, occasionally, sudden, Grass, spotted, feet, boggy, Floor, too, cool, Barefoot, Noon, passed, stooping, feel, Fellow, attended*. If we then look at the doubled letters themselves—*rr llss cc lldd ss tt ee gg oo oo oo oo oo ss oo ee lltt*—we can see that they culminate in a chorus of serpentines and "oo" circles that have emerged from the grasslike *ll*'s before they [ha]lltt.

Given the power of rhyme schemes of all kinds to lend particular semantic and visual weight to the place of unrhymed words, we might see the development of free verse as an unrhymed pause in the greater scheme of rhyme's poetic history.[43] Rhyme endows us with some particular freedoms—among them: the vernacular, including the locality of the poem itself, becomes released from the standard; the monolingual enters into dialogue with the multilingual; sound is opened up by vision, and even released from meaning entirely; expectation is released into surprise; and, perhaps rhyme's greatest gift, pattern is drawn from the forgetting of time. Rhyme is perfect, imperfect, total, and partial at once. To follow Dante, why not allow, in making poems or any other art form, "as much liberty as may be desired"?

orange/strange, chimney/homily, breadth/heath, circle/myrtle, desert/death's hurt, monarch/my ark, month/loath, virtue/eschew, wisdom/his dome

7 / MEETING

It seems safe to say that man would know nothing of inner freedom if he had not first experienced a condition of being free as a worldly tangible reality. We first become aware of freedom or its opposite in our intercourse with others, not in the intercourse with ourselves. Before it became an attribute of thought or a quality of the will, freedom was understood to be the free man's status, which enabled him to move, to get away from home, to go out into the world and meet other people in deed and word. This freedom clearly was preceded by liberation: in order to be free, man must have liberated himself from the necessities of life. But the status of freedom did not follow automatically upon the act of liberation. Freedom needed, in addition to mere liberation, the company of other men who were in the same state, and it needed a common public space to meet them.

—HANNAH ARENDT, "What Is Freedom?"[1]

The poetry of Dante may be considered as the bridge thrown over the stream of time, which unites the modern and ancient world.

—SHELLEY, "Defence of Poetry"[2]

I A Freedom of Association

For English-language poets many etymologies and sources meet in the meaning of *meeting* and words that are, like the lovers of traditional ballad, "well-met": a meeting that fits; a fit or shape that meets or measures; a meeting of minds and makers, to meet the eye of, to exercise a meet judgment. Yet from the messenger speeches of classical tragedy to the perambulations of troubadours and bards, we are familiar with the far wider tradition of the poetic speaker as a figure who brings the news, either immediate or prophetic. Wanderers and minstrels may remain strangers, but they often find welcome and welcoming audiences abroad, including patrons. The wandering ninth-century minstrel-*scôp* of the Saxon Myrgings, Widsith (whose name means "Far Journey"), sang optimistically of this possibility:

> The makar's wierd is to be a wanderer:
> the poets of mankind go through the many countries,
> speak their needs, say their thanks.
> Always they meet with someone, in the south lands or the north,
> who understands their art, an open-handed man
> who would not have his fame fail among the guard
> nor rest from an earl's deeds before the end cuts off
> light and life together.
> Lasting honour shall be his,
> a name that shall never die beneath the heavens.[3]

Yet there is one poet who has explored the possibilities of the poem of meeting more than any other—Dante, whose *Commedia* remains one of world poetry's greatest meeting places. It is not only these traditional aspirations and meanings associated with the poet as stranger that are at work in Dante's legacy, but also a larger poetic structure of encounters and a purpose for poetry as a face-to-face art of emerging insights and mutual transformations. To write a poem is from the outset to intend toward someone who will attend to one's words—to extend the work, to stretch toward another.[4] The powerful conversations we find in classical drama—whether they result in the separations of tragedy or the joinings of comedy—involve speakers who fulfill their roles through speech that is already scripted by the gods themselves. Dante, however, abandons such scripted, ritualized speech and gives a sense of the poetic line as freely expressed and made by a single, developing poetic speaker. In the *Convivio*, Dante had written that the greatest desire of each thing—and the first given it by nature—is to return to its origin,[5] and in the *Commedia* he is gradually drawn to a premature meeting, before he is finished making, with his Maker who is himself uncreated. And Dante will have many significant meetings on his way to this meeting.

The spaces where the poet encounters others in voluntary, free association include the space of the poem itself. Meeting with others, including the stranger, the dead, the dreamed, and the divine, Dante's poet-speaker does not admit impediment, and his poem of meeting comes into relief against a long historical panorama of works in the voices of sailors and soldiers and wanderers facing all-too-real hardship and solitude. These poetic speakers long for reunion—domestic, erotic, or platonic—and the poem itself is the first overture to such a meeting. Alcaeus's lyric fragment 73, for example, describes a ship saying she "has no wish to be struck by a . . . wave and to fight against the rain . . . and . . . battered by a hidden reef" and adds that she wishes "to forget these things and to enjoy being young in company with you all." Horace was much taken with these themes and addresses the Greek poet directly in *Odes* 2.13: "Ille et nefasto te posuit die," describing how he sings "with your golden plectrum of the hardships of your boat, the evil hardships of exile, the hardships of war . . ."[6] The trope of longing for meeting also suffuses this beloved but anonymous English lyric committed to paper in the late fifteenth or early sixteenth century:

> Western wynd, when wyll thou blow,
> The small rayne downe can rayne?
> Cryst, yf my love were in my armys,
> And I yn my bed agayne!

Unlike other medieval and Renaissance poems of similar themes—"Blow, Northerne Wynd," in the Harley Lyrics, or the folk songs "Blow the Wind Southerly" and "Bring Back My Bonny to Me"—this lyric seems to respond on not only thematic but also metrical grounds to a classical source, Tibullus's first elegy in *Book One*:

> quam iuvat immites ventos audire cubantem
> et dominam tenero continuisse sinu
> aut, gelidas hibernus aquas cum fuderit Auster,
> securum somnos imbre iuvante sequi!

In the translation of Robert Jungman, "What delight to hear the winds rage as I lie and hold my love safe in my gentle clasp; or when the stormy south wind sheds the chilling showers, untroubled to seek after sleep, the rain my lullaby!"[7] In such poems the situation of calm, necessary to listening to songs and lyrics, is internalized as a theme.

Dante's masterpiece, however, grows from an exile enforced by a threat of violence; creating a world and peopling it with figures drawn from the realms of the living and the dead, the poet crosses every boundary—earthly, hellish, purgatorial, and heavenly. But the *Commedia* only subtly expresses Dante's homelessness, and it is not longing for Firenze that troubles him. Nor is his great work merely a narrative of pilgrimage and resting places. For later historical pilgrims like Margerie Kempe and fictional ones like those of Chaucer, and perhaps especially the *pícaros* and rogues who make their way from the Renaissance and on to the novel, are all the more themselves wherever they go. This tradition could be said to culminate in the pinball universe of random, yet overdetermined, freedom we find in Ariosto's *Orlando furioso*. In Ariosto's romance, each one of the myriad "accidental" meetings between characters readily is transformed into captivity and back to freedom. Clearly indebted to Dante, Ariosto nevertheless underlines the ways that not meeting is as likely as meeting in such worlds. He thereby gives coincidence great significance, just as he demonstrates that such significance might be arbitrary. Random meetings further the plot of the work but do not result in the psychological or spiritual transformations we associate with the *Commedia* or Dante's earlier work in lyric.[8]

Even so, Ezra Pound is not exactly right when he says the *Commedia* is itself a poem of lyric expression.[9] It is true that the work is intensely subjective; but it is a narrative poem of retrospection and reconsideration. It contains songs, but it is not a song; the speaker expresses himself in the first person, but that person is undergoing serious self-revision, to the point of conversion. When ancient lyric poets like Sappho or Archilochus, using the rhetorical strategy of *priamel*, say "others may think *x*, but I think *y*," they are setting themselves off in relation to other speakers, and particularly other poets, and they are emphasizing the fixed traits of their natures. Dante, however, is crowned and mitered over himself in *Purgatorio* 27, line 142, through a performative act of Virgil—another poet endows him with the intellect and art necessary for self-making.[10]

What could be a lonely solipsism becomes instead a practice of revision. Dante's extraordinary capacity for self-overcoming and self-understanding is revealed especially in the densely hermeneutic gap between the scenes of encounters and the scene of writing. Yet this capacity for reflection is evident in many aspects of Dante's practices as an author. Consider the freedom with which he revisits his own work: he creates a commentary for his early lyrics by reworking them into the *Vita nuova*; he revises the *Vita nuova* and later lyrics in the *Convivio*, and he then revises the *Convivio* in the *Commedia* and revises the *Commedia* in *De monarchia*.[11] Traditional *cante*-fables and other oral forms split up the roles of speaking and singing within a single work. But it was Dante who cleared the way for a poem to contain its own criticism and for the poet to go beyond mere change and novelty to self-knowledge via revision and the exploration of antithetical possibilities. For Dante the poet's task is a great unfinished project within which individual works, or parts of works, might be integral and perfected forms. This is a model for the poet's life's work that has had profound repercussions for the career of every consequent major poet—indeed, this model has come to define what we mean when we speak of a major poet.

Dante's use of the vernacular, his decision to speak intimately to his readers in their own language, is another dimension of the freedom of meeting in his work. There are certain departures from Tuscan: the Provençal of Arnaut Daniel in *Purgatorio* 26; the playful use of Bolognese slang in the meeting with Caccianemico in *Inferno* 18 and Lucchese dialect in the meeting with Bonagiunta in *Purgatorio* 24; the nonsense of Nimrod in *Inferno* 31; the brief explosions of Latin in the greetings of Cacciaguida and the Latin hymns of angels; the swift and marked switch to the *voi* form in Canto 16 of the *Paradiso*; the inclusion, as Osip Mandelstam noted, of many kinds of stammerers, baby-talkers, and tongue-tied lispers.[12] Yet these departures are all, to use one of Dante's own metaphors, like a bit of salt sprinkled on bread.

If we remember that the major revolutions in poetry since the Enlightenment have been shaped as commitments to a more popular, and more expansive, diction—language as it was really spoken by men in Wordsworth's Romanticism, for example, the speech of Polish immigrant mothers in William Carlos Williams's American modernism—we start to see the possibilities for free assembly that Dante has brought us. Things and persons have to be moving on different courses—like astronomical bodies—if they are going to meet. They cannot come from the same place, and a certain freedom of movement must be guaranteed. It is significant that the souls trapped in Hell are immobilized and blinded in their sunless world, and that among all the figures of Purgatory, the poet Sordello, in *Purgatorio* 6 through 9, has the kind of freedom to wander that we find in classical tradition among the souls of Elysium. It is a freedom to find out, to look into, to know and converse.[13]

Yet Dante at the start of the *Commedia* places himself in the precarious position of too much freedom, the position of straying without coordinates—this is above all a spiritual predicament with nothing less at stake than the poet/speaker's soul, but it is also the risk-laden, terrifying, exhilarating situation of pure potential that characterizes beginning to make a poem. As the narrative gradually builds from indeterminacy to predestination, the poet's task is to find a corresponding form. Predominant here is the force of terza rima[14] as a method of winnowing the relation between coincidence and singularity. Like the center of the anchoring loop of thread that allows the lace-maker or embroiderer of flame-stitch to add new strands, as we have seen, the outer rhymes connect the line to what is finished while the inner rhymes expand the work. In Italian, which rhymes as often as not, this is not a matter of finding or making rhymes alone but as well a matter of controlling and avoiding them, of staying untangled. The tension between coincidence and freedom at the heart of the poem of meeting is thereby manifested in Dante's rhyme scheme as well.

The poetry of meeting involves a lived encounter or exchange and so includes an open possibility of transformation by means of language. Visions and beholding may be involved in these poems of meeting, but because the speakers of such poems are not alone, sublime experiences do not lead to silence and speechlessness. Even in the *Paradiso*, where the incommensurability between the experiences Dante has had and his language to speak about them is constantly emphasized, it is the communicability of understanding that is given priority. For example as we read Canto 23 (lines 23–25) of the *Paradiso* and Dante tells us he cannot give us a sense of the radiance of Beatrice's face and eyes ("Pariemi che 'l suo viso ardesse tutto, / e li occhi avea di letizia sì pieni, / che passarmen convien sanza costrutto"), we realize how much his metaphors and similes, whether expressed or withheld, are a form of pedagogy. Early in Canto 17 (lines 7–12), Beatrice explains that even though she always already knows them, Dante should deliberately utter his thoughts

("Manda fuor la vampa / del tuo disio . . . non perché nostra conoscenza cresca / per tuo parlare, ma perché t'ausi / a dir la sete, sì che l'uom ti mesca"). She, too, makes it clear that she values the insights that follow from conversation—she tells Dante that it is through his own expression that he will learn what his thirst is and how it will be quenched.

Central to the sense of a fresh start beginning in darkness is the structure Dante borrows from the story of Aeneas and the Sibyl entering the Underworld—that of a poet accompanied by a sage or elder poet as he undertakes a journey of learning and self-transformation. But Dante's guide is sent by another guide who herself waits in the wings and has been sent by yet other guides. There is no end to the dangers surrounding the poet; nor is there an end to the resources in wait for him. Fairy tales have heroes who have goals in mind—they must find a silver box or a place where the road forks or prepare to slay a dragon. And they have advisers and sages who give them directions and tools for their journeys. But these helpers, unlike Dante's, do not drop what they are doing and travel along with the protagonists for a time.[15]

The poetry of meeting also obliges the poet to commit himself to truth and sincerity in speech. Such poetry draws upon the intensity of the face-to-face meeting and all the consequences lived encounters imply. It therefore is not surprising that the mental, emotional, and spiritual engagement Beatrice mandates within the poem is also transposed to the structure of the poem and that, in turn, the work's auditors and readers are called upon to provide more than a rote or passive response. We remember that as the *Aeneid* begins, Venus comes to Aeneas as a young girl, a huntress. She teases and deceives her son and only gradually shows her identity. Virgil writes, "He knew his mother / And his voice pursued her flight: / Cruel again! Why mock your son so often with false phantoms? / Why may not hand be joined to hand and words / Exchanged in truthfulness?"[16] The ancient gods felt free to lie and trick their subjects in this mode, but the god of the Hebrew Scriptures, as we have seen, makes promises—covenants that must be renewed under other terms when humans break them. And the Christian god is one who both exemplifies and manifests his truth, hence providing a reliable, if at times enigmatic, guide and companion for his earthly subjects.

There are many lying sinners in the *Inferno*, most prominent of them perhaps is the misleading Malacoda,[17] but beyond this episode, there seem to be no other deliberate lies told to Dante on his journey. Souls in blessedness cannot lie, explains Beatrice in *Paradiso* 4, lines 94–96, and an imperative of plain-speaking girds the poem. The prophecies and explanations of Ciacco (*Inferno* 6), Farinata (*Inferno* 10), and Cacciaguida are far clearer, for example, than the inscrutable oracles of the ancients: "per chiare parole e con preciso / latin rispuose quello amor paterno," Dante says of Cacciaguida's terrible words (*Paradiso* 17, lines 34–35). In the end, the reader can have little question that the good faith underlying all significant conversation is the good faith underlying the poem and that the poem itself is designed to reveal the good faith underlying the promise of salvation.

Nevertheless, as the shade of Dido might remind us, meetings, after all, can go in any direction, from indifference to violence. And listening, too, has a moral economy. Dante borrows heavily from Virgil as he creates a hell that, like Tarturus and the surreal landscape of Revelation, is a mineral world of spectacle. There pain and fury inhibit communication. And he creates a Paradise that, like Virgil's Elysium, is a place of unimpeded movement and conversation. The Sibyl advises Aeneas not to know too much about the doom of Tartarus's inhabitants,[18] and Dante's Virgil similarly regulates the encounters his protégé has in hell. On the one hand, Dante stoops to hear Brunetto Latini more clearly in Canto 15 and Virgil tells him to listen well, but on the other Virgil condemns merely voyeuristic listening in Canto 30 and says he'll start a quarrel with Dante if Dante keeps listening to the strife between Master Adam and Sinon.[19] As the astonished shades press toward Dante's living body in Purgatory, Virgil insists that Dante listen but also that he keep moving.[20]

Listening requires an act of will, and the *Commedia* records the poet's growing sense of responsibility and volition toward face-to-face meetings. Whereas Hell and Purgatory require of Dante that he listen and judge when and how to respond, Paradise requires him to speak and be tested. When Dante passes his examination at the end of *Paradiso* 24, St. Peter encircles him, delighted by his successful speech. In the course of the journey, as conditions of speech move from inarticulate howls of pain and suffering to the ideal mind-reading that characterizes meetings in Paradise, Dante also never forgets that the reader follows his ship in her *piccioletta barca*—as he says, "eager to listen."[21]

II The Visitors

We have seen that it is Virgil who gives Dante the means to "crown and miter" himself, and the meetings of poets with other poets in extreme situations are particularly laden with resonant, often prophetic speech. The poet as visitor in this sense returns us to the praise poem as a poem of beholding and listening, yet the *visitor* sees and sees into—he or she is not a supplicant and appears on a human scale. Within the *Commedia*, the meetings Dante has with poets form a discernible pattern of speaking and listening, with the latter including conscientiously refraining from speech. In Canto 4 of the *Inferno*, where Dante is invited to become the sixth intellect in the company of Homer, Horace, Ovid, Lucan, and Virgil, he is so pleased, he so glories in his witnessing, that he decides not to say more about it, concluding, "Silence here is just as appropriate as our speech was there."[22]

In Canto 22 of the *Purgatorio*, Statius appears, expressing his veneration of Virgil and then walking on with the travelers. Dante says simply that those two, Virgil and Statius, were in the lead and he walked alone behind them, listening to their *sermoni*—sermons that taught him much about poetry, though he does not elaborate further. Whereas such a respectful silence accompanies the discourse of the dead poets of antiquity, Dante settles scores and revisits his own poetics in his passages on Bertran de Born, who is stuck in the ninth *bolgia* of Malebolge as a promoter of schisms; Sordello, who is confined, despite his ability to roam, to ante-Purgatory for scandal and violent death; Bonagiunta, who can be found on the terrace of the gluttonous in *Purgatorio* 24; Guido Guinizelli, who is on the seventh terrace of Purgatory because of his lust; and Cavalcanti, who makes a sole, and ambiguously described, appearance.[23] Even when souls have lost their bodies and context is unintelligible, Dante constantly uses surprise as a device of comedy—the surprise of withheld speech, the surprise of score-settling, yet humble, remarks, and the surprise of recognition by means of language and speech alone. Ugolino's plaintive voice in *Inferno* Canto 33 queries simply, "I don't know who you are or in what way you've come down here; and yet you surely seem from what I hear to be a Florentine."[24] The poet who leaves space for listening and evaluation within the poem, who creates a rhyme scheme of contact and avoidance, who lays bare the choices of speaking and not speaking, whose comic timing surprises us and whose sincerity absorbs us, reminds us of his guiding presence. The poem promises immortal fame to those whose stories it inscribes, even as the poet modestly apologizes in Canto 30 of *Purgatorio* for the single instance of his transcription of his own name.[25] We readers, like the poet and Christian pilgrim, have been met more than halfway.

Thousands of English poems mention and cite Dante; they particularly have flourished whenever new translations have become available, starting with the *Inferno* translations of Charles Rogers in 1782 and Henry Boyd in 1785 and the first accurate translations of the *Commedia* in 1805–12 by Henry Cary. Tracing the preoccupation with the story of Francesca da Rimini alone would give us one way of narrating the history of British Romanticism. But the legacy of the poem of meeting seems to be of even greater importance than the record we have of a continual interest, expressed via allusions, in Dante and his texts. A poem always already deeply informed by the presence of past poets and so incorporating these meetings within its form, the *Commedia* in fact lends its structure in a range of ways to many of the poetic masterpieces of world literature.

Although Wordsworth is a poet rarely linked to Dante, the encounters and testimonies that underlie many of his poems are indebted to this structure as well; Wordsworth's sister Dorothy is often his silent ever-present moral compass, as he in turn uses the poems as a way of proleptically guiding her. In Wordsworth we also find a poet who, like Dante, is obsessed with self-revision and the reframing of earlier work.[26] And in Wordsworth's many poems of encounter a consciousness of the poet as interlocutor to others, including other poets, is paramount. At the same time as Wordsworth's encounters borrow from Dante, they also show in fundamental ways the differences between a medieval poet, confident in the afterlife as a place of significant meetings, and a Romantic poet suffering deep uncertainty about the intelligibility of other minds even as he celebrates the depth that ensues from meetings with them. Just as Dante's meetings acquire their power and theological import from the frame narrative that tells of the divine plan the intercession of Mary has enacted for him, so, conversely, Wordsworth's meetings require spontaneity and surprise.

As Wordsworth mentioned to Thomas De Quincey, "The sudden cessation of any kind of intensive observation or expectation leads to an instantaneous, unexpected and penetrating awareness of some other thing or things" falling into view.[27] Many of Wordsworth's poems might exemplify this, from "Lines. Composed a Few Miles above Tintern Abbey, on Revisiting the Banks of the Wye during a Tour, July 13, 1798" to the portraits of single figures such as Lucy and Michael. In *The Prelude*, narrated, like the *Commedia*, in the past tense, we find the meeting with the discharged soldier in book 4, lines 473–78:

> . . . In all he said
> There was a strange half-absence and a tone
> Of weakness and indifference, as of one
> Remembering the importance of his theme
> But feeling it no longer.

Strikingly close to the lines from Coleridge's Dejection Ode we considered above, where the poet can "see, [but] not feel" the beauties of nature, these lines have a quality that often suffuses the speech of Wordsworth's "others"—the discharged soldier no longer remembers "the importance of his theme" and so suffers from a form of writer's block in producing language. Conversely, in book 5's narration at lines 91–99 of the friend's dream of encountering an Arab carrying a seashell, Wordsworth writes that the Arab asks the listener to hold the shell to his ear:

> . . . I did so
> And heard that instant in an unknown tongue,
> Which yet I understood, articulate sounds,
> A loud prophetic blast of harmony,
> An ode in passion uttered, which foretold
> Destruction to the children of the earth
> By deluge now at hand.

This is a promise of translatability, down to the point of genre, the ode, and theme—a broken covenant that recalls the story of Noah. Yet the promise withholds any particular content. Meeting and understanding are presented without a common language. In these episodes, not only are boundaries of language, class, culture, and time traversed but also those between reality and dreams, including the dreams of others.

In two paradigmatic works on this theme of encounter, "The Solitary Reaper" and "Resolution and Independence," Wordsworth further tries to solve the problem of intelligibility that we could say arose most distinctly a generation before his own, in Thomas Gray's "Elegy Written in a Country Churchyard" of 1750.[28] Given Wordsworth's goal of making poems from "the real language of men," these poems enact the refinement of everyday "real" language back into the pure sounds that will be available to the composing poet. The materiality of language in such works reaffirms Wordsworth's strong need for the actual in all of his experience.

"The Solitary Reaper" opens with the aural and visual image of a Highland lass singing by herself in Erse as she reaps the grain in a field. The poet speaker attempts to bridge the distance between himself and this figure of self-sufficiency by summoning a companion, who may be the reader or who may be Dorothy or someone else—we never know, as we never know the actual distances between any speaker/singers in the poem. Turning to this companion, the poet constructs the opening stanza by means of a series of imperatives: "Behold her," "Stop here, or gently pass!" and "O listen!" In the third stanza, as the speaker plaintively asks, "Will no one tell me what she sings?" we vividly realize that in fact no one has been the subject of these imperatives and that the distance between the speaker and the singer remains unbridged. In the last, fourth stanza the speaker shifts to the past tense, which has the effect of placing the solitary maiden at an even greater distance and making her song even less intelligible:

> Whate'er the theme, the Maiden sang
> As if her song could have no ending;
> I saw her singing at her work,
> And o'er the sickle bending;—

I listened, motionless and still;
And, as I mounted up the hill,
The music in my heart I bore,
Long after it was heard no more.

The significance that the discharged soldier has forgotten is what the poet speaker simply cannot know—the meaning of words that are heard or overheard. It is singing itself that Wordsworth *sees* and, listening, internalizes. He never in truth "hears" it. The use of passive tense—"it was heard no more"—underlines the impossibility of a comprehensive form of hearing and directly inverts the use of imperatives at the start of the poem. If semantics are lost, poetry does not suffer, since what these encounters produce is the form's pure music.[29]

The rich potential of such miscommunication reaches its apogee in "Resolution and Independence," where the poet/traveler can hear the sweet voices, answering, of stock-doves, the chattering of jays and magpies, and the "pleasant noise" of water. This sequence of sounds, each linked to the specific identity of its type of "speaker," is taken in during a kairotic "now" in the first two stanzas. But then, mirroring his technique in "The Solitary Reaper," Wordsworth runs the scene by again in the past tense and introduces a kind of static: "I heard . . . or heard them not," he writes. He is overcome by a depressive state: "Dim sadness—and blind thoughts, I knew not, nor could name." These terms are a vivid contrast to the manic, joyful opening lines of the poem, running the initial images past once more but now behind the haze of his state of mind and losing the specificity of names, images, and sounds they had earlier offered.

The speaker is awakened from this state, again in the past tense, by the specific "warbling" of a "sky-lark." With the kind of philosophic mind he celebrated in the Intimations Ode, Wordsworth next reflects on states of "solitude, pain of heart, distress, and poverty." These are presented as abstractions, but Wordsworth brings forward the specific suffering of first Thomas Chatterton, who is presented by name, and then Robert Burns, euphemistically mentioned, as one might substitute an epitaph for the name of a god: "Him who walked in glory and in joy / Following his plough, along the mountain-wide." In the remainder of the poem, as the speaker meets with "a Man before me unawares: / The oldest man he seemed that ever wore grey hairs," he does not break through his reverie so much as incorporate the old man within it.

The encounter with this old man is a remarkable study in Romantic figuration. Drawing on a train of aesthetical ideas, Wordsworth dramatically sets forward the progress of his approach to the figure. First the man is described "as a huge stone [that] is sometimes seen to lie / Couched on the bald top of an eminence." Next "like a sea-beast crawled forth, that on a shelf / Of rock or sand reposeth, there to sun itself." Finally, the speaker draws near enough to say, "His body was bent double, feet and head / Coming together in Life's pilgrimage; / As if some dire constraint of pain, or rage / Of sickness felt by him in times long past, / A more than human weight upon his frame had cast." Thereby at the moment of the speaker's meeting with his human form, the man remains an object shaped by nature, and indeed he is next described as "Motionless as a cloud . . . / That heareth not the loud winds when they call; / And moveth altogether, if it move at all." How motionless is a cloud, especially in the vicinity of winds loud enough to hear, or not? And what would it mean for a human being to move as an entirety? Such motion obviously would have to be driven by an external force.

In sum, this is a description that, despite the solidity of its object, continually narrows its focus and in consequence makes the figure in turn enormous, remote, and hardly volitional. Beyond Wordsworth's impression of the man's age and decrepitude, all of these similes also seem to take precedence over any attributes he might possess. In the consequent stanzas, as an actual conversation between the speaker and the old man begins, we learn of his "gentle answer," "courteous speech," how his "words came feebly, from a feeble chest, / But each in solemn order followed each / With something of a lofty utterance drest— / Choice word and measured phrase." We are given a redaction of what he says, but we do not hear him. And most surprisingly, neither does the poet:

> The old Man still stood talking by my side;
> But now his voice to me was like a stream
> Scarce heard; nor word from word could I divide:
> And the whole body of the Man did seem

Like one whom I had met with in a dream;
Or like a man from some far region sent,
To give me human strength, by apt admonishment.

It is difficult to avoid the ironic conclusion that when the old man, a leech gatherer by trade, finally does speak—of how difficult it is to find leeches, no longer plentiful—that he is commenting on the utter dependence and serious opportunism that the poet/speaker has brought, leechlike, to the situation.

Frederick Garber, in his classic book *Wordsworth and the Poetry of Encounter*, however, puts this relationship in a more positive light, emphasizing that what Wordsworth sought was not an aggrandizement of himself so much as the possibility of making poems from an otherwise inchoate set of experiences. Garber writes that in encounter, "the self comes to meet something outside (some aspect of a person or an object or some thing); it is an event in which the self may break through to a fleeting, incomplete, but definite understanding of something about the world of the other. . . . In the activity of encounter, and coming out of it, is the energy which, controlled and channeled, could lead the experience into the wholeness of shape of a poem."[30] We must further note that the very quality that is impossible to poetry—the paraphrasability that it prohibits—is what Wordsworth brings to the speaker's language as he refines it into his own work. The strange alchemy by which the poet makes paraphrase into poems that cannot be in turn paraphrased all the more emphasizes the purely somatic, lived encounter of Wordsworth with the sounds of the original speech.

Wordsworth frequently meets not only with Chatterton and Burns but also, above all, with Coleridge as he composes his work. It was indeed Coleridge who revived and reinvented the "conversation poem" in this period. When in the 1798 *Lyrical Ballads* Coleridge introduced the genre, he was drawing on the eighteenth-century tradition of the conversation painting that depicted the living and the dead in group portraits. But he was drawing even more deeply from Dante, whose work he had known in English since he borrowed Boyd's translation of the *Inferno* from the Bristol Library in the summer of 1796.[31] Coleridge's Ancient Mariner, too, is a messenger bound by a redemptive vow to be a

Virgil to everyone he encounters—the poem as we have it is one episode of his perpetual journey.

The Dantean encounter poem persists throughout the period and beyond. Dante himself is the guide for Byron's "Prophecy of Dante," composed in 1819 during a period when Byron frequently mentioned in his conversations and letters his feeling of identification with Dante as a poet and political exile.[32] Shelley's final great unfinished work, his terza rima "Triumph of Life" of 1822, is built around an encounter and subsequent journey with the guiding ghost of Jean-Jacques Rousseau.[33] In another realm of Romanticism, the terror of the night journey of Goethe's *Faust* (from part 1, completed in 1806) stems at least in part from our acknowledgment that the protagonist is guided by Mephistopheles, and so Goethe presents a serious parody of, and homage to, Dante's journey with Virgil.

The American tradition of encounter poetry seems to owe something to Byron's picaresque verse pilgrimages with their mixture of libertinage and ethnographic detail; in the twentieth century this line of work leads to the homosocial worlds of the wandering Beats and the New York School poets, who took up as well the Baudelairean motif of the chance meeting. The poems of Frank O'Hara, for example, owe a great deal to a work like Baudelaire's "À une passante":

À une passante

La rue assourdissante autour de moi hurlait.
Longue, mince, en grand deuil, douleur majestueuse,
Une femme passa, d'une main fastueuse
Soulevant, balançant le feston et l'ourlet;

Agile et noble, avec sa jambe de statue.
Moi, je buvais, crispé comme un extravagant,
Dans son oeil, ciel livide où germe l'ouragan,
La douceur qui fascine et le plaisir qui tue.

Un éclair . . . puis la nuit!—Fugitive beauté
Dont le regard m'a fait soudainement renaître,
Ne te verrai-je plus que dans l'éternité?

> Ailleurs, bien loin d'ici! trop tard! *jamais* peut-être!
> Car j'ignore où tu fuis, tu ne sais où je vais,
> Ô toi que j'eusse aimée, ô toi qui le savais![34]

Such poetry of superficial meeting relies on an aesthetics of appearance, speed, and imaginative flight. Far from the heavy-handed coincidences of Renaissance romance plots, it has the beauty of a sketch, a quite literal "brushwork," suggesting to the imagination some further meetings, some further consequences. The final implication that these two strangers share in the same erotic knowledge indicates that what has happened now may have happened before and may happen again and the certain economy between the unique and simultaneous is unmoored.

In contrast, Walt Whitman begins his *Drum-taps* accompanied by the spirit of his city, Manna-hatta, and goes on to meet a procession of figures who have suffered the contrary experiences of violence and compassion during the period of the Civil War. The encounters of William Butler Yeats's Crazy Jane poems similarly can be said to travel, via Wordsworth's Lucy poems especially, back to Dante's meetings with suffering speakers. As the foremost American poet of exile, Ezra Pound relies heavily on Dante for his *Cantos* and calls on Robert Browning and scores of other poets and thinkers to accompany his work in free verse unfolding "50 years of the growth of a poet's mind."

The "Love Song of J. Alfred Prufrock" of T. S. Eliot achieves some of its sense of disorienting solipsism from the way its opening speaker first appears to be a kind of Virgilian guide, saying, "Oh, do not ask, 'What is it?' / Let us go and make our visit."—only to then turn back to the conventions of dramatic monologue alone. In the culmination of the scenes of dialogue and prophecy and the direct allusions to the *Commedia* in *The Waste Land*, Eliot further draws on Dante. The trope of the vanishing guide appears in these haunting lines regarding a mysterious companion:

> Who is the third who walks always beside you?
> When I count, there are only you and I together
> But when I look ahead up the white road

> There is always another one walking beside you
> Gliding wrapt in a brown mantle, hooded.[35]

In her 1924 lyric "The Muse," Anna Akhmatova sees the ghost of Dante's Beatrice and asks her, "Are you the one . . . whom Dante heard dictate / the lines of his Inferno . . . ?" and Beatrice answers yes. During the 1920s and 1930s Akhmatova frequently looks for inspiration to the poet's exile and refusal to return to Florence as a penitent. For both Akhmatova and Osip Mandelstam—of the major twentieth-century Russian poets, the most prominent of those who refused exile—the exiled Dante became a tremendous moral resource. Nadezhda Mandelstam, writing in the second volume of her memoir of the Stalin years, *Hope against Hope*, described how her husband and Akhmatova lived with the constant presence of all poets about them. She writes,

> Both Mandelstam and Akhmatova had the astonishing ability of somehow bridging time and space when they read the work of dead poets. By its very nature, such reading is usually anachronistic, but with them it meant entering into personal relations with the poet in question; it was a kind of conversation with someone long since departed. From the way in which he greeted his favorite poets of antiquity in the Inferno, Mandelstam suspected that Dante also had this ability. . . . In the same way, he thought, one can look for friends and allies across the barriers of both time and space. This would probably have been understood by Keats, who wanted to meet all his friends, living and dead, in a tavern.[36]

Akhmatova identified with all poets throughout history and at the same time remained rooted during the years of Stalin's rule in her little room at Fontanka (Fountain) House in St. Petersburg, under surveillance for a suicide watch and suffering the death and imprisonment of her friends and family. Deliberately choosing confinement over emigration, she continually expanded her empathetic powers of imagination in space and time.

In her poem of 1922 "I am not one of those who left the land," she is referring at once to Dante and to her own situation. This is a translation by Stanley Kunitz and Max Hayward:

I am not one of those who left the land
to the mercy of its enemies.
Their flattery leaves me cold,
my songs are not for them to praise.

But I pity the exile's lot.
Like a felon, like a man half-dead,
dark is your path, wanderer;
wormwood infects your foreign bread.

But here, in the murk of conflagration,
where scarcely a friend is left to know,
we, the survivors, do not flinch
from anything, not from a single blow.

Surely the reckoning will be made
after the passing of this cloud.
We are the people without tears,
straighter than you . . . more proud . . .

Here we find Akhmatova's typical ellipses, meant in this last stanza to reflect the passing of thought and the passing of time until a final reckoning or accounting. In mentioning the poison wormwood infecting the bread of strangers, she alludes to the tragic lines of *Paradiso* Canto 17 (lines 58–60) where Cacciaguida predicts Dante's terrible fate as an exile, saying:

Tu proverai si come sa di sale
lo pane altrui, e come è duro calle
lo scendere e 'l salir per l'altrui scale.

You will come to know the salt-taste
of others' bread and how hard is the path
climbing up and down their stairs.

Akhmatova's ability to experience simultaneously the presence of all of world literature is something that characterized the ambitions of other modernist poets, such as Pound and Eliot, but her powers of empathy reached just as strongly into the all-too-present suffering of those about her, and during the darkest years of her life we find her early poems of lyric encounter transposed to poems of meeting and witness. Consider the famous opening to what is perhaps her best-known poem, her *Requiem* of 1935 to 1940, which recounts the experience of women who waited outside Stalin's prisons with packages for their loved ones—including Akhmatova bringing packages to her imprisoned son Lev. In the prose paragraph, "instead of a Preface," which she attached to the poem on April 1, 1957, she wrote, here, too, in the Kunitz/Hayward translation:

> In the terrible years of the Yezhov terror I spent seventeen months waiting in line outside the prison in Leningrad. One day somebody in the crowd identified me. Standing behind me was a woman, with lips blue from the cold, who had, of course, never heard me called by name before. Now she started out of the torpor common to us all and asked me in a whisper (everyone whispered there):
>
> "Can you describe this?"
>
> And I said: "I can."
>
> Then something like a smile passed fleetingly over what had once been her face.

Requiem was first published in 1963 in Munich. It did not appear in Russia until 1987. As Akhmatova wrote within the poem:

> No foreign sky protected me,
> no stranger's wing shielded my face.
> I stand as witness to the common lot,
> survivor of that time, that place.

The poem is in ten numbered sections with an additional verse epigraph of 1961, the prose preface of 1957, a verse dedication of 1940, the prologue of 1935, and a final epilogue. As the sequence proceeds, Akhmatova links the suffering of the women outside the prison to the suffering of other women in history—among them the Virgin Mary at the site of the crucifixion and the wives of the troops who in 1698 mutinied against Peter the Great and were tortured and killed. In the last part of the epilogue, she imagines proleptically a future memory of this time and the role she will have played as a witness and messenger. She writes of the forgotten women who have suffered in that place and of their names and what they said to each other. Feeling them "drawing near," she describes particular features of their walks and gestures, their words and glances, and vows to memorialize them even "if a gag should blind my tortured mouth, / through which a hundred million people shout." As the poem closes, she gives directions for her own memorial, asking that it be placed "here, where I endured three hundred hours / in line before the implacable iron bars."

From this period forward, Akhmatova's work progressed by means of the resources of world culture—literary allusions, correspondences, and subtexts—features of an early twentieth-century European and Anglo-American modernism from which she was largely shut off.[37] She burrowed deep into the recesses of modern and ancient literatures to create many-layered structures for her poems. She gave a clue to this process in her final work, *Poem without a Hero*, writing, "But the box has a triple bottom." The box was a Florentine chest filled with letters, dolls, and fragmented souvenirs of the past that her friend the actor Olga Sudeikina had left in the little room at Fontanka House years before as she left the country.

It was from this chest that Akhmatova constructed *Poem without a Hero*, her great final epic of reunions. Using what she found there and drawing on her memories, she created a parade of characters from the bohemian world of the Stray Dog Café, where she had first read her poems and found her literary community in the cabaret culture of St. Petersburg between 1910 and 1914. In costume, as ghostly mummers, these figures come to visit her on New Year's night of 1940. She builds allusions with more than one source, setting up meetings between poets who might draw strength and sympathy from one another: Mandelstam echoes Pushkin; the dandies of the Stray Dog echo Byron's Don Juan; the theatrical roles Olga played, such as a goat-legged dancer or the figure of Psyche, echo both the conventions of Greek tragedy and myth and the "harlequinade" theatrical experiments of Vsevolod Meyerhold, who was imprisoned and tortured in 1939 and executed February 1, 1940.

Committed to memory in small sections during furtive meetings with her few remaining friends, *Poem without a Hero* is a text shot through with ellipses. In a little lyric Akhmatova composed in 1955 about the poem and subtitled "lines wandering around in the manuscript copy," she wrote:

I fear neither death nor shame.
It is secret writing, a cryptogram
A forbidden method.
Everyone knows along what edge
I am somnambulistically treading
And toward what house I'm heading.

Once a set of censored verses is reinserted, we can read, in the last sections of the work, descriptions of the torture and imprisonment of the Stalin years and of the natural beauty she encountered in 1941–44 when she was an evacuee in Tashkent. A kind of metempsychosis gives the *Poem without a Hero* powers of reanimating the dead, and of giving past forms, despite their suppression in the present, safe passage into the future. She writes:

Who met whom, and when and why,
Who perished and who survived
And who is the author and who is the hero . . .
It's the devil's own work, rummaging through this chest . . .
But how does it come to pass
That I am totally guilty of everything . . .

The boundaries between realities are breached in this phantasm of masks, disguises, and portraits brought to life.

In this last great work, Akhmatova's imagination contains and continues the lives of those she has lost and, in fear and delight, comes full circle, during the horrors of war, to its ancient origins. Even so, there is no celebration or reconciliation in this "poem without a hero"—it is a powerful and serious critique of the mistaken idealism of the heroic. She writes of the powers inherent in a congregating imagination in a late reflective poem from 1961, here in the translation of Judith Hemschemeyer:

No, we didn't suffer together in vain,
Without hopes of even drawing a breath.

We took an oath, we voted—
. . . No, not under the vault of alien skies
And not under the shelter of alien wings—
I was with my people then,
There, where my people, unfortunately, were.

The tavern of Akhmatova's and Mandelstam's imaginations, like the remembered world of the Stray Dog Café, is a kind of watering hole.[38] Perhaps the poetry of meeting has its origin in human and animal gathering places by water, just as the journey of water has its source in springs and wells. Beatrice spoke of the *sete* of Dante when she asked him to articulate his thoughts, and poets are always thirsty—they need water in order to breathe, and the sound of it underlies the flow of their words, which always spill in rhythm and in time. Composing poets are like the birds Dante describes in the *Paradiso* 18 (lines 73–75) who, refreshed by a riverbank, rise up to form their circles, *V*s, and other shapes: "E come augelli surti di rivera, / quasi congratulando a lor pasture, / fanno di sé or tonda or altra schiera. . . ."

In closing, then, we might consider the crux formed by the imagery of water and life in the *Commedia* and the meaning of the metaphor of the *radice* or root that recurs in these poems of exile and meeting. Within the world of Dante's thought, the relation between air and water, or we could say inspiration and flow, is linked to the influences of the stars. In his treatise on air and water, Dante resolved the question of why the earth is higher than water despite its heavier weight by concluding that the northern stars have drawn up the earth of the continents. Yet Dante also held that springs, habitats of the muses, developed from the condensation of vapor or air, not from water rising.[39]

In the *Commedia*, the waters of the Acheron, marking the boundary to Hell, the waters of the Styx, the Phlegethon, the Cocytus, and even the little *fiumicello* that gives safe passage across the desert of blasphemers, sodomites, and usurers[40] are all associated with punishment. The *fiumicello* runs red; along with the rivers of Hell, it comes from the tears of the Old Man of Crete—specifically from those silver, brass, iron, and earthen parts of him that represent the ages of man. These waters may provide transport, but they are not life-giving. As part of the ecology of a world of drained souls, they indicate at once the flow of blood sacrifice, the poisonous runoff of sewers, and a mineral hardness.

Virgil had placed the Lethe among these rivers of Hell, but Dante has the river of forgetting stem not from rising waters but from the pure and changeless fountain of a spring—out of one side of that spring flows Lethe, erasing the memory of sins, and out of the other flows the poet's own remarkable invention—the river of the memory of good deeds, Eunoe. Washed in the waters of Lethe and Eunoe successively, now flanked by Beatrice and Statius, Dante is remade and renewed in that enleaved place, the Earthly Paradise, as he says, like a new tree putting out new shoots—the laurel or triumph of life. This moment in *Paradiso* Canto 32, lines 52–60, is the culmination of a successive flowering of the imagery of the poem. In the *Inferno* (4, lines 118–20) a green meadow turns out to be merely enameled; branches are dead and twisted like thorns (13, lines 4–6). But in the progress of the *Purgatorio*, the organic world of life cyclically emerges: the image of newborn leaves first appears in the flashing wings of the angels of ante-Purgatory. Here on the threshold of Paradise, like the triumph of a laurel wreath, it becomes an attribute of Dante's completion of this part of his journey. Green, as no reader can forget, mantles the living flame of Beatrice's red garment as the green leaf enfolds the red bud in spring—the rosy color, less red than roses and deeper than violet, of the flowering tree of the Earthly Paradise.

In Shelley's own "Triumph of Life," the narrator/poet has a striking first encounter with his guide, Rousseau. Watching the sad pageantry of history, the narrator is despondent, and then he suddenly hears a voice cry "Life!" He turns, and this is what he discovers:

> . . . what I thought was an old root which grew
> To strange distortion out of the hill side
> was indeed one of that deluded crew,
>
> And that the grass which methought hung so wide
> And white, was but his thin discoloured hair,
> And that the holes he vainly sought to hide,
>
> Were or had been eyes . . .

Shelley, in his usual ingenious way, has noticed something very important about his source text, the *Commedia*: the concept of *radice* or root is vital to the poem of exile. A journey underground to sources of life and means of nourishment and knowledge echoes especially two important and pivotal scenes. First there is the almost comic reappearance of Beatrice at *Purgatorio* 32, lines 85–87. As Dante looks around to find her ("Ov' è Beatrice?"), there she is, seated on the roots of the newly flowering tree. And second, Cacciaguida's stunning pronouncement in *Paradiso* 15, lines 88–90: "O fronda mia in che io compiacemmi / pur aspettando, io fui la tua radice"—I was your root. Dante remedies his uprootedness, via the springs of memory and allusion, by showing that his true roots are not in the literal earth but in language and, for Dante, faith as expressed in and for language. The lesson learned by those poets who follow Dante, each exiled by circumstances of geography, war, or alienation, is that the poetry of the past is our root and birthright; it is always waiting in the future to meet us.

8 / PERSONS AS MAKERS

My lines and life are free; free as the rode,
Loose as the winde, as large as store.
—GEORGE HERBERT, "The Collar"

But he is a master, isn't he? A master?
—STALIN TO PASTERNAK, with reference to Mandelstam

I Conditions of Making

There is a fine balance between freedom of means and freedom of reception. In the twentieth century, as artists struggled against both the iron powers of totalitarianism and the softly insidious powers of advertising, we find some tragic responses and poignant statements to this effect. Between 1925 and 1930, Osip Mandelstam in particular found himself unable to write poetry at all because of the state's insistent demand for patriotic displays in verse. Then, between 1931 and 1934, in the period after his intense studies of Dante that we have considered, the poet again began writing. In or around November 1933 he composed by memory a poem commonly known as "Epigram to Stalin" or "The Kremlin Mountaineer," reciting it to friends in private settings as its only means of "publication." As we have seen, this was a strategy of "writing" by memorization that Akhmatova also followed during the years of her internal exile and the first means of publication for her great *Poem without a Hero*. But for Mandelstam this strategy brought about a swift and disastrous consequence—one of his interlocutors reported the work to Stalin's police, and he was arrested and sent into exile, first to Cherdyn and then to Voronezh. This relatively "mild" punishment is believed to have been brought about by Stalin himself. In a telephone call to Mandelstam's friend Boris Pasternak, Stalin repeatedly worried about Mandelstam's destined reputation, asking, as our epigraph records, whether the poet was a master and so the author of a poem assured of immortality that would thereby simultaneously assure Stalin's own eternal infamy. After Mandelstam's punishment expired in 1937, he was arrested again in May 1938 and sentenced to hard labor. Two years later, according to his official death certificate, he died of heart failure.[1]

What was this poem that served as a death sentence? Here is a translation by Robert Tracy:

> We live, but we do not feel the land beneath us;
> Ten steps away and our words cannot be heard,
>
> And when there are just enough people for half a dialogue—
> Then they remember the Kremlin mountaineer.
>
> His fat fingers are slimy, like slugs,
> And his words are absolute, like grocers' weights.
>
> His cockroach whiskers are laughing,
> And his boot-tops shine.
>
> He has a rabble of skinny-necked leaders around him,
> He plays games with the aid of those who are only half human,
>
> Who twitter, who mew, who whimper.
> He alone bangs and thrusts.
>
> Decree after decree, he hammers them out like horseshoes—
> One in the groin for him, in the forehead for him, for him one over the eyes, one in the eyes for him.
>
> When he has an execution, it's a special treat
> And the Ossetian chest swells.[2]

Whatever paranoia led Stalin to worry that Mandelstam's artistry, if not his bravery, was something to be feared, the poet follows a strategy of satirizing in most bitter terms not only the ruler but also the situation of poetic production and reception. The disembodied, ungrounded speakers of the opening cannot be heard, nor can they sustain any public speech or mode of contestation. After the first four lines the poem is dominated by the material reality of the dictator, whose title could not be more aptly employed. The executioner is a parody of the poet/maker—fingers too fat and slick to work, words like 35-pound weights. Stalin is not called by his proper name, but Mandelstam includes some personal insults beyond these physical descriptions—his "Ossetian" chest makes him a particular kind of bumpkin and strips him of his claim to more "refined" Georgian origins. And every Russian schoolchild knows a poem by Korney Chukovsky in which a huge cockroach with a mustache terrorizes other animals in a forest until a courageous little sparrow not only stands up to him but eats him.[3]

Mandelstam, one of the strongest and most learned lyric poets of the early twentieth century in any language, must rely on name-calling and cartoonish imagery as a last stand against that dictation that circumscribes all powers of free speech and free association. As article 58 of the Stalin-era "Criminal Code" stated that anyone who knew of a "criminal group" was a member of such a group and obliged to report it, anyone also could be arrested, as Akhmatova's son Lev was twice in 1935, for "conversations at home."[4] Despite the eventual wide acclaim for Mandelstam's satire, Nadezhda Mandelstam understood well that Stalin's regime destroyed not only her husband's life but also his work. She wrote in her second memoir, *Hope Abandoned*, "He was cut off before he had come to maturity—he was a slow developer—and he was still in the process of reaching it. His voice came through not because he was being hounded and smothered, but in spite of it. If it had not been for the 'different channel' he would most likely have become a poet in the philosophical mold. Once he had freed himself for a moment from themes which imposed themselves (and here I would include the 'Kremlin Mountaineer'), he wrote his 'Octets.' I believe these show us the poet he was not allowed to become."[5]

These eight-line poems, gathered under the title "Vos'mistisija," or the Octets cycle, were composed as a set in 1933 in Moscow and numbered later by the Mandelstam scholar Clarence Brown. Some of them have been brilliantly, if freely, translated by Donald Davie, and Davie has described them as "forms that are 'bent in,' rounded, sounding a full bell-note. . . . The form of the bent-in and the rounded-upon-itself is the most ancient and constant of all European understandings of the beautiful—it is what long ago recognized in the circle the image of perfection." [6] Here are two octets in Davie's translation that give some sense of his insights:

(73)
Those plaguy, needling games of ours, where stooks
Of jackstraws figure, phials whence we drink
Illusions of causality! These hooks
With which we touch on Quantities, we think,
Are deathly playthings; one small figure catches
On to another as the hook is cast
Over, and snags. The child, though, sleeps. The vast
Universe sleeps, where cradled Eternity watches.

(75)
To get past harping on the laws of Nature
the blue-hard eye has pierced to the Law behind:
Lodged in the earth's crust, zany is God's own creature
And upthrust, grubbed from the breast, his groan is mined.
The aborted foetus, deaf, something can bend it;
Like a forge-ahead road it is bowed back, hooped to a horn
—The plenty of bent-in Space, to apprehend it
Takes up the pledge of the petal's, the cupola's form.[7]

The octets suggest a paired compression of the quatrains of a song, on the one hand, and a Platonic frame, where circular gestures and forms undergird all the poet observes, on the other. The stooks, which are usually encircled bunches of grain, here are encircled jackstraws, the narrow strips or sticks used to play a game where the straws are heaped and then pulled out one by one without making the whole set collapse. Evoking the fasces and sickle at once, the translation lets the stooks suggest two kinds of twentieth-century extremism, binding them in a metaphor of chance and uncertainty. The circling catch of stray elements is revealed as well in the repeated allusions to causal arguments, which hook phenomena to their origins, as in the snagging motion of a fishing line. A sleeping child and an aborted fetus both curve toward themselves, as does a looping road or cornucopia or petal or cupola—or the universe encircled by an equally cradled eternity.

Image by image, octet by octet, Mandelstam creates a panoply of exacting forms, each bearing the perfection of a circle, and all related. Yet to read these poems is to find oneself resisting sequence; each octet seems to begin again, to underscore, to refuse any teleology of motion or plot. The poems are masterpieces of the extreme situation—resolutely fashioned one after another in a climate where making could be halted at any time. They are the antithesis of the repetitions of hard labor, the sentence of days and years that in truth cannot possibly be "lived out."

In 1939, the year of Meyerhold's torture, the year after Mandelstam's death, Kenneth Burke wrote a little fable in his essay "The Calling of the Tune":

> A piper who had insisted upon the right to call his own tune became unhappy when everyone began saying to him, "I don't care what tune you play." He discovered that he wanted them to care tremendously—and to make them do so, he tried outrageous tunes. Though insisting upon his professional immunity, he didn't want to be too damned immune, since complete tolerance would imply the unimportance of his craft. He simultaneously wanted separation and integration. He wanted the joyous marriage of "you must" and "I will."

Two years later W. H. Auden declared, "Since the breakdown of patronage in the eighteenth century, the artist has been the extreme case of the free individual, the one for whom, more than for any other, society has become open and untraditional; and in the second place, since art by its nature is a shared, a catholic, activity, he is the first to feel the consequences of a lack of common beliefs, and the first to seek a common basis for human unity."[8] In each of these statements we find symptoms of the rising hegemony of popular and commercial forms of culture, forms that came to dominate the productions of artists and to replace their role in unifying and congregating audiences. Burke, with his deep interest in the communicative value of art, indicates the sterility of an artistic alienation from, and abandonment of, the audience, and Auden, with his own interests in ethics and politics, indicates the disastrous consequences for artists when the public sphere has been fragmented.

The punishment of hard labor, so obviously an intensification of work's power to wear away and wear down the human body that we found in Ovid's myths, is also of course a punishment of mind. In such circumstances of work and labor, there is perhaps no more vivid contrast than the one that arises by comparing Kant's description of the artist/genius—"genius is the inborn predisposition of the mind [*ingenium*] through which nature gives the rule to art"[9]—to Marx's description of the worker alienated from the products of his labor in his *Economic and Philosophic Manuscripts of 1844*. Marx writes:

> First, the fact that labor is *external* to the worker, i.e., it does not belong to his intrinsic nature; that in his work, therefore, he does not affirm himself but denies himself, does not feel content but unhappy, does not develop freely his physical and mental energy but mortifies his body and ruins his mind. The worker therefore only feels himself outside his work, and in his work feels outside himself. He feels at home when he is not working, and when he is working he does not feel at home. His labor is therefore not voluntary, but coerced; it is *forced labor*. It is therefore not the satisfaction of a need; it is merely a *means* to satisfy needs external to it. Its alien character emerges clearly in the fact that as soon as no physical or other compulsion exists, labor is shunned like the plague. External labor, labor in which man alienates himself, is a labor of self-sacrifice, of mortification. Lastly, the external character of labor for the worker appears in the fact that it is not his own, but someone else's, that it does not belong to him, that in it he belongs, not to himself, but to another.[10]

Yet these two accounts are quite consistent with one another in that Marx views self-legislation as vital to creativity and authentic being just as Kant does. Marx is reliant, too, on Hegel's story of the bondsman. The artist has nurtured within himself a natural inclination to make his own rules and formulate his own judgments, and this inclination is precisely what has been taken from the alienated worker—what he or she has been forced to sacrifice in order to survive. Art arises from amateur domains as it arises from professional ones; the constant accreditation of art practices, whether by the state or by communities of artists, is a formula for formulas; and the iron-bound traditions of closed societies, including programmatic avant-gardes, can keep art within the realm of craft.

The value we assign to art epitomizes our distinction, as Arendt notes, between *labor*, which becomes erased back into time and nature, and *work*, which has some manifested consequence. We further distinguish between objects made for some explicit and foreseen purpose, which are works of craft, and those objects we make without any purpose other than their actualization and apprehension, which are works of art. Implicitly, and for better or worse, this distinction carries over into our sense of a life worth living—a life that counts in some way precisely because artworks give us an opportunity to judge what counts and what doesn't count.

At the same time, we could say that all work is inevitably erased back into time and history and that we often do not hold persons and artworks to be singular and thereby irreplaceable. Forms made of matter break down or accrue into either other forms or formlessness, and aside from the ordinary vicissitudes of history, we face the inevitable fact of the eventual destruction of our solar system. On a more intelligible scale, we reject, ignore, neglect, ruin, and even destroy works of art more often than we might like to acknowledge. And we have an economic system that is willing, in the interest of short-term gain, to destroy not only the physical and mental health of individual workers but also, in utter self-defeat, the resources of the earth itself.

Concepts of planned obsolescence and replacement, the operations of profit's sublimity, are as counter as they could be to the values of singularity and saturated meaning I have been pursuing. Those values find intense expression as early as Shelley's "Defence" with its anthology of liberational hopes for poetry in history. Among such hopes, Shelley prophetically indicates that poetry might be a counterforce to overconsumption as he captures the disorienting effects of a world of things cut off from nature. He writes, in a strange transposition of Platonic Forms into the materials of rhythm and order: "The functions of the poetical faculty are two-fold: by one it creates new materials of knowledge, and power and pleasure; by the other it engenders in the mind a desire to reproduce and arrange them according to a certain rhythm and order which may be called the beautiful and the good. The cultivation of poetry is never more to be desired than at periods when, from an excess of the selfish and calculating principle, the accumulation of the materials of external life exceed the quantity of the power of assimilating them to the internal laws of human nature. The body has then become too unwieldy for that which animates it."[11] He further desires that poetry will be part of the "highest political hope that it can enter into the mind of man to conceive"—the abolishment of "personal slavery," and he adds that the "freedom of women" will continue to produce the poetry of sexual love, turning love into a religion.[12]

II Production and Reproduction

Liberty, like luck, may most often be figured as a "lady" in the West, but the aleatory and spontaneous are gifts of a deity to her mortal devotees. More often, the differences between labor and work, regardless of how worthwhile it might be to maintain them in the interest of the nonalienation of our making, are, from the outset, set out starkly in gendered terms that make the labor of childbirth the paradigm for gratuitous suffering. The contemporary Italian philosopher Adriana Cavarero has been especially concerned with the denigration of birth in favor of concepts of immortality in ancient philosophy and of the finitude of death in modern philosophy. She has traced the influence of a female labor and male work in the entire Western philosophical tradition to the writings of Plato, arguing that "Plato's text is so much more significant for the fact that it belongs to the beginnings of philosophy, to the dawn of an age of envy whose results were about to be consolidated into a system and which still revealed the matricidal expropriation that sustains them."

Cavarero is thinking of the theme and role of maieutics in Plato's texts—the lessons on the path to beauty, away from human reproduction to the productions of art to the ideal Forms, offered by the midwife Diotima in the *Symposium*, and Socrates's own self-definition as a "midwife" of thought. In the *Theaetetus* (150b) he writes: "Now my art of midwifery is just like theirs in most respects. The difference is that I attend men and not women, and that I watch over the labour of their souls, not their bodies." And several passages later: "There is another point also in which those who associate with me are like women in child-birth. They suffer the pains of labour, and are filled day and night with distress; indeed they suffer far more than women. And this pain my art is able to bring on, and also to allay" (151a-b).[13] Caverero points out how in these examples, "traces of the technical language pertaining to conception and motherhood persist in the tradition," despite the homosocial bond that in fifth- and fourth-century BC Greece has already begun to characterize the transmission of philosophy as a practice.[14] She observes that "in philosophical discourse spoken by men, the act of engendering something that is not subject to being engendered (because it is eternal) indeed partakes of human life. It is a sort of *genesis* freed from transience, since, paradoxically, the nature of the philosophical child is *ageneton*, 'not born,' insofar as it exists from the beginning of time and forever."[15] Socrates is able to denigrate women in more than one way: by suggesting that philosophy is not something women, who labor with their bodies rather than their souls, engage, and by contending that the suffering of the thinking philosopher is greater than that of a woman giving birth.

The contrast between labor and work in the Hebrew scriptures' account of Genesis and the expulsion from Eden is no less strikingly gendered and appropriative of women's maternity. The first man is not born, but made, by a god who is invisible, whose face may not be seen, but whom we nevertheless continually find to be imagined as a male; the first woman is created by the same male god. In one Genesis account, as we have seen, she is wholly formed; in the other she is pulled from the rib of the first man. We remember that at the violation of the interdiction not to eat of the fruit of the tree of good and evil, the god intervenes expressly to stop Adam and Eve from eating from the second tree in Eden: the tree of life, which grants immortality.

In the Platonic tradition, as Cavarero argues, women are denigrated because they give birth to mortal forms—the inverse of the immortal and eternal truths of the Forms. The struggles of Adam and Eve in the Hebrew scriptures are comparably mired in death, in Eve's case, and materiality, in Adam's. At the expulsion Eve is condemned to pain in childbirth; we take it for granted that childbirth is her task, even though no children have yet been born by wholly human means. Adam is condemned to pain in work; he will meet with resistance as he fashions his world from nature. Adam may be driven by hunger, but the earth will yield up its fruits to him, and such fruits will be a consequence of his agency. Eve's agency is indeterminate; it is not clear that she will intend to bear children—we know only that she will suffer as a side effect of their arrival—but surely if she were the agent of her own procreative powers, she might want to avoid the pain of childbirth and could do so without suffering the starvation she and Adam would face if they neglected their tasks of cultivation.

For Cavarero such divisions of tasks, whether obvious or subtle, indicate a persistent theme of what we might call "womb envy" in Western myth and thought. Even Zeus gives birth a try—producing Athena from his head and Dionysus from his thigh. If we imagine these are atavistic concerns needing to be brought up to date, we have only to consider a passage in Étienne Gilson's mid-twentieth-century treatise *The Arts of the Beautiful*, where the philosopher writes of "the universally recognized analogy between artistic production and the biological functions of reproduction." Gilson explains: "One speaks of the conception and birth of a work of art. It is accepted as an obvious fact that the works of the same artist bear the mark of their origin and, in a way, resemble him, as children resemble their parents. For the same reason, they also look alike; they constitute a sort of 'family' and have a family look as a result. These expressions, and similar ones, bring out the fatherly feeling of the artist for his works. Painlessly, but far from effortlessly, the artist generates his works like children to whom he feels bound by quasi-physiological ties. Indeed, the artist may carry them within himself for a long time before they are born." Gilson concludes by adding a statement that "biological analogies with art are so many and so visible that it would be tedious to list them. Besides, differences would likewise have to be taken into account, for nature begets and art makes. . . . The main difference between the two orders is that, like all properly human operations and unlike mere animal reproduction, art implies knowledge and freedom."[16]

Given the differences between a reproduction that is willed and one that is not, the gendering of female birth and male making is a false transposition of nature into culture, even though it is only in cultural terms that we can make sense of it. Let us look a little more closely at this phenomenon—one that has kept at a minimum the development of women artists and the appreciation of the products of women's art making and perpetuated a division of labor of course not only in the realm of art but also just as universally in the realm of childrearing.[17] Gilson's implicit assumption that artistic making is a fatherly enterprise and biological making a motherly one is hardly a surprising update of Diotima's discourse in Plato's *Symposium*. But Gilson himself, in other pages in *Arts of the Beautiful*, suggests that the "domain of poetics in all its forms" is the only order where human beings are masters of their work. We cannot create ex nihilo, so we do not produce being, and we discover the good and the true only to the extent that we can find intelligibility in what nature provides us.[18] We need not accept that the persistent, impossible desire for the eternal is anything less than human, and we can take up the invitation of renewal because of, not despite, the fact of our mortal finitude.

The tie between mortality and the need to make anew, to turn to "a new song," has a basis in biological reproduction itself and reveals a much more fundamental problem with the concept of singularity when it is applied to living beings. In a particularly insightful passage in *L'évolution créatrice*, Bergson wrote: "It may be said of individuality that, while the tendency to individuate is everywhere present in the organized world, it is everywhere opposed by the tendency towards reproduction. For the individuality to be perfect, it would be necessary that no detached part of the organism could live separately. But then reproduction would be impossible. For what is reproduction, but the building up of a new organism with a detached fragment of the old? Individuality therefore harbors its enemy at home. Its very need of perpetuating itself in time condemns it never to be complete in space."[19] To the extent that we make artworks that are singular, we are able to produce the finitude of a perfected form. As each singular artwork is animated by its place in the long history of art making in general, the work's integrity is a matter of promethean influences and epimethean aftereffects.

The finitude of the individual artwork, folded within the potential infinity of the project, is analogous to the finitude of the person within the potential infinity of humanity. The tension between individuality and reproduction is analogous to the tension between creativity and necessity—there is no just reason to organize the world as, for quite different reasons, Diotima and contemporary "family values" advocates suggest, by establishing a division of labor between those who produce and those who reproduce. Nor is there a just reason to draw a separation between laboring for necessity and creating for pleasure. A respect for human faculties of reasoning, judging, creating, caring, and inventing demands that these be activities that everyone has the time and space to pursue. They are indeed at the core of the Enlightenment's open concept of the "pursuit of happiness"—a pursuit made possible by the possession of life and, in consequence, the possession of liberty.

III The Self's Materials and the Person's Reception

There are both an artificial and an artifactual direction to thinking about freedom as something made. Our human capacities for freedom of motion and association are not quite like those we find in other creatures, which, so far as we know, do not undergo the same processes of deliberation and reconsideration that we bring to these spheres. And our freedom is not only immanent: we also exemplify or manifest our freedom, judging it as a state that can be more or less, always seeking to expand its powers. In thinking about the philosophy of art and aesthetics, my concern has been with a positive freedom. The volitional and underdetermined qualities of making that I have emphasized heighten the fundamental condition of the free act as that which could have been otherwise, including left undone. Projecting reception when composing, reflecting on intention when receiving, giving over to rhythm and coincidence, imagining worlds, overcoming received habits of perception, reframing categories and frames of understanding—such practices emerge from the interface between a desiring body and a willing intellect.

Artworks exist in and for themselves and beyond the intentions of their makers to the extent that they command their own perpetually incomplete project of hermeneusis; it is their very objecthood that makes them available to interpretation. They are a record of all the choices made as they came to be, yet they become the repository of all the possible meanings with which they can be invested. They exist as a force in the long history of our efforts to represent the world to ourselves and, in the process, to humanize ourselves.

Indeed, throughout Western thought an abiding and intrinsic connection between the singularity of works of art and the singularity of persons is maintained. We hold to a sense that persons and works of art have integrity in and for themselves; and art as the artifact of a person remains the paradigm for art in our world: as early as the first quarter of the fifth century BCE, in the chorus of Euripides's *Andromache*, we can find an emphasis on the efficacy of the singular artist: "When a pair of craftsmen draft one hymn, the muses always cause strife."[20]

The numerous contemporary artists who work in collaboration—we might think of Anne and Patrick Poirier, Gilbert and George, or, on another scale, the four-person Ant Farm Collective—represent an alternative to this paradigm yet also extend it in the sense that they realize an erotic and/or utopian merger of the singular and collective will.[21] Collaboration also becomes tied to features of the mode of production—the more complex the materials and techniques of the artwork, the more its scale goes beyond the possibilities of an individual body's strengths and skills, the more likely a collaborative effort will be required. If the "truth" of production lies in the fact that all artworks are collaborative because they are created out of every influence and energy that goes into them, dance troupes and filmmaking crews typically organize themselves around the name of an "auteur" or other person who does the primary work of composing, and even mega-architectural firms emphasize a "face" or personality that organizes the public's perception of the work. Meanwhile, works of literature and paintings are rarely made by more than one person, but a printmaker's singular vision is most often realized by means of equipment that is owned by institutions and shared among individuals.

Whenever we hold to a creative singularity that will meet with minds alike and unlike in the field of reception, we continue to invest the figure of the artist with free powers despite the fact that, unlike other persons of high status, the artist does not maintain those powers by an implicit or explicit threat of violence. Psychoanalysis has given us a model of the relation between our desire to know and our relation to objects in the world as involving aggression and incorporation. Even if we believe that our engagement with the world is underlain by aggressive fears or projected, hence a priori, desires, the fundamental gestures of production and care characterizing art making and reception nevertheless stand at odds with these initial conditions. A boy cannot build and destroy a sand castle at the same time, and when destroying is a reversible action, remedied by building another castle—or another anything—building develops into skill. The story of the continuity of human making, whether set out in the dialectical utopianism of Hegel and Marx or told by neurologists or art historians, thereby gives us a somewhat different picture from the one offered by Freud and his disciples—one where our intervention in nature, including our own nature, is driven by the need to create and contemplate objects outside and beyond ourselves both for their own sake and for the sake of changing ourselves.

Causal explanations are again of little help here. For example, Pierre Bourdieu, who holds to antecedent social causes of all human behavior, including art making, has described the artist as a "producer of the fetish which is the work of art," claiming that "the artist's status is a consequence of constituting the artistic field (which includes art analysts, beginning with art historians, even the most critical among them) as the locus where the belief in the value of art and the artist's power of valuable creation is continually produced and reproduced."[22] But before such value is produced and reproduced—the value of individual works, and inherently the value of individual artists as the sources of such works—the artwork itself must be made. And if artworks are made only according to preexisting values, Bourdieu finds himself in a circular argument about production that merely reifies social causes from the outset. In a Bourdieuian world of art production, where form and content have already been deprived of any organic or emergent possibilities, there would on the face of it be no need for forms: we could summarize or otherwise convey by the most efficient means the social messages art is meant to transmit. In this world there also would be no need for content, for whatever an art work might "say" would already exist in social life. Such sociological arguments thereby turn out to be theological ones, for the disappointing conclusion that all art has a social—in the case of Bourdieu, class-based—explanation could be avoided only by some superhuman form of creation. An imaginary nostalgia for creation ex nihilo suffuses such theories of social cause, just as a somewhat more credible nostalgia for the manifested intentions of craftmanship suffuses any theory of biological cause.

Nevertheless, Bourdieu reminds us that philosophical aesthetics tends to "forget the historical process through which the social conditions of freedom from 'external determinations' get established; that is, the process of establishing the relatively autonomous field of production and with it the realm of pure aesthetics or pure thought whose existence makes it possible." Creative freedom may be as inalienable as any other freedom of our persons, yet Bourdieu is convincing when he implies that we do not have a world—or do not yet have a world—where everyone exercises, or is able to exercise, such liberty.

The very language of "subjectivity" tends to elide the differences between agency and passivity, the volitional and nonvolitional, that which we subject to our making and those forces that subject us in turn. We have traditions of self and character out of literary humanist traditions that frame subjectivity as a matter of *Bildung* or development. And we have traditions of the self as something worked on out of Nietzschean concepts of the shaped life and Freudian concepts of a structure driven by desire and modified by self-knowledge. In these frames, the self develops toward mastery and self-mastery—we do not picture ourselves as mere material worn down by the world, diminished in and by time. The theological and legal concept of the person as the embodiment of integrity, subject to respect and endowed with inalienable rights, further complicates, and in many ways enriches, our frame for subjectivity and the perspectives available within that frame. By freeing subjectivity of particularity and distributing it universally, the concept of the person suggests a being bearing inalienable rights and deserving of justice.

Here the relations between the negative freedoms that would enable the conditions for leisure and concentration under which art might be made and the positive freedoms that art making itself involves come into focus. The production of art intensifies our sense of the open possibilities of a composing, contingent, reflexive, transforming agency we associate with "selves." The reception of art analogously underlines our sense of the integrity of "persons," their expressions and presence as occasions for respect and attentive apprehension regardless of our knowledge of the particular circumstances of production. Artists continue to model the face-to-face situations that are the basis of all ethical encounters, yet their works take place in situations free of the consequences of such lived meetings and so open up the imagination to new kinds of associations and responses.[23]

Until human beings are free of a causality brought about entirely by nature or by conditions of political and social denigration that keep them perpetually bound to goals not of their own making, the positive freedom of art making is only one of many forms of liberty that will remain unavailable to them. This thralldom is not only a matter of the poverty and physical dependence that always have characterized hierarchical human social forms. Even as little is done to remedy these inequities and handicaps, new varieties of impoverishment have been brought about by the unthinking acceptance of technology. Now, more than at any other time in history, we seem likely to lose touch with the realm of nondetermined, we might say "nondedicated," time and space—not in the sense that we suffer from necessity without respite, for our means of existence in the first world are certainly more to hand than ever before, but because of the relentless purging of boredom from our everyday existence. It has been our choice to let machines demand our attention rather than free it.[24]

Once the culture of rest or *otium* vanishes, it is not easy to fall into a mood or a daydream. To play, to create free, even random comparisons, to risk error and "give it a try," all require independence from both the true urgencies of hunger and shelter and the imaginary urgencies of entertainment. Indeed, perhaps weather has served as the cause of so many poetic moods simply because the contemplation of weather without anxiety or distraction is an index to the degree of leisure in which makers find themselves. From the account of God's rest on the seventh day in Genesis, to the long afternoons of pastoral literature from Theocritus forward, to Marx's optimistic plan for a workday that would be brief enough to allow workers time to develop their artistic, imaginative, and utopian inclinations, the case already has been made for the intersection of creativity and respite. Such conditions of leisure and concentration are preconditions for the making of art, preconditions even more fundamental than any specifically social ones.

Yet the means and modes of art do come under economic and social terms as well, for the poet does not require the space and physical resources of the painter or sculptor, let alone the goldsmith. Precious works can be made out of precious materials or "airy nothings," and from any number of substances in between. If the conditions for art making are not wholly determined by space and means, they are also not wholly determined by investments of time. The more tedium in the work—the more likely the question "how long did it take you to make that?"—the more likely the ephemerality of the work's value. There is a certain economy to elegance, and efficiency of means and profundity of concept are recurring qualities of works that endure.

With her emphasis on "natality," Arendt provided an account of why the singular new is necessary not only to individual self-legislation but also to the collective evolution of human values. The very last words of her long meditation *The Life of the Mind* are a commentary on Augustine's idea that birth marks the entry of a new being into the world and hence that the purpose of divine creation in Genesis was to make possible a new beginning: "Human beings, new men, again and again appear in the world by virtue of birth. . . . [This] seems to tell us more than that we are *doomed* to be free by virtue of being born; no matter whether we like freedom or abhor its arbitrariness, are 'pleased' with it or prefer to escape its awesome responsibility by electing some form of fatalism. This impasse, if such it is, cannot be opened or solved except by an appeal to another mental faculty, no less mysterious than the faculty of beginning, the faculty of Judgment."[25] There Arendt famously breaks off her discussion, in a project on judgment that she was unable to complete before her death. Yet by emphasizing the familiar existential claim that we are "condemned," here "doomed," to freedom, Arendt indicates a great deal about our relation to judgment. If we are not the necessary consequences of a series of antecedent causes; if our birth is not only the continuation of a biological process of species development but, by means of our own powers of signification, the marking of a new situation and a new relation to time, then our freedom is, on the crest of our natural being, a frame for action.

Arendt particularly valued actions in the public sphere that were spontaneous—those that boldly set out possibilities whose novelty echoes the potential of natality itself. In her 1961 essay "What Is Freedom?" she wrote, "Since the whole problem of freedom arises for us in the horizon of Christian tradition on one hand, and of an originally anti-political philosophic tradition on the other, we find it difficult to realize that there may exist a freedom which is not an attribute of the will but an accessory of doing and acting."[26] In seeking out a form of freedom that is not a matter of the will at odds with the determinism of humankind's fallen nature, or a matter of claiming, as philosophers from Thomas Aquinas to Kant have, that the conscience has priority over external rules and norms, Arendt concertedly aestheticizes political action.

In this line of thought, Arendt separates political action from the sphere of the social, arguing that embedding the political in the social creates a deadening and instrumental politics, one always proceeding under the paradigm of "the enormous family which has only one opinion and one interest."[27] Hence, for Arendt any rule-governed, nonspontaneous form of political action would be far too compromised by prior values. She implies that prior values always are, in their deep structure, derived from a concept of patriarchy—and any new beginning requires a genuine departure from the status quo.[28]

The noninstrumentality of artistic making becomes more explicitly the paradigm for political action in a second claim Arendt makes that politics should not be viewed allegorically; just as Kant's genius must give the rule to art, so Arendt suggests that the political actor benefits from a "loss of standards": "the loss of standards . . . is only a catastrophe for the moral world when one assumes that individuals are not capable of judging things in themselves, that their power of judgment is not adequate to an original judgment; one cannot expect of them anything more than the application of known rules."[29] Elsewhere she similarly suggests that politics viewed as the fabrication or making of a prior concept—a practical application of prior sets of rules—is contrary to true political action: political actors must "know not what they do";

their actions are spontaneous, and the consequences of such actions promote judgment. In a set of rapid arguments in "What Is Freedom?" in favor of principled action as the exercise of freedom, Arendt argues that "action, to be free, must be free from motive on one side, from its intended goal as a predictable effect on the other. . . . This is not to say that motives and aims are not important factors in every single act, but they are its determining factors, and action is free to the extent that it is able to transcend them."[30] For Arendt, speech and action are inaugurating, creating out of the arbitrariness of their beginnings unpredictable outcomes that lead to judgments that lead to further inaugurations.

If Arendt obviously is vulnerable to critiques of the aestheticization of politics, she also calls into question the integrity of such a critique. She argues that "the creative process is not displayed in public and not destined to appear in the world. Hence the element of freedom, certainly present in the creative arts, remains hidden; it is not the free creative process which finally appears and matters for the world, but the work of art itself, the end product of the process." She aligns Greek democracy's "space of appearance" with performance—a "kind of theater where freedom could appear."[31] Freedom of speech and freedom of association are preconditions linking the political and aesthetic, but the conflation of politics and art making in this domain of Arendt's thought does not do justice to either action. Spontaneity in politics abandons the ethical potential of weighing the relation between intentions and consequence—inventing new standards and methods for the distribution of power in a world of perpetual revolution might sufficiently reduce the effects of such consequences, and perhaps, although she does not say so, this is what Arendt had in mind.

But one of the greatest resources of art is its reversibility—that control over time and consequences that Arendt herself celebrated in our faculties for promising and forgiving. The finitude of form of individual artworks within the ongoing open history of art in general allows for a far greater range of possibilities than the spontaneous transposition of an aesthetic model to actions in the world. When human beings intervene in the fabric of nature at the level of molecules and cells, for example, it is only by doing so within a finite sphere, characterized by reversibility, that they can be saved from disaster. Irreversibility is the standard for damage as reversibility is the standard for healing. The limited sphere of art making allows for erring as a kind of opening, and the successive attempts the artist makes all accrue toward further richness in the emerging form and further knowledge of nature.

The freedom of the artist is not a privilege of occupation but rather something that anyone can exercise under certain conditions. These are a bounded time and space not dedicated to prior ends, an openness to mood and a self-composed independence from it, a willingness to let the imagination play against the determinations of form, and a commitment to choosing and judging anew. The finite experiences of art making, as untied as they can be to causes and consequences, are by definition attempts or tries, yet in their long history they give the fullest account we have of human striving and dreaming and provide the fullest arsenal of resources for action.

In our own time we are faced with an emergency regarding the future of the earth—that humus out of which both science and religion tell us we are ourselves made. We have confused our part for the whole, but perhaps the knowledge of parts and wholes, the freedom to act and the freedom to judge that art can provide, might help us become, inversely, a resource for that nature we have heretofore depleted. To learn the artist's necessity of starting again is to glimpse the power of such beginnings.

THE SAND CASTLE

Care in destruction is a form of self-deception,

and fury is blind,
or even the precision destruction
of a sand castle,

there is no such thing as
a precision bomb,

the formal finitude of made things overcomes
our respect for what we have made

often that our desire to destroy
is the dark
side of the news he brought.

Unwilling or unable to be
the curator of his creation,
the boy swiftly

returned it to its elements,
that is, to
its pure potential.

Once the skills used in making the castle
were internalized, they were ready
to be used again.

As if what he had been practicing
all along was a mode of
memorization or,

better, learning, returning

the power of the form back to
himself, the boy seemed
to be,

using all his physical
might to do so, by destroying
the mere thing.

But could not realize an interior,
acquire an interiority in being
a memory alone,

did this object that implied,
one he felt could be replaced

easily, was his castle
a work of craft

rather than art, we cannot
give value to our making,

always present as the potential
for unmaking, or at least

we have to making, for
without the freedom of reversibility

enacted in unmaking,
we have to making,

that boy has represented
for me a certain relation.
Since then.

And he skipped off to wherever he was going next
he grinned (to himself, to me, I couldn't tell)

But the boy was delighted
"the lone and level sands stretch far away"

"Ozymandias," I thought of the end
of Shelley's
"come to grief," as we say, startled,

feeling that something beautiful had.
Then not distinguishable at all,

barely distinguishable from the sand surrounding them
as the castle's sandy walls and towers

his arms and legs flailing like a gritty
whirligig, he kicked with all his might,
reaching it.

Turned again, and raced back to his castle,
stopped, ran back a few yards, turned,
smacked his hands together,
then he stood.

And still the boy worked on,
smaller children began to whine for their supper,

bony driftwood into emptied buckets
and spilled the day's find of shells

and sunbathers shook out their towels.
Darker than the sky,
streaked the horizon,

then darker blue,
strips of red, orange meanwhile.

It would be there tomorrow.
Or a patrolling jeep wheeled over it, or a pair
of lovers stumbled across it, and unless

in the dark a drunk,
his castle would be safe,

even as the tide came in—
he had chosen his site carefully as well—

revisions made with the tips of his fingers,
the point of minor additions and deletions

were thrown aside, for his work had reached
his blunter instruments, shovels and buckets.

Where the windows would be
indentations carved
by a spoon's edge to show,

turrets, moats, interior walls,
who was building an elaborate sand castle,

maybe eight, maybe nine
years old, I could catch sight of a boy,

beyond the periphery of its oblong shadow,
I was reading under a beach umbrella and

but one late summer afternoon
which coast, or which sea,

I don't remember where.

ENDNOTES

CHAPTER ONE

1. Paul Ricoeur, *Philosophie de la volonté* (Paris: Aubier, 1950), 453–86. Translated by Erazim V. Kohák as *Freedom and Nature: The Voluntary and the Involuntary*, vol. 1 (Evanston, IL: Northwestern University Press, 1966), 485–86.

2. R. W. Dyson translates this passage as follows: "In order that there might be this beginning, therefore, a man was created before whom no man existed." From Augustine, *City of God against the Pagans* (Cambridge: Cambridge University Press, 1998), 532. For a discussion of the relevance of Augustine's notion of beginnings to medieval literature more generally, see the work of my colleague D. Vance Smith, *The Book of the Incipit: Beginnings in the Fourteenth Century* (Minneapolis: University of Minnesota Press, 2001), 16.

3. Pico della Mirandola, "Oration on the Dignity of Man" (a title later applied and not Pico's own), in *The Renaissance Philosophy of Man*, ed. Ernst Cassirer, Paul Kristeller, and J. H. Randall (Chicago: University of Chicago Press, 1948), 223–25.

4. See the discussion of Kant's concepts of transcendental freedom as the power of spontaneity and practical freedom in relation to the negative and positive valences of the will in Heidegger's Freiberg lectures: Martin Heidegger, *The Essence of Human Freedom*, trans. Ted Sadler (London: Continuum, 2005), 18–20.

5. Isaiah Berlin, "Two Concepts of Liberty," in *Four Essays on Liberty* (London: Oxford University Press, 1969; new ed. 2002), 118–72. In "Two Concepts," Berlin traces the largely spatial arguments by which John Locke, John Stuart Mill, Benjamin Constant, and Alexis de Tocqueville argue for "a certain minimum area of personal freedom" in negative freedom as a stay against the powers of the state (128–31). Positive freedom is rooted in the sense of "being one's own master" and the possibilities of self-realization. Berlin analyzes its relation to the schizophrenic image of a being split between transcendence and the passions, with the former reigning over the latter (134). In "From Hope and Fear Set Free," in Isaiah Berlin's *Concepts and Categories: Philosophical Essays* (London: Hogarth; Oxford: Oxford University Press, 1980) (reprinted in Berlin, *Four Essays on Liberty*, 2002 ed.), Berlin criticizes theories of freedom (the Stoics, Spinoza, Bradley, and Stuart Hampshire) that "confine freedom to self-determination." He also corrects his earlier argument in "Two Concepts" to say, "It is the actual doors that are open that determine the extent of someone's freedom, and not his own preferences" (193). He further

notes that knowledge may make us free, but if knowledge tends more and more to knowledge of determinism, a certain paradox results (197). But surely the conclusion we might draw from this is that the quality of whatever freedom we might experience in a determined world has all the more resonance and significance.

6. Immanuel Kant, *Critique of the Power of Judgment*, ed. Paul Guyer (Cambridge: Cambridge University Press, 2000), 332–33.

7. For a contrary reading to this tradition of self-transcendence, see Slavoj Žižek's commentary on F. W. J. von Schelling's *Ages of the World*: "Is therefore the God prior to the primordial contraction, this pure gaze that finds enjoyment in contemplating its own nonbeing, also not a fantasy formation at its purest? Schelling emphasizes again and again the passage of the pure *Seinkönnen* of the primordial Abyss into the contracted Ground cannot be accounted for and deduced; it can only be described (narrated) *post festum*, after it already took place, since we are not dealing with a necessary act but with a free act that could also not have happened—however, does this not amount to an implicit admission of the fact that its status is that of a retroactive fantasy?" *The Abyss of Freedom / Ages of the World: An Essay by Slavoj Žižek with the Text of Schelling's "Die Weltalter" (Second Draft, 1813)*, trans. Judith Norman (Ann Arbor: University of Michigan, 1997), 91n11.

8. Epictetus, *The Discourses, as Reported by Arrian*, vol. 1, ed. and trans. W. A. Oldfater (New York: Grove, 2007; repr. from the two-vol. ed., London: Heinemann, 1925). For a discussion of Epictetus on freedom, see Orlando Patterson, *Freedom*, vol. 1, *Freedom in the Making of Western Culture* (New York: Basic Books, 1991), 191, 281.

9. Hannah Arendt, "What Is Freedom," in *Between Past and Future: Eight Exercises in Political Thought* (New York: Viking, 1961), 143–71, 146–47.

10. Friedrich Wilhelm Joseph Schelling, "Philosophical Investigations into the Essence of Human Freedom and Related Matters," in *Philosophy of German Idealism*, ed. Ernst Behler, trans. Priscilla Hayden-Roy (New York: Continuum, 1987), 256. A more recent translation of Schelling, with an introduction that emphasizes his contributions to theodicy, is F. W. J. Schelling, *Philosophical Investigations into the Essence of Human Freedom*, trans. Jeff Love and Johannes Schmidt (Albany: State University of New York Press, 2006). For a compelling contemporary meditation on the politics and aesthetics of withdrawal, see Anne-Lise François's *Open Secrets: The Literature of Uncounted Experience* (Stanford, CA: Stanford University Press, 2007).

11. Heidegger, *Essence of Human Freedom*, 94; Hannah Arendt, *The Human Condition*, 2nd ed. (Chicago: University of Chicago Press, 1988), 244.

12. Stuart Hampshire, *Freedom of the Individual* (New York: Harper and Row, 1965), 38–39.

13. Aristotle, "De poetica," in *The Basic Works of Aristotle*, ed. Richard McKeon (New York: Random House, 1941), 1479 (sec. 1459a).

14. Kant, *Critique of the Power of Judgment*, 186. I will return to Kant's concept of genius in my chapter "Forming."

15. Georg Simmel, *The Philosophy of Money*, ed. David Frisby, trans. Tom Bottomore and David Frisby (London: Routledge, 2004), 64.

16. Alfred Gell, "The Technology of Enchantment and the Enchantment of Technology," in *Anthropology, Art and Aesthetics*, ed. J. Coote and A. Shelton (Oxford: Clarendon, 1992), 49.

17. See Hannah Arendt's *The Life of the Mind* (New York: Harcourt, 1971), 32, for Merleau-Ponty's discussion of the sensual and the mental. Arendt believes that there is in fact a *somatic* barrier between body and mind and that thought is foundationless.

18. See Simon Grote's "Pietistische *Aisthesis* und moralische Erziehung bei Alexander Gottlieb Baumgarten," *Aufklärung* 20 (2008): 175–98, and the larger argument of Grote's dissertation in the Department of History at the University of California, Berkeley, "Moral Philosophy and the Origins of Modern Aesthetic Theory in Scotland and Germany," 2010. See also Jerome Stolnitz, "On the Origins of 'Aesthetic Disinterestedness,'" *Journal of Aesthetics and Art Criticism* 20 (1961): 131–43. Stolnitz traces to Anthony Ashley Cooper, the third Earl of Shaftesbury, the idea that "genuine moral and religious concern are with what is intrinsic and that they are therefore terminal. They are not instrumental and therefore anticipatory," and he goes on to link these conditions to those appropriate to the apprehension of artworks (132–33).

19. In Plato's *Ion*, Socrates points out that Ion cannot speak of Homer with any art or knowledge if he also cannot speak of other poets with such authority, for "the art of poetry is surely one whole" (12). Later in the dialogue, Socrates mentions that Homer can't know such acts as charioteering or medicine without being a charioteer or a doctor, and so on from cowherd to general. See *Ion, Hippias Minor, Laches, Protagoras*, trans. R. E. Allen (New Haven, CT: Yale University Press, 1996), 19–22. In book 10 of the *Republic*, Plato famously argues that "all poetic imitators have no grasp of the truth" (271); furthermore, "poetic imitators put a bad constitution in the soul of each individual by making images far removed from the truth and by gratifying the irrational part. . . . Imitation . . . is able to corrupt even decent people" (Plato, *Republic*, trans. G. M. A. Grube [Indianapolis: Hackett, 1992], 276). Arguments against rhetoric in *Gorgias* include the claim that "if someone stripped off the tune, rhythm, and meter from every poetic composition, would what is left turn out to be anything other than speeches? And he mentions "a rhetoric we do not altogether admire, for we assert that it is a flattering one." He further explains

that cooking is like rhetoric, that popular speaking is "flattery and shameful," that the flattery of rhetoric has "no consideration of better or worse," and that the function of tragedy is to "gratify the mob of spectators" (Plato, *Gorgias and Phaedrus*, trans. James H. Nichols [Ithaca, NY: Cornell University Press, 1998], 98–99). See also Plato, *Symposium*, trans. Alexander Nehamas and Paul Woodruff (Indianapolis: Hackett, 1989), 51. Two essays by Christopher Janeway provide helpful surveys of the complexities and discontinuities of Plato's positions: "Arts and Crafts in Plato and Collingwood," *Journal of Aesthetics and Art Criticism* 50, no. 1 (Winter 1992): 45–54, and "Craft and Fineness in Plato's *Ion*," *Oxford Studies in Ancient Philosophy*, vol. 10, ed. Julia Annas (Oxford: Clarendon, 1992), 1–23.

20. Claude Tresmontant, *La préscience de Dieu, la prédestination et la liberté humaine* (Paris: François-Xavier de Guibert, 1996), 42: "Du point de vue du platonisme e du néo-platonisme, il n'y a pas de liberté incrée e créatrice, parce qu'il n'y a pas de création. Il y a procession nécessaire et éternelle à partir de l'Un, sans que l'Un le veuille, comme le dit Plotin." In contrast, Tresmontant emphasizes the "fundamental mystery" that human beings possess their own creative liberty (67–70). Tresmontant also remarks upon Henri Bergson's revival of the Hebrew concept of creation—a counter to Leibnitz's sense of predestination: "Ce que Bergson a découvert, c'est que justement la réalité n'est nullement préformée, mais qu'elle est en genèse, en régime d'improvisation géniale, creation géniale et continué d'imprévisible nouveauté" (79).

21. *Basic Works of Aristotle*, ed. McKeon. *Physics*, trans. R. P. Hardie and R. K. Gaye, bk. 2, pp. 236–39; *Ethica Nicomachia*, trans. W. D. Ross, 6.4, p. 1025. The discussion of error is in 6.5, p. 1027.

22. The question of nothing is taken up as the central crux of being in Heidegger's "What Is Metaphysics?" Martin Heidegger, *Basic Writings*, ed. and trans. David F. Krell (New York: Harper Collins, 1997), 90–110. Heidegger quotes Hegel's *Science of Logic*: "Pure Being and pure Nothing are therefore the same," contending that "from the nothing all beings as beings come to be"—hence in response to *ex nihilo nihil fit*, that *ex nihilo omne ens qua ens fit* (108). In Schelling's 1804 "System of Philosophy in General," this question is answered by the theological claim that "God, by virtue of his self-affirmation, is also immediately the total whole, the universe, not merely as that outside of which nothing is, but also that wherein all possibility is actuality. . . . The total universe is the self-affirmation of God" (in *Idealism and the Endgame of Theory*, trans. and ed. Thomas Pfau [Albany: State University of New York Press, 1994], 166). See the discussion of Schelling's notion of the "non-ground" as the moment before God's self-appearance in self-making in Werner Marx, *The Philosophy of F. W. J. Schelling*, ed. and trans. Thomas Nenon (Bloomington: Indiana University Press, 1984), 67–69. Hannah Arendt traces this

insight to Plato's *Sophist*: "The will's autonomy, its complete independence from things as they are, has only one limitation—it cannot deny Being altogether. As Plato conveys Parmenides's interdiction, we cannot think that which is not. We can hold that God created Being *ex nihilo*, but we cannot conceive this nothing" (Arendt, *Life of the Mind*, 130). The question also arises in Leibnitz's 1697 essay "On the Ultimate Origin of Things." Bergson, in his *L'évolution créatrice*, makes a passionate argument against a number of philosophical commonplaces regarding the "void" or "the nought," arguing, "Negation . . . differs from affirmation properly so called in that it is an affirmation of the second order; it affirms something of an affirmation which itself affirms something of an object." In Bergson's system, the continual psychological desire to strive after what is absent and to make it present drives the creation of an idea of negation that, by virtue of its created status as word, idea, invention, is always already affirmative ("The Idea of 'Nothing,'" in *Creative Evolution*, trans. Arthur Mitchell [New York: Henry Holt, 1911; repr. New York: Dover Books, 1988], 272–98). Only very recently, Fermilab scientists have been able to glimpse that there was a slight predisposition toward matter over antimatter in the first moments of the universe, as described in this bulletin from the Brookhaven National Laboratory: http://www.bnl.gov/bnlweb/pubaf/pr/PR_display.asp?prID=1139 (accessed May 20, 2010). This fascinating discovery of how something prevails over nothing only displaces and intensifies the question of why that should be the case.

23. To my knowledge, the most extensive meditation of the impact of the story of creation from the Hebrew (and Christian) scriptures on Western philosophy is Hans Jonas's "Jewish and Christian Elements in Philosophy: Their Share in the Emergence of the Modern Mind," in *Philosophical Essays: From Ancient Creed to Technological Man* (Englewood Cliffs, NJ: Prentice Hall, 1974), 21–44. Jonas sees the long progress of the syncretic Western combination of classical rationalism, generalism, and theory, on the one hand, and Hebrew voluntarism, individualism, and activism, on the other, as reaching a particular intensity in "Kant's majestic effort to synthesize voluntarism and rationalism. That synthesis appears in the categorical imperative (surely of Hebrew vintage), grounded in the autonomy of the moral will (a transformed Christian conception), but objectively valid because this will is itself reason and thus universal (a classical conception)" (43–44).

24. I follow here the introductory account of creation stories by Mineke Schipper, "Stories of the Beginning: Origin Myths of Africa South of the Sahara," in *Imagining Creation*, ed. Markham Geller and Mineke Schipper (Leiden: Brill, 2008), 103–8, 125.

25. Hesiod, *Theogony*, trans. M. L. West (Oxford: Oxford University Press, 1988), 6: "First came the Chasm." West notes that "the Chasm" is the literal meaning of Greek *Kaos* and does not contain an idea of confusion or disorder (64n116). See

also the discussion of the *Timaeus* in Augustine, *City of God* 11.21: "Just as He moves all temporal things without any temporal motion of His own, so does He know all things with a knowledge that does not occupy time." Augustine goes on to claim that God receives no "addition" from his works, since his knowledge is already perfect (*City of God against the Pagans*, 475).

26. Bernhard W. Anderson, "Introduction: Mythopoeisis and Theological Dimensions of Biblical Creation," in *Creation in the Old Testament*, ed. Bernhard W. Anderson (Philadelphia: Fortress, 1984), 13.

27. The Hebrew scriptures are named after their source texts and the ways those texts refer to the Deity: among them, the P, or Priestly, source text uses the terms Elohim and El Shaddai, meaning "God Almighty," to refer to the divinity; the J, or Jehovah, source text, uses only Jehovah (Yahweh) in speaking of God; and the E text also uses Elohim but tends to introduce angels and dreams. Genesis is an amalgam of the P and J texts.

28. Walther Eichrodt, "In the Beginning: A Contribution to the Interpretation of the First Word of the Bible," in Anderson, *Creation in the Old Testament*, 65–73 (70): "The God who stands apart from [creation] in his sovereign freedom . . . an eternal God who, unlike the pagan deities woven into their cosmogony, truly possesses transcendental majesty and justly claims absolute power over the created world."

29. *The Anchor Bible: Genesis*, ed. E. A. Speiser, vol. 1 (New York: Doubleday, 1964). Speiser emphasizes in his commentary (8–13) the Mesopotamian origins of the Genesis account. However, despite the nearly identical unfoldings of the phenomena of creation, the initial situations of the Babylonian creation epics and Genesis are significantly different: in the Babylonian account, divine spirit and cosmic matter are coexistent and coeternal, but in the Hebrew Genesis, divine spirit creates cosmic matter and exists independently of it. The Creator thereby is not absorbed in the frame of creation (10).

30. *The JPS Torah Commentary on Genesis*, ed. and commentary by Nahum M. Sarna (Philadelphia: Jewish Publication Society, 1989), 5: "The Hebrew stem *b-r-* is used in the Bible exclusively for divine creativity. It signifies that the product is absolutely novel and unexampled, depends solely on God for its coming into existence, and is beyond the human capacity to reproduce—it always refers to the completed product and never to the material of which it is made." For a broad overview of the implications of the Hebrew creation story, see Nahum M. Sarna's additional study *Understanding Genesis* (New York: Jewish Theological Seminary of America and McGraw Hill, 1966).

31. Because I am interested in the philosophy of art and not in theological debate, I have emphasized the prevailing tradition of creation out of nothing in my

discussion. We see the concept in the scriptural passages I have just mentioned, but Hans Jonas writes, "The createdness of matter was, to my knowledge, first explicitly asserted in the 3rd century by Origen (*De principiis*, II, c. 1, 4), and Augustine implies it in his strong emphasis on creation "out of nothing" (*De civ. Dei*, XIV, 11; *ibid* XII, 25). The Jewish (like the Islamic) thinkers of the Middle Ages were divided on the issue. Gabirol, still a Neoplatonist, derives both matter and form from God; but only the forms originate in his will and express the divine spontaneity, while matter emanates from his nature and expresses its necessity. . . . Maimonides . . . firmly asserts the creation from nothing, while Gersonides after him as firmly denies it and (like Averroes) argues that matter is not derivable from God, but preceded his creation." Jonas emphasizes that for Maimonides's doctrine of a creation *ex nihilo* it follows that God, as the Creator of the universe, knows all its particulars ("Jewish and Christian Elements in Philosophy," 36n14, 37n16).

32. Hermann Gunkel, "The Influence of Babylonian Mythology upon the Biblical Creation Story" (1895 text), in Anderson, *Creation in the Old Testament*, 25–52 (32): In Genesis 1 the deity conquers the waters, indicating a Babylonian source text. In Genesis 2, the deity creates the waters, indicating a Canaanite source text. In the first the waters are chaos, and in the second, the renewal of life. Gunkel explains that the notion of Chaos does not fit well with the Jewish concept of a freely acting Creator. The theme of chaos is found in the creation myths of not only Babylonia but also India, Greece, Egypt, and Phoenicia.

33. Sarna, *JPS Torah Commentary* (7): "'God said' means 'God thought' or 'God willed,' emphasizing an effortless and absolute sovereignty."

34. Ibid. (6): "Other texts [too] point to creation by means of divine fiat. Thus Psalm 33:6 and 9 declare 'By the word of the Lord the heavens were made / by the breath of His mouth, all their host. . . . / For he spoke and it was; / he commanded, and it endured.' The postbiblical 2 Esdras has the same notion: 'I said, O Lord, You have indeed spoken from the beginning of creation and on the first day You said: 'Let heaven and earth be made,' and Your word accomplished the work." (Esdras is a book of the Septuagint canonical in Eastern and Oriental orthodoxy but regarded as apocryphal by Jews, Catholics, and most Protestants. Josephus quotes it extensively.)

35. Anderson in "Introduction" (17): "created" as the emphasis indicates that creation is before genealogy—hence prehistorical and even pretemporal. Sarna, *JPS Torah Commmentary* (8), disagrees with other commentators, such as Anderson, in contending that the verb *-s-h*, used in verses 7, 16, and 25, simply means divine intention become a reality. It does not represent a tradition of creation by deed as opposed to word, he contends, referring to Psalm 33:6 as evidence and ar-

guing that the distinction between create (*b-r-*) and make (*-s-h*) is indiscriminate. He argues that in verse 22, when the Lord God fashioned Eve from Adam's rib, "built" is the literal meaning of the verb and the only time it is used in the creation narrative. Widely used in Near Eastern poetic traditions for the action of the deity in creating humankind, it fits well with the Hebrew *tsela*, "rib," which is used as an architectonic term for building texts. Even so, we might then ask why two different words in fact appear, and what do we make of the claims of Psalm 8 and the book of Isaiah?

36. Discussion of the two accounts, their sources, and differences can be found in Claus Westermann, "Biblical Reflection on Creator-Creation," in Anderson, *Creation in the Old Testament*, 90–117 (94). For the history of the P, J, and E texts, see Speiser's introduction to the *Anchor Bible: Genesis*.

37. Westermann ("Biblical Reflection," 97) discusses the meaning of these earthly metaphors. Sarna (*JPS Torah Commentary*, 17) writes in his Torah commentary that the verb here is *va-yitser*, used for the action of a potter in molding clay into a shape. Man is portrayed thereby as the work of God's hands.

38. In Sarna's commentary (*JPS Torah Commentary*, 7), separation, or differentiation, is the second modality of creation. Calling or name-giving is associated with both creation and domination, for the bestower of names has power over the object. Other examples of this issue can be found in Psalm 8:3, "thy heavens, the work of thy fingers"; 8:6, "the works of thy hands"; and Psalm 136:5, "To him who by understanding made the heavens." In a passage on the folly of idolatry in Isaiah 44:24: "Thus says the LORD, your Redeemer, who formed you from the womb: 'I am the LORD who made all things, who stretches out the heavens alone, who spread out the earth.'"

39. Gunkel writes of these questions of the deity's agency and actions ("Influence of Babylonian Mythology," 27): "God himself did not 'create' the plants and trees of the earth, but rather the earth caused them to spring forth at the command of God. This turn of phrase is all the more noteworthy in that it has no obvious parallel with the other acts of creation. One is certainly justified in seeing here a reflection of the mythological way of viewing the earth. It is easy to explain why this feature has been retained; it is anchored in the view that, just as the earth once brought forth its vegetation, so it does anew each spring." Sarna's commentary (*JPS Torah Commentary*, 9) suggests, "This creative act constitutes an exception to the norm that God's word directly effects the desired product. Here the earth is depicted as the mediating element, implying that God endows it with generative powers that He now activates by his utterance. The significance of this singularity is that the sources of power in what we call nature, which were personified and deified in the ancient world, are now emptied of sanctity. The pro-

ductive forces of nature exist only by the will of one sovereign creator and are not independent spiritual entities, as in the fertility cults of the ancient Near Eastern religions."

40. Maurice Merleau-Ponty, "Freedom," in *The Phenomenology of Perception*. trans. Colin Smith (London: Routledge, 1989), 439.

41. Jean-Paul Sartre, *The Psychology of Imagination* (New York: Citadel, 1966), 246: "Contrary to what could be believed, the imaginary world [of a dream] occurs as a world without freedom: nor is it determined, it is the opposite of freedom, it is fatal."

42. See the discussion of "self-preservation," meaning a minimal condition of reassimilation to life, in Fred Rush, "Literature and Politics," in *Handbook of Philosophy and Literature*, ed. Richard Eldridge (London: Oxford University Press, 2009), 514n7. Elaine Scarry's pathbreaking study of pain as unmaking and creation as making in *The Body in Pain: The Making and Unmaking of the World* (New York: Oxford University Press, 1987) is a far more extended argument regarding the dynamic between suffering and making. Looking at the genealogical passages in Genesis, Scarry notes that the Genesis stories are "always attentive to creation and procreation, to genesis and to numbers" (187), and she reads the recurrent birth imagery—including images of wells and altars—in these passages as the counterpart to divine creation at the book's beginning.

43. Speiser note for the *Anchor Bible* (5n4). Anderson ("Introduction," 15) writes, "This . . . is not an ethical judgment but an aesthetic one."

44. Gunkel ("Influence of Babylonian Mythology," 30) translates "good" as successful.

45. F. W. J. Schelling, *Philosophical Investigation into the Essence of Human Freedom*, trans. Jeff Love and Johannes Schmidt (Albany: State University of New York Press, 2006) 18.

46. Speiser note for *Anchor Bible* (7–8n2).

47. The contrast to the Babylonian myth is noted by George M. Landes, "Creation and Liberation," in Anderson, *Creation in the Old Testament*, 135–51 (146–47).

48. Jonas ("Jewish and Christian Elements in Philosophy," 28–30) emphasizes the impact of this dimension of Muslim thought, beginning with the ninth-century arguments of the philosopher Kalam: "Everything, from the color of a blossom to the order of the stars, could as well—that is to say, without contradiction—be other than it actually is. The nature it actually has represents a choice from among all the possible alternatives; strictly speaking, from an infinite range of possibilities. But choice is a matter of the will. Thus the logical evidence of the world is more in accord with its having been called forth by the free spontaneity of divine will than with its having emanated or otherwise derived from

the divine essence. God could have willed the world to be other than it is, or not have willed it at all. And the world itself proclaims its createdness by its intrinsic contingency."

49. Schelling writes on the last pages of the second draft of the *Weltalter* (see 181–82 in Žižek, Norman translation):

> That primordial deed which makes a man genuinely himself precedes all individual actions: but immediately after it is put into exuberant freedom, this deed sinks in the night of unconsciousness. This is not a deed that could happen once and then stop: it is a permanent deed, a never-ending deed, and consequently it can never again be brought before consciousness. . . . Likewise that will, posited once at the beginning and then led to the outside, must immediately sink into unconsciousness. Only in this way is a beginning possible, a beginning that does not stop being a beginning, a truly eternal beginning. . . . That deed once done is done for all eternity. The decision that in some manner is truly to begin must not be brought back to consciousness: it must not be called back, because this would amount to being taken back. If in making a decision, somebody retains the right to reexamine his choice, he will never make a beginning at all. . . . The will is like the jealous God of the Old Testament, who tolerated no gods but himself, and his expression or word is this: I am the only one and there is no other but me.

In the essay "Monotheism" in his *History of Ideas* (New York: Scribner's, 1969), 187–211, George Boas traces monotheism as a concept to the figure of Moses and argues similarly that it is Yahweh's autotelic "I am what I am" that sets in motion the separation of divine intellect from the physical world (189).

CHAPTER TWO

1. Ludwig Feuerbach, *The Essence of Christianity*, trans. Marian Evans (London: Trübner, 1881), 105–6.

2. Rainer Maria Rilke, "The Ninth Elegy," in *The Selected Poetry of Rainer Maria Rilke*, ed. and trans. Stephen Mitchell (New York: Random House, 1984), 200. Here are the lines in the original German:

> . . . Zwischen den Hämmern besteht
> unser Herz, wie die Zunge
> zwischen den Zähnen, die doch,
> dennoch, die preisende bleibt.
>
> Preise dem Engel die Welt, nicht die unsägliche, *ihm*
> kannst du nicht großtun mit herrlich Erfühltem; im Weltall,

wo er fühlender fühlt, bist du ein Neuling. Drum zeig
ihm das Einfache, das, von Geschlecht zu Geschlechtern gestaltet,
als ein Unsriges lebt, neben der Hand und im Blick.
Sag ihm die Dinge. Er wird staunender stehn; wie du standest
bei dem Seiler in Rom, oder beim Töpfer am Nil. . . .

3. Ibid., 234–35.

4. In a discussion of what Augustine's theory of being and its connection to praise borrows from these ancient Greek notions, Hannah Arendt goes on to say, "This notion [the necessity for praise] was a kind of philosophical justification of poetry and the arts; world-alienation, which preceded the rise of Stoic and Christian thought, succeeded in obliterating it from our tradition of philosophy. . . . It ends with the era of suspicion of Nietzsche: When men could no longer *praise*, they turned their greatest conceptual efforts to *justifying* God and his Creation in theodicies." She points out that poets never quite accepted this world alienation and cites the end of "Precious Five," a 1950 poem by her friend W. H. Auden:

That singular command
I do not understand,
Bless what there is for being,
Which has to be obeyed, for
What else am I made for,
Agreeing or disagreeing?

Hannah Arendt, *The Life of the Mind* (New York: Harcourt, 1971), section on "Willing," 2:92; the Nietzsche discussion follows on 97. W. H. Auden, "Precious Five," in *Collected Poems*, ed. Edward Mendelson (New York: Modern Library, 2007), 588–89.

5. The most important Western myth to address this contrast between blessings and curses remains the Oresteia, the tale of the cursing Furies who emerge as the Eumenides. Meanwhile, the path from existence to essence is in turn well exemplified by the Western emphasis upon conversion accounts; we might think of the progression in Augustine's *Confessions* from narrative to praise.

6. See Paul Beauchamp, *Création et séparation* (Paris: Desclée de Brouwer, 1969), 50: "l'homme adore ce qu'il fait au lieu d'adorer qui l'a fait."

7. *OED*, *thank*. The first, obsolete meaning is "thought." Under *think* the authors of the *OED* show the sliding pronunciation between the *a* and the *i* but do not indicate a sliding semantic. They contend that the original meaning of *think* "may thus have been to cause [something] to seem or appear [to one's self]."

8. Gilles Deleuze and Félix Guattari, *What Is Philosophy*, trans. Hugh Tomlinson and Graham Burchell (New York: Columbia University Press, 1991), 37.

9. Wallace Stevens, "Of Bright & Blue Birds & the Gala Sun," in *Complete Poetry and Prose* (New York: Library of America, 1997), 225.

10. Joan Breton Connelly, *Portrait of a Priestess: Women and Ritual in Ancient Greece* (Princeton, NJ: Princeton University Press, 2007), 179.

11. A redistribution of values as well as goods seems to be an inherent part of this economy. In her study of ancient Greek priestesses, for example, Connelly describes the evidence that the priest as a slaughterer had no special role in this ritual. Worshipers could pray over and deposit sacrificial items even if priests were not present (ibid., 181). In Hebrew tradition, the blood of the offering must be burned or washed away, but never ingested. See Leviticus 6.

12. Denis Feeney, *Literature and Religion at Rome: Cultures, Contexts and Beliefs* (Cambridge: Cambridge University Press, 1998), 120.

13. This list of sounds comes from those mentioned in Psalms 33, 47, 66, 67, 71, 90, 95, 100, and 144.

14. Nahum Sarna, *On the Book of Psalms: Exploring the Prayers of Ancient Israel* (New York: Schocken, 1993), 9.

15. Gary A. Anderson, in *Sacrifices and Offerings in Ancient Israel*, Harvard Semitic Monographs (Atlanta: Scholars Press, 1987), 15–19, discusses the conflicting scholarly accounts of Israelite and Canaanite sacrifices as "food for the gods." Psalm 50, for example, explicitly says that the god needs no food, and "in both Israel and Mesopotamia, certain literate groups inveighed against overly anthropomorphic characterizations of the deity." G. S. Kirk raises an analogous theological problem regarding animal sacrifice in his essay "Pitfalls in the Study of Greek Sacrifice," in *Le sacrifice dans l'antiquité* (Genève: Fondation Hardt, 1981), 41–80. He argues, at least hypothetically, that the evidence from Homer indicates a "progressive *de-incarnation* of the Olympian gods," for as much as they may enjoy the savor of burning animal fat, they eventually feed on only ambrosia and nectar—necessary to the special substance that flows in their immortal veins instead of the mere blood that runs in human veins (78–79).

16. Allen Ginsberg, *Kaddish and Other Poems, 1958–1960* (San Francisco: City Lights Books, 1961), 11–12.

17. Georges Bataille, *The Accursed Share*, vol. 1, *Consumption*, trans. Robert Hurley (New York: Zone Books, 1991), 25–26 (translation of *La part maudite* [Paris: Les Éditions de Minuit, 1949], 31).

18. That the praising speaker intends his or her judgment to be taken up by others and to enter into the general economy of values is sometimes indicated by grammar as well as content. For example, in Hebrew and in Greek, hortative moods are used to transmit a sense of concerted action not yet accomplished—in Hebrew the cohortative has a first-person imperative form; in Greek, where there

is no first-person imperative, the hortatory subjunctive is a first-person plural tense. We find these moods in the Hebrew scriptures and the New Testament at such moments as Hebrews 10:22: "Let us come forward to the holy of holies with a true heart in full assurance of faith." Or in Hebrews 12:1: "Let us run the race that is set before us." And in John 4:7: "Beloved, let us love one another." Although it is translated into English as "let us," it indicates situations of rousing, exhorting, or exciting—to commence, to spur oneself on, to self-rouse or self-rally—thereby underlining all the more the inner agency of the praiser's expression. Of most importance, the mood indicates an enthusiasm for the proposition of the statement; it is performative in the self-reflexive sense of expressing encouragement or discouragement to engage the suggestion it is making. This autotelic dimension of the hortative distinguishes it from the use of "let me" or "let us" in the sense of actually asking for permission. See Moses Stuart, *Hebrew Grammar* (Andover, MA: Codman, 1823), 304.

19. Hesiod, *Theogony*, trans. M. L. West (Oxford: Oxford University Press, 1988), 6.

20. C. H. Bullock, *An Introduction to Old Testament Poetic Books* (Chicago: Moody Press, 1985), 123: "not all the psalms have a liturgical origin, and . . . many were probably never used at all in the liturgy of the Temple." Bullock relies upon Sigmund Mowinckel, *The Psalms in Israel's Worship*, trans. D. R. Ap-Thomas, 2 vols. (Nashville: Abingdon, 1962), 1:22. A. W. Bulloch, in *Callimachus: The Fifth Hymn* (Cambridge: Cambridge University Press, 1985), 4–8, places Callimachus's hymn, following the Homeric hymns and works of Theocritus, Herodas, and Sappho, in a tradition of literary and not cultic hymns. Yet he emphasizes at the same time that Callimachus also records details that were "thoroughly characteristic of actual ritual" (8). See also G. W. Williams, *Tradition and Originality in Roman Poetry* (Oxford: Clarendon, 1968), 156–57. Williams outlines some of the conventions Horace and Catullus borrow from hymns and prayers, and, like Bulloch, he emphasizes that "to all intents and purposes the hymn or prayer is a literary form, and to that extent artificial. It is already found with recognizable conventional characteristics in Homer. It has reached the form and dimensions of an independent work in the Homeric hymns: these contain a formal opening and ending, with invocatory address to the deity and references to his powers and attributes; between these there is usually an extended account of some legend of the god" (156). He adds that in Latin those actual cult hymns and prayers that have been preserved are not literary, and "have survived without being intelligible" (157). Feeney (*Literature and Religion at Rome*, 38–40) summarizes the debates on the literary versus cultic origin of classical hymns. He also discusses the nostalgic search for cultic origins of Lesbian poetry in his essay "Horace and the Greek Lyric Poets," in *Horace 2000: A*

Celebration: Essays for the Bimillennium (Ann Arbor: University of Michigan Press, 1993), 55–56. Stella P. Revard's *Pindar and the Renaissance Hymn-Ode: 1450–1700* (Tempe: Arizona Center for Medieval and Renaissance Studies, 2001) is a useful guide to Renaissance criticism's views of the classical tradition, yet she follows this criticism's assumptions about ritual origins with little distance upon them, writing, "There is a direct line of descent from Homeric Hymn to Pindaric ode, so too there is a link between Pindar and the Alexandrian poets of the late classical and the early Christian era. Although more than a century and a half separates Pindar and Callimachus, although each represents a very distinctive culture and approaches poetic composition in a personal idiosyncratic way, their hymn-odes belong to a common choral tradition" (132). She goes on to point out that Callimachus's compositions are "literary compositions" that imitated the "choral formulas" of "earlier lyric traditions.".

21. Helene P. Foley (*The Homeric Hymn to Demeter* [Princeton, NJ: Princeton University Press, 1994], 29.) says the dates are 650–550 BCE; for Apostolos N. Athanassakis, editor of *The Homeric Hymns* (Baltimore: Johns Hopkins University Press, 1976), the date is fifth century.

22. Athanassakis, ed., *Homeric Hymns*, 61.

23. Two treatises, generally concerned with epideictic oratory of praise or blame, and most likely dating to the late third or early fourth century AD, are usually ascribed to the orator/sophist Menander. In the first treatise he writes: "In my opinion . . . it would be better to make an accurate distinction [between genealogical and mythical hymns]. I hold that all genealogies and all hymns involving genealogical elements proceed by means of mythical circumstances, whereas it is not true that all mythical hymns proceed by means of genealogies. Consequently, the class of mythical hymns will be the more generic, and that of genealogical hymns the more specific." See Menander, *Rhetor*, ed. D. A. Russell and N. G. Wilson (Oxford: Oxford University Press 1981), 17. For a discussion of this passage and controversies about the function of the hymns, see Jenny Clay, *The Politics of Olympus: Form and Meaning in the Major Homeric Hymns* (Princeton, NJ: Princeton University Press, 1989), 3, 6. Menander's writings on hymn form are also discussed in Hans Färber, *Die Lyrik in der Kunsttheorie der Antike* (Munich: Neuer Filser Verlag, 1936), 29–30.

24. Most editions of the "Hymn to Demeter" draw out an interpretation arguing for its expression of the official cult legend of the Eleusinian mysteries. However, in an important article from 1986, Kevin Clinton convincingly argues against this commonplace. Clinton holds that on internal evidence alone the hymn is probably not from Attica or written for an Athenian audience but rather was "the restatement of a traditional pious subject, showing no especial interest in the actual cult-

myth that was used at Eleusis." "The Author of the Homeric *Hymn to Demeter*," *Opuscula Atheniensia* 16, no. 4 (1986): 43–49. I am grateful to my colleague Froma Zeitlin for drawing my attention to this work.

25. The problem of irreverence arises as well in the *Republic*, when Plato cites with approval hymns addressed to the gods and condemns those that are not. See G. M. A. Grube's translation of the *Republic* (Indianapolis: Hackett, 1992), 278. But this is a distinction hard to maintain, and Plato himself approves of hymns addressed to the gods on sociopolitical grounds that belie their special designation. See Feeney, *Literature and Religion at Rome*, 41, for a commentary on this issue.

26. *If Not, Winter: Fragments of Sappho*, trans. Anne Carson (New York: Vintage, 2002), 3.

27. Mark Payne has pointed out that in the Quiché Mayan *Popol Vuh* similarly "the gods make human beings specifically to praise them, and remake them several times until they are able to do so to their satisfaction" (personal correspondence, January 2011).

28. *Greek Lyric: An Anthology in Translation*, trans. and ed. Andrew M. Miller (Indianapolis: Hackett, 1996), 47.

29. He as well follows Pindar, who wrote at *Pythian* IX (76–79), in the translation of Anthony Verity:

> Great prowess always brings forth many words,
> but when the list is long discriminating people
> prefer to hear a few themes amplified;
> Appropriateness in all things equally is best.

The Verity translation of *Pythian* IX is from Pindar, *The Complete Odes*, ed. Stephen Instone, trans. Anthony Verity (Oxford: Oxford University Press, 2007), 78. See the discussion of the Callimachus hymn in Elroy Bundy, "The 'Quarrel' between Kallimachus and Apollonius," *California Studies in Classical Antiquity* 5 (1972): 39–92, and Andrew Beer's extensive account of the poem's poetic and ritual context in "Tradition and Originality in Callimachus's 'Hymn to Apollo,'" *Frankfurter elektronische Rundschau zur Altertumskunde* 1 (2006): 1–7 (http://www.fera-journal.eu).

30. Callimachus, *Hymns and Fragments*, trans. A. W. Mair, Loeb Classical Library (Cambridge, MA: Harvard University Press, 1969), 36–135. Cleanthes, "Hymn to Zeus," trans. James Adams in *The Stoic and Epicurean Philosophers*, ed. Whitney J. Oates (New York: Random House, 1940), 591–92.

31. J.-P. Vernant, *Mythe et société en Grèce ancienne* (Paris: F. Maspero, 1974), 186.

32. Jean-Marie Schaeffer, *Art of the Modern Age*, trans. Steven Rendall (Princeton, NJ: Princeton University Press, 2000), 88. In his recent book *Philosophy the Day after Tomorrow* (Cambridge, MA: Harvard University Press, 2005), Stanley

Cavell follows out an argument in various contexts regarding "the capacity and right to praise," which he sees as "an essential topic of the examination of our acknowledgment of the existence of others" (3). Cavell writes in relation to Shakespeare that "the skeptical problem of the existence of others takes the form of raising the possibility of praise, of finding an object worthy of praise, and proving oneself capable of it" (37). His further thoughts on *epideixis* follow from the studies of Joel Fineman's *Shakespeare's Perjured Eye: The Invention of Subjectivity in the Sonnets* (Berkeley: University of California Press, 1986). Cavell is especially interested, whether he is looking at the speeches of Mark Antony or the dances of Fred Astaire, in the ways that "tainted praise" becomes a kind of curse, emphasizing that the curse is an error or deviation from what he sees as the intersubjective function of praise. See also the chapter on praise in Robert von Hallberg's even more recent volume *Lyric Powers* (Chicago: University of Chicago Press, 2008), 40–60. Here, von Hallberg explores several further dimensions of praise—the role of praise in alerting the dead, who face oblivion, to the achievements of the living (46) and the question whether praise is appropriate in a world of suffering and wrong (53). As he cites Cavell's claim that praise is a safeguard against skepticism, his argument is characterized by a persistent skepticism regarding the merits and motives of praise.

33. Pindar, *Nemean Odes, Isthmian Odes, Fragments*, trans. William H. Race, Loeb Classical Library (Cambridge, MA: Harvard University Press, 1997), 47.

34. Here is the full opening: "I am not a sculptor, so as to fashion stationary / statues that stand on their same base. / Rather, on board every ship / and in every boat, sweet song, / go forth from Aigina and spread the news (ibid., 47).

35. Ibid., 49.

36. Ibid.

37. *The Odes of Pindar*, trans. C. M. Bowra (London: Penguin, 1969), 99. He may be asking for a greater payment in this passage, but the meaning is not clear (see 100n).

38. Leslie Kurke in *The Traffic of Praise* (Ithaca, NY: Cornell University Press, 1991) has explained of Pindar scholarship that "what earlier scholars had read as obscure historical allusion or sheer incoherence, we have learned to recognize as the masterful ellipses, manipulations, and baroque elaborations of a consummate poet composing for an audience that shared his complete familiarity with the conventions of praise" (10).

39. *Odes of Pindar*, 72.

40. Hilary Mackie, in *Graceful Errors* (Ann Arbor: University of Michigan Press, 2003), 10–11, describes such gestures and what she calls "encomiastic futures" as

devices Pindar uses to create an impression of impromptu spontaneity. Mackie also discusses at length the significance of excess in Pindar's repertoire of themes. She argues that Pindar's concern is not that too much praise might lead to the envy of the athlete by other men, as likely as this emotion might be, so much as a concern with a performative balance between the subjective response of the audience to the praise being offered and the amount of praise necessary to generate the just amount of *kudos* (16–21). A similar economy, she contends, must be delicately maintained in relation to the envy of the gods (24–27).

41. Bundy, in "'Quarrel' between Kallimachus and Apollonius," lists a series of deictic, self-conscious gestures by which hymnists can both amplify and apologize at once. These are (1) forms of *praeteritio*, including *recusatio*; (2) aporetic passages where a speaker reveals himself at an advantage or disadvantage before his theme; (3) break-off formulas, abandoning a theme that requires more or less elaboration than has been given to it; (4) protestations intended to counter real or imaginary objections or to allay suspicions; (5) ascriptions of poetic inspiration in *prooimia*, transitions, or epilogues to the Muses or other patrons of song or the theme; (6) use of exempla and quotations from authority; and (7) any other programmatic passages.

42. Mackie, *Graceful Errors*, 63.

43. Andrew Ford, in *Homer: The Poetry of the Past* (Ithaca, NY: Cornell University Press, 1992), 48, writes: "The singer or bard had his hidden knowledge and knows paths we do not." Mackie has emphasized that the wishes and prayers for the future that are uttered frequently by the odist are also a way of making offerings to the gods, crediting them with the present victory and ones to come. See *Graceful Errors*, 91–105.

44. In addition to the many instances of the theme of "the new song," or closing commands and promises regarding the new, novelty is emphasized by several formal qualities of pattern and surprise in the Hebrew scriptures. For example, the acrostic poems in Psalms 9–10, 25, 34, 37, 111, 112, 119, and 145, and in Proverbs 31:10–31, repeat the same Hebrew letter at the beginning of verses, half-verses, or stanzas in the order of the letters of the alphabet; in this sense each letter is generative, as in the acrostic form of the book of Lamentations, where the first four chapters are composed by having each verse begin with a new letter of the alphabet. In chapter 3, the same letter begins three verses in succession, a pattern that continues to be followed. Irregularities in Lamentations and the Psalms become visible against a pattern of expectations. See the discussion of these examples in Bullock, *Introduction to the Old Testament Poetic Books*, 47. This book provides an often useful commentary on the poetry of the Hebrew scriptures, but it is marred

in several places by ethnocentrism and flights of purely speculative theological explanation, as in the Bullock's claim that the "New Testament" helps us understand the Psalms because "the Holy Spirit opened up the deeper dimensions of the words (*sensus plenior*) through the New Testament spokesmen" (129).

45. Kurke, *Traffic of Praise*, 71–72.

46. *Nemean VI* declares that both men and gods find their origin in "one mother": Gaia, the Earth. On the maieutic powers of Eileithyia in relaiton to athletic victory and the rebirth of a house's reputation, see ibid.

47. Paul Fry, *The Poet's Calling in the English Ode* (New Haven, CT: Yale University Press, 1980), 56.

48. George Shuster, *The English Ode from Milton to Keats* (New York: Columbia University Press, 1940), 134, 170–73.

49. Shuster points out that Pindar's reputation for "wildness" became so prevalent that in the eighteenth century "primitive" poems by newly encountered and remembered traditions—from Lapland song to Norse and Welsh, Anglo-Saxon and Native American forms—all became labeled "odes" (ibid., 162).

50. G. W. F. Hegel, *Aesthetics: Lectures on Fine Art*, trans. T. M. Knox, 2 vols. (Oxford: Clarendon, 1975), 2:1140.

51. Ibid., 2:1141–42.

CHAPTER THREE

1. David Smith, "Report on Voltri," in *David Smith*, ed. Garnett McCoy (New York: Praeger, 1973), 160.

2. "[A] man is capable of being in uncertainties, mysteries, doubts, without any irritable reaching after fact and reason." Letter to George and Tom Keats, December 21–27, 1817, in *The Letters of John Keats*, ed. Maurice Buxton Forman, 2 vols. (Oxford: Oxford University Press, 1931), 1:77. In *The Phenomenology of Moods in Kierkegaard* (The Hague: Martinus Nijhoff, 1978), Vincent McCarthy usefully explains Kierkegaard's arguments against the "superficial profundity" of Romantic poets on the topic of moods. "He who lives religiously has an infinity *within*, and this is the alternative open to one who presently lives poetically and fantastically, with an infinity outside himself in the form of infinite (unrealizable) possibilities. Kierkegaard associates Romantic irony with boredom here—'bliss without enjoyment,' 'the negative unity into which opposites appear'" (24). For Kierkegaard the artist can overcome and master irony by developing a coherent view of life, and each poem will be a moment in the development of that view (28).

3. Martin Heidegger, *Being and Time*, trans. John Macquarrie and Edward Robinson (New York: Harper and Row, 1962), 173, 175, 195. Gilbert Ryle, *The Concept of*

Mind (New York: Barnes and Noble, 1949), 83. See the discussion of these passages in McCarthy, *Phenomenology of Moods*, 120–27. For further discussion of "the pervasiveness of mood" in Heidegger, see Bruce Ballard, *The Role of Mood in Heidegger's Ontology* (London: University Press of America, 1991), 30–34.

4. Étienne Gilson, *The Arts of the Beautiful*, no trans. listed (New York: Dalkey Archive, 2000; reprint of Charles Scribner ed., New York, 1965), 73–74.

5. Percy Shelley, "A Defence of Poetry," in *Shelley's Poetry and Prose*, ed. Donald H. Reiman and Neil Fraistat (New York: W. W. Norton, 2002), 531.

6. Coleridge famously wrote in his 1816 commentary on the poem composed nineteen years before (1797–99) how in the summer of 1792 he fell asleep over the description of "the Khan Kubla's palace" in Samuel Purchas's book *Purchas, His Pilgrimage*. He continued to compose in his dreaming state, sleeping for about three hours and creating perhaps two to three hundred lines. He awakened with a vivid memory of this production and took out his pen, ready to write down the lines, when a knock on the door "from a person on business from Porlock" interrupted his mood and his composition. After an hour's absence, he returned and found he had only eight to ten scattered lines in mind. From these he created the fifty-four lines of the existing poem, which he calls in 1816 "a fragment." Coleridge makes a similar claim regarding the less dramatically interrupted yet nonetheless halting composition of "Christabel," another poem begun in 1797, continued in 1800 and again in 1816, and never in fact completed.

7. In *The Shape of Time: Remarks on the History of Things* (New Haven, CT: Yale University Press, 1962), George Kubler writes more extensively about these models of inspiration (49–50). He describes the notion of "the invisible chain" of influence from otherworldly sources down to poets, painters, church fathers, and saintly scholars. Here he relies in part on the research of A. M. Friend Jr., "The Portraits of the Evangelists in Greek and Latin Manuscripts," pt. 1, *Art Studies* 5 (1927): 115–50; pt. 2, *Art Studies* 7 (1929): 3–29. Kubler writes,

> The artist is not a free agent obeying only his own will. His situation is rigidly bound by a chain of prior events. The chain is invisible to him, and it limits his motion. He is not aware of it as a chain, but only as *vis à tergo*, as the force of events behind him. The conditions imposed by these prior events require of him either that he follow obediently in the path of tradition, or that he rebel against the tradition. In either case, his decision is not a free one: it is dictated by prior events of which he senses only dimly and indirectly the overpowering urgency, and by his own congenital peculiarities of temperament. . . . The theme of possession by the work in hand is evident in many artistic biographies; the individual is driven in every action by forces of an intensity absent from other lives; he is possessed by his vision of the possible, and he is obsessed with the urgency of

its realization, in a solitary posture of intense effort, traditionally represented by the figures of the poet or the muse. (50–51)

8. Susanne Langer, *Feeling and Form* (New York: Charles Scribner's, 1953), 240–41.

9. Paul Valéry, *The Art of Poetry*, ed. Jackson Mathews (Princeton: Princeton University Press, 1989), 61: "I was suddenly *gripped* by a rhythm which took possession of me and soon gave me the impression of some force outside myself. It was as though someone else were making use of my *living-machine*. Then another rhythm overtook and combined with the first, and certain stronger *transverse* relations were set up between two principles."

10. Emmanuel Levinas, "Reality and Its Shadow," in *The Levinas Reader*, ed. Seán Hand (London: Blackwell, 2001), 133, first published in 1948 in *Les temps moderne*. In Kant's *Anthropology from a Pragmatic Point of View*, ed. Robert B. Louden (Cambridge: Cambridge University Press, 2006), 67, Kant suggests something of the passivity of mood regarding composition. He describes how music "can put a poet or philosopher into a mood in which he can snatch and even master thoughts agreeable to his vocation or avocation." He attributes this phenomenon to situations "when sense, through a manifold that of itself can arouse no attention at all, is distracted by some other object that strikes it more forcibly, thought is not only facilitated, but also enlivened." Writing in the same text of the *furor poeticus*, he says "the poet [as opposed to the prose writer] . . . must snatch the propitious moment of the mood of his inner sense as it comes over him, in which lively and powerful images pour into him, while he behaves merely passively, so to speak" (81).

11. Enid Starkie, in her beautiful biography *Arthur Rimbaud* (New York: New Directions, 1961), records this information in two places (231 and 254–55).

12. Leo Spitzer, *Classical and Christian Ideas of World Harmony*, ed. Anna Granville Hatcher (Baltimore: Johns Hopkins University Press, 1963), 5; the discussion of *Stimmung* as being "in the moment" can be found later (139n).

13. Plato, *Protagoras*, in Plato, *Ion, Hippias Minor, Laches, Protagoras*, trans. R. E. Allen (New Haven, CT: Yale University Press, 1996), 185 (326a4–b6). In *The Republic* (398–401d) Plato endorses the educational role of music in similar terms.

14. Spitzer, *Classical and Christian Ideas*, 6–9.

15. Ibid., 33–35.

16. Ibid., 76.

17. Ibid., 128.

18. Arthur Schopenhauer, *The World as Will and Idea*, trans. R. B. Haldane and J. Kemp, 4th ed. (London: Kegan Paul, 1896), 1:323. See also his discussion of artworks of small compass made under the pressure of inspiration: "The work which

is completed in the inspiration of its first conception, and as it were unconsciously dashed off, like the melody which comes entirely without reflection, and quite as if by inspiration, and finally, also the lyrical poem proper, the mere song, in which the deeply felt mood of the impression, and the impression of the surroundings, as if involuntarily pours itself forth in words, whose metre and rhyme come about of their own accord—that all these, I say, have the great advantage of being purely the work of the ecstasy of the moment, the inspiration, the free movement of genius, without any admixture of intent and reflection" (3:180–81).

19. Ibid., 1:323.

20. Achim von Arnim and Clemens Brentano, comps. and eds., *Des Knaben Wunderhorn: Alte deutsche Lieder*, 3 vols. (orig. Heidelberg/Frankfurt, 1806; repr. Stuttgart: Philipp Reclam, 1987, 2006), 1:263–64. Marjorie Perloff recently has offered this translation:

Departure from Bremen
Spoken

Oh Bremen, now must I leave you,
Oh you most wonderful of towns
And within your walls must I leave you
My most beautiful of crowns.

We have often sat together
Many a beautiful moonlit night
Gave up so much sleep together
And spent our time as we found right.

My trunk rolls off, the morning cools
Ah, the streets are now quite bleak,
And what my heart must now endure
I nevermore may speak.

Once again my journey took me
Where my sweetheart was looking down,
So that she'll remember me always
I fire two pistol shots at the ground.

Soon there rise in your narrow alleys
Little clouds of wind-driven dust
My sighs these are, which carry
Dry leaves to lay at your feet.

So now I am really on shipboard,
My trunks I see on the deck,
When the sailor blew his whistle,
There was no more looking back.

I see the storm wind roaring
Oh my ship is sailing fast,
If it goes down to the bottom,
My suffering will end at last.

21. Robert E. Thayer, *The Origin of Everyday Moods* (New York: Oxford University Press, 1996), 50.

22. Ana Adan writes in a study, "Mood Rhythmicity and Individual Differences," that "there are certain endogenous mechanisms of generation and oscillatory control that allow circadian rhythms to appear even though the organism is not receiving information from the rhythmic variations in the environment. But it is also thought that endogenous or environmental phenomena interact with those and modulate their manifestations." Her primary example is that individuals can adjust to periods of light and darkness different from the twenty-four-hour period, but independently of the environment a cycle of light and darkness sensitivity continues—she includes the astonishing example of lungs, livers, and other tissues that are grown isolated in dishes and yet continue to respond to circadian rhythms. In *Causes, Role and Influences in Mood States*, ed. Anita V. Clark (New York: Nova, 2005), 36–37.

23. For a discussion of the heartbeat and rhythm, see Andrzej Szczeklik, *Catharsis: On the Art of Medicine*, trans. Antonia Lloyd-Jones (Chicago: University of Chicago Press, 2005), 55–67.

24. Adan, "Mood Rhythmicity," 52.

25. Raimbaut de Vaqueiras, "Kalenda maya," trans. W. D. Snodgrass, in *Lark in the Morning: The Verses of the Troubadours*, ed. Robert Kehew (Chicago: University of Chicago Press, 2005), 252–53.

26. John Keats, "Ode to a Nightingale," in *The Complete Poems*, ed. John Barnard (London: Penguin, 1988), 346.

27. Percy Bysshe Shelley, "Stanzas Written in Dejection—December 1818, Near Naples," in *Shelley's Poetry and Prose*, ed. Donald Reiman and Neil Fraistat (New York: W. W. Norton, 2002), 135.

28. "Mediocritie in Love Rejected," in *Poems by Thomas Carew Esquire, one of the gentlemen of the privie-chamber and Sewer in Ordinary to His Majesty* (London: I.D. for Thomas Walkley, 1640), 19.

29. Henry Vaughan, "The Storm," in *The Complete Poems*, ed. Alan Rudrum (London: Penguin, 1976), 178. Long before the river sonnets of William Lisle Bowles and William Wordsworth, Vaughan deserves the crown as the English poet laureate of water. In Vaughan's early poem "To the River Isca" (*Complete Poems*, 70–72), he composes a hymn to the local river Usk, beginning with a survey of what bodies of water have meant to earlier poets:

When *Daphne's* lover here first wore the *bays*,
Eurotas' secret streams heard all his *lays*.
And holy *Orpheus*, Nature's *busy* child
By headlong *Hebrus* his deep *hymns* compiled,
Soft *Petrarch* (thawed by *Laura's* flames) did weep
On *Tiber's* banks, when she (*proud fair!*) could sleep;
Mosella boasts *Ausonius*, and the *Thames*
Doth murmur SIDNEY'S *Stella* to her *streams*;
While *Severn* swoln with *joy* and *sorrow*, wears
Castara's smiles mixed with fair *Sabrin's* tears
Thus *poets* (like *nymphs*, their *pleasing themes*)
Haunted the *bubbling springs* and *gliding streams*,
And *happy banks!* whence such *fair flowers* have sprung,
But happier those where they have *sate* and *sung*!
Poets (like *Angels*) where they once appear
Hallow the *place*, and each succeeding year
Adds *reverence* to't, such as at length doth give
This aged faith, *that there their genii live*.

30. Henry Vaughan, "The Waterfall," in *Complete Poems*, ed. Rudrum, 306–7.

31. Langer, *Feeling and Form*, 330.

32. Stephen Spender, "The Making of a Poem," in *Creativity*, ed. P. E. Vernon (London: Penguin, 1970), 62–63. This state of suspension resembles the use of such suspension in phenomenological method, as Joseph Kockelmans describes Edmund Husserl's use of the concept of the *epoché*—"the suspension of judgment in regard to everything that, in the transition from the not yet evident to what is evident is to be left out of consideration because it cannot be accepted without further examination, or because no adequate evidence can be achieved in its regard." Joseph J. Kockelmans, *Edmund Husserl's Phenomenology* (West Lafayette, IN: Purdue University Press, 1994), 118–19.

33. See Mark A. Ellenbogen, "Stress, Psychopathology and the Regulation of Mood and Cortisol Levels," in Clark, *Causes, Role and Influence of Mood States*, 12:

"Some stimuli are given priority or emphasis over others. Once a focal point is selected, attention functions to highlight the information that is most relevant to present functioning, often referred to as the 'spotlight' metaphor. Attention amplifies information processing of the stimulus or stimulus characteristics to which we are attending . . . for example, visual attention to color, shape or size of a stimulus array augments neuronal activity . . . in the extrastriate region specialized for processing of that attribute. Thus, attentional mechanisms serve to select information for further processing and thus represent the first step between environmental input and behavioral response. Further, attentional mechanisms seem to be independent of sensory modality or function, in that attentional networks important for amplifying the production of verbal content appear to be the same ones important in emotional informational processing."

34. Timothy Clark observes, in his important 1997 book *The Theory of Inspiration: Composition as a Crisis of Subjectivity in Romantic and Post-Romantic Writing* (Manchester: Manchester University Press, 1997), that instead of thinking that inspiration causes enhanced creativity, we might consider that "any transformed state of mind accompanies or follows the emergent words and the sense of proleptic reception that they produce. That is to say that any emergent material that seems of a quality to trigger some sense of anticipation, the corroborating of personal fantasy, intention, or ambition, will necessarily be accompanied by a sense of ease and confidence. The crucial affective dimension of inspiration . . . should be characterized in privative terms, i.e., as the removal of blocking agents. There may be a release from inhibitions, possibly accompanied by a sense of speed, or of being overwhelmed by all the emergent possibilities that proliferate in the space of composition" (31).

35. Orhan Pamuk, *Snow*, trans. Maureen Freely (New York: Alfred A. Knopf, 2004), 86.

36. G. W. F. Hegel, *Phenomenology of Spirit*, trans. A. V. Miller (Oxford: Oxford University Press, 1977), 131.

37. William N. Morris, *Mood: The Frame of Mind* (Berlin: Springer-Verlag, 1989), 189–90.

38. Keats, "In Drear-Nighted December," in *Complete Poems*, 217.

39. Immanuel Kant, *Critique of the Power of Judgment*, trans. and ed. Paul Guyer (Cambridge: Cambridge University Press, 2000), 186, 203.

40. Giambattista Vico, *New Science*, trans. David Marsh (London: Penguin, 2001). See particularly "Poetic Metaphysics as the Origin of Poetry, Idolatry, Divination, and Sacrifices," 144–49, and the extended discussion of "poetic logic," 157–206.

41. Shelley, "Defence," 512.

42. I. A. Richards, *The Philosophy of Rhetoric* (Oxford: Oxford University Press, 1936), 90, on metaphor as vital to all language; 97–138 for discussion of tenor and vehicle.

43. Ibid., 125.

44. Quintilian, *The Orator's Education, Books 6–8*, ed. and trans. Donald A. Russell (Cambridge: Harvard University Press, 2001), 8.6, 425–69. Quintilian defines a trope as "a shift of a word or phrase from its proper meaning to another, in a way that has positive value" (425). He sees the function of metaphor as adding "to the resources of language by exchanges or borrowings to supply its [language's] deficiencies, and (hardest task of all) it ensures that nothing goes without a name" (427). Quintilian establishes the distinction between simile as a comparison and metaphor as a substitution (429) and goes on to discuss synecdoche, metonymy, antonomasia, onomatopoeia, catachresis, metalepsis, epithets, allegory, periphrasis, hyperbaton, and hyperbole—the last a form of lying.

45. Monroe Beardsley's "The Metaphorical Twist," *Philosophy and Phenomenological Research* 22, no. 3 (March 1962): 293–307, explores the competing claims of an "object-comparison" theory of metaphor, whereby a metaphor depends upon the comparison of the actual qualities of two actual objects, and a "verbal-opposition" theory, whereby a tension arises between the central meanings of a word and the marginal meanings. In this tension lies what he calls "the metaphorical twist," or shift from designation to connotation—a semantic distinction arises between two levels of meaning, and the semantic field, the range of connotation, is thereby transformed. This can, in fact, result in a new view of the actual qualities of actual objects, and so the two theories are not mutually exclusive.

46. Ibid., 304n.

47. Spitzer, *Classical and Christian Ideas*, 23.

48. Friedrich Nietzsche, *The Birth of Tragedy and Other Writings*, ed. Raymond Geuss and Ronald Speirs (Cambridge: Cambridge University Press, 2004), 29. The Schiller letter to Goethe, sent from Jena, March 18, 1798, is translated in *Correspondence between Goethe and Schiller*, trans. Liselotte Dieckmann (New York: Peter Lang, 1994), 107. Schiller is describing his work on what will be his *Wallenstein* trilogy and writes, "The preparations for such a complicated whole as a play start a strange motion in the mind. Even the very first action is no small trifle, namely, to find a sure method for the entire thing in order not to stumble pointlessly around. I am now working only on the skeletal structure and I find that, in drama just as in humans, everything depends on it. I would like to know how you handled this in similar cases. To my mind, the emotional component is at first without a definite

and clear object; this forms itself only later. A certain musical mood precedes, and only after this does the poetic idea follow."

49. Schopenhauer, *World as Will*, 333.

50. Ibid., 338.

51. Antoine Arnauld, *The Art of Thinking: Port Royal Logic*, trans. James Dickoff and Patricia James (New York: Bobbs-Merrill, Library of Liberal Arts, 1964), 38.

52. Victor Zuckerkandl, *Sound and Symbol: Music and the External World*, trans. Willard R. Trask, Bollingen Series 44 (New York: Pantheon, 1956) 157–58.

53. Ibid, 314.

54. Friedrich Nietzsche, "Dichters Berufung / The Poet's Call," in "Appendix: Songs of Prince Vogelfrei," in *The Gay Science: With a Prelude in Rhymes and an Appendix of Songs*, trans. Walter Kaufmann (New York: Vintage Books, 1974), 351–55. The next stanza begins "Wie mir so im Versemachen"—"I kept making verses"—and indeed he makes five more stanzas, asking himself successive questions and meditating on poetry making: Is he a poet? What is he wasting his time for—aphorisms or images? If rhymes are arrows, they are killing him. Are poets sick? They seem to rhyme beyond their will. In each stanza, the woodpecker answers with the refrain "Ja, mein Herr, Sie sind ein Dichter"—"Yes, my good man, you are a poet."

55. Augustine of Hippo, *Confessions*, trans. R. S. Pine-Coffin (London: Penguin, 1961), 177–78: "What is true of the whole psalm is also true of all its parts and of each syllable. It is true of any longer action in which I may be engaged and of which the recitation of the psalm may only be a small part. It is true of a man's whole life, of which all his actions are parts. It is true of the whole history of mankind, of which each man's life is a part."

56. For an extensive discussion of how mood is a means of understanding or grasping musical form, and how music itself produces moods in its listeners, see Jenefer Robinson, "Emotional Responses to Music: What Are They? How Do They Work? And Are They Relevant to Aesthetic Appreciation?" in *The Oxford Handbook of the Philosophy of Emotion*, ed. Peter Goldie (New York: Oxford University Press, 2010), 651–80.

CHAPTER FOUR

1. William Wordsworth, *Poems*, ed. John O. Hayden (London: Penguin, 1977), 1:978n.

2. See W. J. B. Owen, introduction to William Wordsworth and Samuel Taylor Coleridge, *Lyrical Ballads, 1798*, ed. W. J. B. Owen (Oxford: Oxford University Press, 1969), xiv. Coleridge writes of this division in the *Biographia Literaria*, ed. James

Engell and Walter Jackson Bate, 2 vols. in one (Princeton, NJ: Princeton University Press, 1983), 2:6–7.

3. William Wordsworth, *The Prelude: The Four Texts (1798, 1799, 1805, 1850)*, ed. Jonathan Wordsworth (London: Penguin, 1995). In the 1805 version, "things" is followed by a hyphen and "herself" is written "itself."

4. *Collected Letters of Samuel Taylor Coleridge*, vol. 2, *1801–1806*, ed. Earl Leslie Griggs (Oxford: Clarendon, 1956). 782.

5. *The Notebooks of Samuel Taylor Coleridge*, vol. I, *1794–1804*, ed. Kathleen Coburn (Princeton, NJ: Princeton University Press, 1957), 1607.

6. Samuel Taylor Coleridge, *The Friend*, in *Complete Works*, ed. W. G. Shedd, 7 vols. (New York: Harper, 1856), 2:464.

7. See "Excursus Notes" in Samuel Taylor Coleridge, *Aids to Reflection*, ed. John Beer (Princeton, NJ: Princeton University Press, 1997), 563. Beer cites Coleridge's *Marginalia*, ed. George Whalley (Princeton, NJ: Princeton University Press, 1980), 1:585.

8. In this sense, the ode bears some resemblance to *Pythian* V with its apostrophe to Kastor, the "gold charioted lord. / After the storm-shower / He smiles fair weather down on your happy hearth." See Pindar, *The Odes*, trans. C. M. Bowra (London: Penguin, 1969), 182; see also the discussion in Leslie Kurke, *The Traffic in Praise: Pindar and the Poetics of Social Economy* (Ithaca, NY: Cornell University Press, 1991), 68–69.

9. By now there is a vast literature on this poem: we know about its antecedents in Coleridge's letters and drafts and the many changes Coleridge made to its conclusion. Incomplete quotations from the poem appear in letters to William Sotheby and Robert Southey from July 1802, to Thomas Wedgewood in October of that year, when it was published in the *Morning Post*, to Sir George and Lady Beaumont from August 1803, and to his brother George the following October. The ode has resonances from the dual Wordsworth-Coleridge project "The Mad Monk" and Wordsworth's "Resolution and Independence," as well as the first four stanzas of Wordsworth's "Ode: Intimations of Immortality from Recollections of Early Childhood," and the Dejection Ode is itself the source of language in the later extended version of the Intimations Ode. Coleridge's epigraph from "Sir Patrick Spence" alters all the known versions of that early ballad, and the conclusion's section on a lost child in a storm draws from an incident in early childhood when Coleridge himself was lost on a stormy night. (See R. A. Benthall, "New Moons, Old Ballads and Prophetic Dialogues in Coleridge's 'Dejection: An Ode,'" *Studies in Romanticism* 37 [Winter 1998]: 593–601.) It is worth noting that Dorothy Wordsworth's journals habitually record the appearance of the moon, referring to it as "crescent," an "auld moon," "a silver boat," "a perfect rainbow," "horned," "contract-

ing," "sailing," and "like a gold ring snapped in two." Dorothy Wordsworth, *The Grasmere and Alfoxden Journals*, ed. Pamela Woof (Oxford: Oxford University Press, 2002), 5, 15, 33, 38, 47, 76, 96, 97, 136, 141, 143, 150, 152. Thomas Otway's play "The Orphan," added as a citation in late versions of Coleridge's drafts of the storm section, does not in fact tell the story of a lost child but does have an unmentioned subtitle relevant to Coleridge's state of mind at the time: "The Unhappy Marriage." See Thomas Otway, *The Orphan*, ed. Aline MacKenzie Taylor (Lincoln: University of Nebraska Press, 1976). In sum, the Dejection Ode exists in so many versions that it is difficult to say what it is. The work has a changing title as well, from its initial "A Letter to____" to the 1817 *Sibylline Leaves* version, "Dejection: An Ode." And a poem such as "The Day Dream" is so closely related that it is not quite accurate to say it is a separate work.

10. See *Coleridge's Dejection: The Earliest Manuscripts and the Earliest Printings* (Ithaca, NY: Cornell University Press, 1988). For further discussion of the substitutions in the many versions of the poem, see in Coleridge, *Poetical Works*, vol. 2, *Poems (Variorum Text)*, pt. 2, ed. J. C. C. Mays, in *The Collected Works of Samuel Taylor Coleridge* (Princeton, NJ: Princeton University Press, 2001), Mays's Variorum notes to "A Letter to ____," 861–75; "Dejection: An Ode," 884–97; and "The Day Dream," 897–99.

11. John Worthen's recent study *The Gang: Coleridge, the Hutchinsons and the Wordsworths in 1802* (New Haven, CT: Yale University Press, 2000), 104, 312n15, argues against the likelihood of either a mutually romantic or realized sexual relationship between Coleridge and Sara Hutchinson—a suggestion that has often been made by earlier biographers including Holmes, Whalley, and Ashton. Of course, for the purposes of understanding Coleridge's choice of poetic form, as opposed to understanding the motivations of his actual actions in history, the terms of his imaginative life are as relevant, perhaps more relevant, than are the terms of his realized life. The rewriting of a letter to Sara Hutchinson into an ode that is most often read as addressed to her bears a parallel to Coleridge's much earlier rewriting of his letter poem to his wife Sara in September 1795, a poem first called "Epistle" and later retitled "Ode to Sara [Fricker], Written at Shurton Bars, Near Bridgewater, in Answer to a Letter from Bristol."

12. Richard Holmes, *Coleridge: Early Visions* (New York: Pantheon, 1989), 318–20; Worthen, *The Gang*, 136–54, 275–93.

13. There is in fact a direct analogue to Ben Jonson's famous enjambment across the section headings at lines 84–85 of his Pindaric "To the Immortal Memory and Friendship of that Noble Pair Sir Lucius Cary and Sir H. Morison" (*Complete Poems*, ed. George Parfitt [New Haven, CT : Yale University Press, 1975], 214):

And there he lives with memory: and Ben
THE STAND
Jonson! Who sung this of him, ere he went

Jonson's use of an interpolation within the poem and at midsignature (as in his frequent use of "Ben: Jonson") was a way of inscribing a monumental aura about his name; for Coleridge the underlining Greek pseudonym seems to call on an exterior or reflective judgment that stops the flux of substitutions and declares the work's completion.

14. *Biographia Literaria*, 2:66–67. Here Coleridge includes several passages of thoughts on the problem of translating Pindarics and transcribes Cowley's opinions on Pindaric translations. In early November 1791, Coleridge wrote in a letter that he had been "reading Pindar, and composing Greek verse, like a mad dog," and a few months later he won a prize at Cambridge for his "Sors Misera Servorum in Insulis Indiæ Occidentalis," a Sapphic ode on the West Indian slave trade (*Poetical Works*, 72–84). Another possible antecedent for the structure of the Dejection Ode is the model from the Pauline epistles where letter writing involves thanksgiving passages interspersed with "joyful intercessions." The thanksgiving as a specific poetic genre was still extant in the seventeenth century but then seems to have become absorbed into the ode with the advent of neoclassicism. See Peter O'Brien, *Introductory Thanksgivings in the Letters of Paul* (Leiden: E. J. Brill, 1977), 20–46, 62–104.

15. D. Wordsworth, *Journals*, 16, 17, 19, 235.

16. William Hazlitt, *Selected Essays of William Hazlitt, 1778–1830*, ed. Geoffrey Keynes (New York: Random House, 1948), 517.

17. Of great significance to Coleridge is the idea that imaginative forms require not merely equivalence but also combinative, or what he called "esemplastic," powers. This theme is mentioned in the Dejection Ode, in the second epode, where he describes the "shaping spirit of imagination." See *Biographia Literaria*, 1:295–306.

18. We remember that by the time of Shelley's "Defence," "to compose" had a negative implication of too much controlling intention: "When composition begins, inspiration is already on the decline, and the most glorious poetry that has ever been communicated to the world is probably a feeble shadow of the original conception of the poet" (Percy Bysshe Shelley, "A Defence of Poetry," in *Shelley's Poetry and Prose*, ed. Donald H. Reiman and Neil Fraistat [New York: W. W. Norton, 2002], 504).

19. For a discussion of the differences between odes "on" and odes "to," see Paul Fry, *The Poet's Calling in the English Ode* (New Haven, CT: Yale University Press,

1980), 27: "Whereas an 'ode on' simply announces a topic, sometimes carrying in its title the lapidary suggestion that it is literally inscribed on its object, an 'ode to' claims to be a poem of address."

20. See Samuel Taylor Coleridge, *The Complete Poems*, ed. William Keach (London: Penguin, 1997), 553–57; Mays Variorum edition, 887–97.

21. Immanuel Kant, *Critique of the Power of Judgment*, trans. and ed. Paul Guyer (Cambridge: Cambridge University Press, 2000), 192–94.

22. Ibid., 43n21. My understanding of this dimension of Kant's work relies in part on Paul Guyer, *Kant and the Experience of Freedom: Essays on Aesthetics and Morality* (Cambridge: Cambridge University Press, 1993), 158–59.

23. "The affinity of all appearances (near or remote) is a necessary consequence of a synthesis in the imagination that is grounded *a priori* on rules. The imagination is therefore also a faculty of synthesis *a priori*, on account of which we give it the name of the productive imagination." Immanuel Kant, *Critique of Pure Reason*, trans. Paul Guyer and Allen W. Wood (Cambridge: Cambridge University Press, 1998), 240; for further discussion of the distinction between the reproductive and productive imagination, see 238–41. In *Art of the Modern Age*, Jean-Marie Schaeffer discusses why artistic genius expresses itself through the productive imagination (trans. Steven Rendall [Princeton, NJ: Princeton University Press, 2000], 41).

24. Coleridge's theory of imagination is most fully laid out in chapter 13 of volume 1 (295–306) of his *Biographia Literaria*, "On the Imagination or Esemplastic Power," and continued in chapter 14 of volume 2 (15–16), in "Definition of a Poem and Poetry." For an excellent contextualization of these concepts in relation to British Empiricism and German Idealism, see Mary Warnock, "Coleridge and Wordsworth, Theory and Practice," in *Imagination* (Berkeley: University of California Press, 1978). 72–130.

25. *Complete Works*, ed. Shedd, 1:437–38.

26. *Aids to Reflection*, 227–28, 556–57, 557n.

27. Coleridge, *Poetical Works*, vol. 1, *Poems (Reading Text)*, pt. 2, ed. Mays, in *Collected Works*, 778.

28. Kurke, *Traffic in Praise*, 4.

29. Richard Holmes in *Coleridge: Early Visions* says Coleridge was himself usually absent during the births of his children (122–23, 282), and though he was devoted to his children as they grew, recording, for example, detailed notes about Hartley's development (182), he also referred in his letters to his wife Sara's "breeding" (322).

30. *Collected Works of Samuel Taylor Coleridge: Lectures, 1808–1818*, ed. R. A. Foake (London: Routledge, 1987), 5:222.

31. Even so, like Aristotle with his concept of imagination as mental re-

presentation, Plato also acknowledged that thought is dependent on the power of producing mental images—including the geometrical aspect of his own philosophy.

32. Boethius, *The Consolation of Philosophy*, trans. Victor Watts (London: Penguin, 1999). Boethius argues in the Stoic mode that "the human mind cannot die" (32) and, correlatively, that "you cannot impose anything on a free mind" (38). He writes of the power of not only the reason but also the imagination, which "in the absence of the senses . . . can still survey all sensible objects not through sensory but through imaginative perception" (128). He also claims that all creatures who enjoy the innate powers of reason also have the freedom to will (118). The *Consolation* as a whole is a compendium of the powers of mind at the point of death.

33. Sidney wrote, "Only the Poet, disdaining to be tied to any such subjection, lifted up with the vigor of his own invention, doth grow in effect another nature, in making things either better than nature bringeth forth, or, quite anew: forms such as never were in nature, as the *Heroes, Demigods, Cyclops, Chimeras, Furies*." Sir Philip Sidney, *A Defence of Poetry*, ed. Jan Van Dorsten (Oxford: Oxford University Press, 1966).

34. Joseph Addison, Richard Steele, and others, *The Spectator in 4 Volumes* (London: J. M. Dent, 1913), no. 420, July 2, 1712, 3:89.

35. Addison, *Spectator*, no. 421, July 3, 1712, 3:92.

36. Ibid., 3:93.

37. David Hume, *A Treatise of Human Nature*, vol. 1, *Of the Understanding* (London: John Noon, 1739), sec. vii, 461, 464.

38. Hume, *Essays and Treatises on Several Subjects* (London: A. Millar, 1758).The *Philosophical Essays concerning Human Understanding* of 1748 was later given the title under which it appears in this volume, *An Enquiry concerning Human Understanding*. This passage comes from part 2, "Of the Origin of Ideas," 289–91.

39. George Ludwig Collins, notes from Kant's 1784–85 lectures on moral philosophy, in Immanuel Kant, *Lectures on Ethics*, trans. Peter Lauchlan Heath, ed. Jerome B. Schneewind (New York: Cambridge University Press, 1997), 139.

40. This manifold being is addressed as "it" in the third person and as "thou" in the second person—in the latter practice borrowing the familiar form that is used in the collects of the Book of Common Prayer, a point noted by Donald Reiman and Sharon B. Powers in *Shelley's Prose and Poetry*, ed. Reiman and Powers (New York: W. W. Norton, 1977), 93n2. I have relied on their version of the text (93–95). Reiman and Powers explain that the *Examiner* text of the poem, published in Leigh Hunt's magazine of the same name in 1817, required three slight revisions. Stuart Curran had discovered, in studying the Silsbee notebook, which has been at Harvard since 1902, that Shelley himself had corrected in 1819 two errors in the text:

the first was at line 27 of the third strophe: "Therefore the names of Demon, Ghost, and Heaven" should read "Therefore the name of God & ghosts; and heaven"; the second change appears in line 58 just before the climax of the poem: not "News of birds and blossoming" but "News of buds and blossoming." A third change, from "doth" to "dost" at the start of the second strophe, is one Reiman has made for grammatical reasons, since the second-person familiar form is coherent with the rest of the sentence that follows.

41. Shelley uses the term "Intellectual Beauty" in his *Symposium* translation as follows: "Contemplating thus the universal beauty no longer would he, like some servant in Love, unworthily and meanly enslave himself to the attraction of one form, nor one subject of discipline or science, but would turn towards the wide ocean of Intellectual Beauty." *"The Symposium" of Plato: The Shelley Translation*, ed. David K. O'Connor (South Bend, IN: St. Augustine's, 2002), 56. Plotinus, "On the Intellectual Beauty" (Eighth Tractate), in *The Enneads*, trans. Stephen McKenna (London: Penguin, 1991), 410–24. Inspired by Diotima's speech in *The Symposium*, Plotinus nevertheless adds an Aristotelian twist to the relation the arts bear to beauty, writing, "The arts are not to be slighted on the ground that they create by imitation of natural objects; for, to begin with, these natural objects are themselves imitations; . . . they give a bare reproduction of the thing seen, but go back to the Reason-Principles from which nature itself derives, and, furthermore that much of their work is all their own: they are holders of beauty and add where nature is lacking" (411). He adds, "The artist himself goes back, after all, to that wisdom of Nature which is embedded in himself . . . [a wisdom that is] a unity working out into detail" (416).

42. "Four Hymnes," in *The Poetical Works of Edmund Spenser*, ed. J. C. Smith and E. De Selincourt (London: Oxford, 1960), 585–99. Two of the hymns, written in Spenser's youth, are addressed to Love and Beauty, and in 1596 he decides "by way of retraction to reforme them, making instead of those two Hymnes of earthly or naturall love and beautie, two others of heavenly and celestiall." "Dedication to 'Four Hymnes' " (586).

43. Mary wrote in her diary, "I go to bed soon, but Shelley and Jane sit up and for a wonder do not frighten themselves." On one particular night Shelley describes how Jane, thinking someone has unaccountably moved a pillow in her room, wears "the lineaments of terror that could not be contained; her hair came prominent and erect; her eyes were wide and staring, drawn almost from the sockets by the convulsion of the muscles; the eyelids were forced in, and the eyeballs, without any relief, seemed as if they had been newly inserted, in ghastly sport, in the sockets of a lifeless head. This frightful spectacle endured but for a

few moments—it was displaced by terror and confusion, violent, indeed, and full of dismay, but human." Richard Holmes, *Shelley: The Pursuit* (New York: Penguin, 1987), 258–61.

44. With Thomas Jefferson Hogg, in winter 1811 Shelley published a pamphlet, "The Necessity of Atheism," which grew out of Hogg's arguments for atheism—called by Shelley a "cudgel for Xtianity." See ibid., 48–50.

45. Kant, *Critique of the Power of Judgment*, 192.

46. Ibid., 144–48. Kant earlier writes of how the sublime "does violence to our imaginations, but is nevertheless judged all the more sublime for that" (129).

47. As Paul Ricoeur has noted in his studies of metaphor as a process, writing particularly in the context of a critique of Colin Turbayne's theory of metaphor, there is a heuristic function to any metaphorical expression, and the "as if" dimension of the expression tends over time to drop away. Ricoeur objects to Turbayne's notions of the "use and abuse" of metaphor, holding instead that the tension between literal "what is" and metaphorical "as if" expresses "the construction of the world by and with feeling." *The Rule of Metaphor: Multi-disciplinary Studies of the Creation of Meaning in Language*, trans. Robert Czerny with Kathleen McLaughlin and John Costello (Toronto: University of Toronto Press, 1977), 251–55.

48. Schaeffer, *Art of the Modern Age*, 26.

CHAPTER FIVE

1. This futile, and irreducibly temporary, sense of mastery is the reason Kierkegaard argued that "aesthetic existence is under the category of necessity even when it boasts of its freedom. It flees inner freedom and directs itself to the manipulation of the exterior world." See Vincent McCarthy's *Phenomenology of Moods in Kierkegaard* (The Hague: Martinus Nijhoff, 1978), 52. This argument is thereby the antithesis of Arendt's belief, which I discussed in the first chapter, that claims for an absolute inner freedom of the mind are merely reactions to, and withdrawal from, the actuality of external impediments to freedom.

2. Ovid, *Metamorphoses*, trans. A. D. Melville (Oxford: Oxford University Press, 1986, 2008), 3. Here is the original Latin from the Loeb Classical Library (Cambridge, MA: Harvard University Press, 1984), 8:

natus homo est, sive hunc divino semine fecit
ille opifex rerum, mundi melioris origo,
sive recens tellus seductaque nuper ab alto
aethere cognati retinebat semina caeli.

quam satus Iapeto, mixtam pluvialibus undis,
finxit in effigiem moderantum cuncta deorum,
pronaque cum spectent animalia cetera terram,
os homini sublime dedit caelumque videre
iussit et erectos ad sidera tollere vultus.

3. Ovid, *Metamorphoses*, ed. Melville, 12. From the Loeb edition (28):

. . . discedite templo
et velate caput cinctasque resolvite vestes
ossaque post tergum magnae iactate parentis!

4. Ovid, *Metamorphoses*, ed. Melville, 13. Loeb edition (30):

et iussos lapides sua post vestigial mittunt.
saxa (quis hoc credat, nisi sit pro teste vetustas?)
ponere duritiem coepere suumque rigorem
mollirique mora mollitaque ducere formam.
mox ubi creverunt naturaque mitior illis
contigit, ut quaedam, sic non manifesta videri
forma potest hominis, sed uti de marmore coepta
non exacta satis rudibusque simillima signis,
quae tamen ex illis aliquo pars umida suco
et terrena fuit, versa est in corporis usum;
quod solidum est flectique nequit, mutatur in ossa,
quae modo vena fuit, sub eodem nomine mansit,
inque brevi spatio superorum numine saxa
missa viri manibus faciem traxere virorum
et de femineo reparata est femina iactu.
inde genus durum sumus experiensque laborum
et documenta damus qua simus origine nati.

5. A frieze at Ostia Antica, dedicated to Hephaestus and most likely from the second century AD, has recently been rejoined after part of it was scattered as a consequence of private excavations in the eighteenth century. Read from right to left, it tells a number of stories of unusual births and confirms the connection between Hephaestus, artifice, and reproduction. The first image shows the birth of Athena from the brain of her father, Zeus; confronted by this miraculous birth, Eileithyia, goddess of childbirth, is shown in the next frame fleeing in terror; then Hera, who generated Hephaestus alone, is shown next to a toddler Hephaestus who is taking uncertain steps; as Hera realizes the child's deformity, she throws

him down, in disgust, from Olympus. In the moment of his fall head first, the little boy is already wearing the short tunic and cap of a craftsman—the tools of his trade plummet around and with him. He is falling to the island of Lemnos, where a young armed Athena awaits him. A series of full-length portraits follows: Hermes, Helios, Athena, Zeus, Hera, Apollo, Aphrodite, Ares, and Poseidon. The narrative then is reintroduced and concludes with a somewhat syncretic representation of the Attic myth of the life of Erichthonios, who was born of Hephaestus and Gaea (Earth) and nursed by Athena. Erichthonios is portrayed, like many of the offspring of Gaea, as a serpent.

6. *Oxford English Dictionary*, online updated 2nd ed., 1989 (accessed November 2010).

7. In Jean-Marie Schaeffer's incisive account of the genesis of the "speculative theory of art" in *Art of the Modern Age*, trans. Steven Rendall (Princeton, NJ: Princeton University Press, 2000), he writes of this Platonic insistence that mimesis cannot be a route to ontological revelation (93). Schaeffer emphasizes Aristotle's allegiances to Plato on this point and writes in a note (318n63) of the passage in book B in the *Physics* (2.8.199A) where "Aristotle maintains that art has the power to achieve what nature by itself is incapable of realizing." Schaeffer emphasizes, "This thesis in no way endows art with a function of ontological revelation." It is not necessary, however, to claim that art has a *function* of ontological revelation to follow Aristotle's point that art brings into being what otherwise would not be; is it not the case, for example, that the function of the imitation of an action in tragedy is to reveal a truth that is not evident in the unfolding of the represented events in time? Aristotle's *Poetics* indicates, by the very peripeteia of the protagonist, that there is no tragic insight in life, which is merely suffered—such insight is provided only in plots, which are grasped in their unity.

8. I am indebted here to Michael Podro's succinct discussion of the artist's freedom as one of "composition" on the one hand and "composure" on the other. See his discussion of Alberti, Aristotle, and Schiller as promoting freedom in composition, and of Kant, Hegel, Gottfried Semper, and Alois Riegl as promoting freedom of composure, or self-making, in *The Critical Historians of Art* (New Haven, CT: Yale University Press, 1982), 5–7.

9. G. W. F. Hegel, *Phenomenology of Spirit*, trans. A. V. Miller (Oxford: Oxford University Press, 1977), 118–19.

10. See Jean Hyppolite's commentary on the liberty of Stoicism in *Genesis and Structure of Hegel's Phenomenology of Spirit* (Evanston, IL: Northwestern University Press, 1974), 182–83.

11. G. W. F. Hegel, *Aesthetics: Lectures on Fine Art*, trans. T. M. Knox (Oxford: Clarendon, 1975), 1:5, 31.

12. Edward Young, *Conjectures on Original Composition in a Letter to the Author of Sir Charles Grandison*, 2nd ed. (London: Millar and Dodsley, 1759), 11–12.

13. Edward Young, *The Works of Dr. Edward Young*, 6 vols. (London: Mallard, Durfey, Nelson, et al., 1779), 6:95.

14. Richard Sennett's recent study *The Craftsman* (New Haven, CT: Yale University Press, 2008) is concerned with the craftsman's relation to materials, the adjustments that must be made in encountering surprises, and the pursuit of quality. Yet Sennett does not take up the fundamental distinction between craft and art based on the former's prior determination of use. His brief discussion of one of Benvenuto Cellini's salt cellars (67–68) mentions that "in transcending any mere functional purpose" the work calls "attention to it and to its maker," yet this is the only indication that such a distinction might be important. Studies of craftsmanship often become mired in defensive arguments regarding the hierarchy of craft and art, but it is clear that originality, as Sennett indicates throughout his study, is a dimension of craft just as it is of art. Nevertheless, the free determination of the work, without any particular template shaped by functional need, makes art a different enterprise from craft. Art's enterprise in relation to craft's is analogous to the distinctive functions of poetry and speech, and no less complementary or mutually influential.

15. See Rhonda Roland Shearer, "Marcel Duchamp's Impossible Bed and Other 'Not' Readymade Objects: A Possible Route of Influence from Art to Science," *Art and Academe* 10, no.1 (Fall 1997): 28–62 and 10, no. 2 (Winter 1998): 76–94. Shearer's claim—that none of the ready-mades seem to be examples of actual manufactured goods—is embedded in a larger argument about Poincaré's ideas of probability and the ways that Duchamp's three-dimensional works, under certain perspectives and combinations of perspectives, acquire a "four dimensional' coherence in relation to one another. In other words, works we have seen as typifying mass production in fact create idiosyncratic worlds that exist only within the system of relations between themselves. See also Leslie Camhi, "Did Duchamp Deceive Us?" *Art News* 98 (February 1999): 98–102.

16. In Germano Celant, *Art Povera* (New York: Praeger, 1969), 109.

17. David Smith, "Report on Voltri," in *David Smith*, ed. Garnett McCoy (New York: Praeger, 1973), 156–63. For an exploration of Serra's work, see *Richard Serra Sculpture: Forty Years*, ed. Kynaston McShine and Lynne Cooke (New York: Museum of Modern Art, 2007).

18. Immanuel Kant, *Critique of the Power of Judgment*, translated and edited by Paul Guyer (Cambridge: Cambridge University Press, 2000), 220.

19. George Kubler, *The Shape of Time: Remarks on the History of Things* (New Haven, CT: Yale University Press, 1962), 15.

20. Alfred Gell, "The Technology of Enchantment and the Enchantment of Technology," in *Anthropology, Art and Aesthetics*, ed. J. Coote and A. Shelton (Oxford: Clarendon, 1992), 49.

21. The theme of the bouquet in Stevens's poems, like the theme of still life, appears in many more works than those I am mentioning here. Indeed, perhaps his most sustained study of these issues is in his "The Man on the Dump" (*Complete Poetry and Prose*, 184–86), where the dump itself becomes a kind of metabouquet. The poem begins by making this connection explicitly:

> Day creeps down. The moon is creeping up.
> The sun is a corbeil of flowers the moon Blanche
> Places there, a bouquet. Ho-ho . . . The dump is full
> Of images. Days pass like papers from a press.
> The bouquets come here in the papers. So the sun,
> And so the moon, both come, and the janitor's poems
> Of every day . . .

The relation between parts and wholes that preoccupies so much of Stevens's works is beautifully realized in this poem, where the *the*ness, the definite articulation of things in their being, is brought up against their capacity to form new things in aggregation.

22. In the poem "Of Bright & Blue Birds & The Gala Sun," mentioned earlier in relation to poetry and cognition, Stevens refers to a "bright *scienza* outside ourselves." Stevens read H. P. Adams's *The Life and Writings of Giambattista Vico* (1935) and wrote inside the back dust jacket a quote from p. 72: "scienza nuova a great liberation of creative power." See Eleanor Cook's description of this book, which is in the library of the University of Massachusetts at Amherst, in *A Reader's Guide to Wallace Stevens* (Princeton, NJ: Princeton University Press, 2007), 157.

23. Theodor Adorno, in his *Aesthetic Theory*, trans. Robert Hullot-Kentor (Minneapolis: University of Minnesota Press, 1997), 155, makes this point in relation to montage alone, contending that it is in modernist film and collage work that the synthetic element is broken down and the "aesthetic principle of construction" revealed. He powerfully contends that montage marks the end of an aesthetics of mood, particularly that promulgated by Impressionism. But the aesthetic of the fragment in Romanticism seems to me to begin this process fairly close on the heels of the development of a concept of organic form in the writings of the Schlegel brothers and Coleridge. And as we saw in my discussion of mood, poets are as likely to compose out of the force of breaking from, or interrupting, a mood, establishing their form against it, as not. Indeed, we have seen that the state of mood in aesthetic experience does not require a form.

24. Étienne Gilson, *Forms and Substance in the Arts*, trans. Salvator Attanasio (Normal, IL: Dalkey Archive, 2001), 19. Presumably a new means like film comes under the narrative and dramatic arts for Gilson.

25. Out of the unparaphrasability of poetry, Kant generates its true value as linguistic expression. See Kant, *Critique of the Power of Judgment*, trans. and ed. Guyer, 203–4.

26. Ibid., 192.

27. "Poetry is the universal art of the mind which has become free in itself and which is not tied down for its realization to external sensuous material; instead it launches out exclusively in the inner space and the inner time of ideas and feelings." Hegel's *Aesthetics*, 1:89.

28. Friedrich von Schiller, "Naïve and Sentimental Poetry," in *"Naïve and Sentimental Poetry" and "On the Sublime": Two Essays*, trans. Julius A. Elias (New York: Frederick Ungar, 1967), 165–66.

CHAPTER SIX

1. "As for the organisation of rhymes, in so far as they are used in the *frons* or the *cauda* it seems that as much liberty as may be desired must be allowed." Dante adds, "But the effect will be particularly beautiful if the endings of the last lines cause the stanza to fall silent on a rhyme." Dante, *De vulgari eloquentia*. ed. Pio Rajna (Florence: Società Dantesca Italiana, 1960); Dante, *De vulgari eloquentia*, trans. Stephen Botterill (Cambridge: Cambridge University Press, 1996).

2. G. W. F. Hegel, *Aesthetics: Lectures on Fine Art*, trans. T. M. Knox (Oxford: Oxford University Press, 1998), 2:1137. Hegel discusses the various advantages of Spanish meters, the French alexandrine, and German and English meters on p. 1174. The independence of rhyme from language practices is evident in English in the ways a "gendered" system of differences is carried over in the conventions of masculine and feminine word endings in rhyme while it is dropped in the everyday use of articles. By contrast, in Romance languages a masculine or feminine rhyme can be made by means of a noun of the opposite gender—in English such a difference can be effected only through semantics.

3. *Poetics*, trans. Ingram Bywater, in *The Basic Works of Aristotle*, ed. Richard McKeon (New York: Random House, 1941), 1463–64: "The distinction between historian and poet is not in the one writing prose and the other verse—you might put the work of Herodotus into verse, and it would still be a species of history; it consists really in this, that the one describes the thing that has been, and the other a kind of thing that might be. Hence poetry is something more philosophic and of graver import than history."

4. Andrzej Szczeklik, *Catharsis: On the Art of Medicine*, trans. Antonia Lloyd-Jones (Chicago: University of Chicago Press), 55–67.

5. One of the most thoughtful and provocative arguments about such issues of "traditional" and "free" prosody in translation is Yves Bonnefoy's 1979 rejoinder to Joseph Brodsky's contention that strongly metered Russian poetry, such as that of Mandelstam, was ill-served by free verse translation. Bonnefoy describes the French alexandrine with its symmetrical halves as particularly suited, as a closed system, to metaphysical and idealized worlds—the Racinian world of "rational and intemporal exchange between the archetypes of the mind." In his translations of Shakespeare, Bonnefoy initially decided against using the alexandrine, but he also found that following the Shakespearean line led him to a recurring emphasis on eleven syllables—a pattern of six and five that began freely, without preconception as to meter, and ended quite close to Shakespeare's own. Bonnefoy concludes that this encounter between "the absolute and life" led to a flexible meter that would at times even expand to an alexandrine as "an indication of plenitude." Yves Bonnefoy, "On the Translation of Form in Poetry," in *Companion to Contemporary World Literature from the Editors of World Literature Today*, ed. Pamela A. Genova (New York: Twayne / Thompson Gale, 2003), 10–11.

6. Here is another prose version from a recent translation by David Kovacs:

> Do you know the nature of our mortal life? I think not. How could you? But listen to me. Death is a debt all mortals must pay, and no man knows for certain whether he will still be living on the morrow. The outcome of our fortune is hid from our eyes, and it lies beyond the scope of any teaching or craft.

Euripides, *Cyclops; Alcestis; Medea*, trans. D. Kovacs, Loeb Classical Library (Cambridge, MA: Harvard University Press, 1994).

7. William Harmon, "Rhyme in English Verse: History, Structures, Functions," *Studies in Philology* 84, no. 4 (Fall 1987): 365–66. See also Eduard Norden's discussion of *homeoteleuton* in *Die Antike Kunstprosa: vom VI. jahrhundert v. Chr. bis in die zeit der Renaissance*, 2 vols. (Leipzig: Teubner, 1898), 1:51–52 (in ancient rhetoric) and 2:871–82 (in medieval texts and the genesis of rhyme).

8. Helen Waddell, ed., *Medieval Latin Lyrics* (New York: Henry Holt, 1929). 68. Here is her translation (69):

> **The Day of Wrath**
> Day of the king most righteous,
> The day is nigh at hand,
> The day of wrath and vengeance,
> And darkness on the land.

Day of thick clouds and voices,
Of mighty thundering,
A day of narrow anguish
And bitter sorrowing.

The love of women's over,
And ended is desire,
Men's strife with men is quiet,
And the world lusts no more.

9. The description of Celtic poetry in this section relies on a series of articles in the *Princeton Encyclopedia of Poetry and Poetics*, ed. Alex Preminger and T. V. F. Brogan (Princeton, NJ: Princeton University Press, 1993), on Irish poetry, Celtic prosody, generic rhyme, and Indo-European prosody. Throughout this study, I have been indebted as well to the general entry "Rhyme." For a complex system of rhyme analogous to Irish poetics—one that recognizes both external rhyme, between end syllables of lines, and internal rhyme within certain clusters of syllables in each line, see Thomas John Hudak, "Internal Rhyme Patterns in Classical Thai Poetry," *Crossroads* 3, nos. 2–3 (1987): 94–105.

10. Ezra Pound, *The Spirit of Romance* (New York: New Directions, 1968), 30. Dante's praise is in *De vulgari eloquentia* (2.2).

11. F. R. P. Akehurst's empirical study of restrictions on rhyme words in troubadour verse in "Incantatory Value of Words in the Provençal Troubadours" (in *Court and Poet*, ed. Glyn S. Burgess [Liverpool: Cairns, 1981], 59–68) underlines an argument made by Robert Guiette, "D'une poésie formelle en France au Moyen Âge," *Revue des sciences humaines* 54 (1949): 61–68. This article was later expanded into a monograph: Robert Guiette, *D'une poésie formelle en France au moyen âge* (Paris: A.-G. Nizet, 1972). Guiette's argument: "given the social requirement for discretion, the poet sings not the love which he experiences, but an ideal love": "le thème n'est qu'un prétext. C'est l'oeuvre formelle, elle-méme, qui est le sujet" (the theme is only a pretext. It is the formal work itself that is the subject).

12. Here is an unrhymed translation by K. Foster and P. Boyde from *Dante's Lyric Poetry* (Oxford: Clarendon, 1967) of the poem as it appears in Dante Alighieri's *Rime* (approx. 1283–1308):

XXXIX, Dante da Maiano to Various Makers of Rhyme
You who are intelligent, consider this vision
and please show its true meaning.
It was like this: a fair woman, in gaining
whose favour my heart takes much pleasure,

made me a gift of a green leafy garland;
and charmingly she did so. And then
I seemed to find myself clothed
in a shift that she had worn.
Then I made so bold as gently to embrace
her. The fair one did not resist, but smiled;
and as she smiled I kissed her repeatedly.
I will not say what followed—she made me
swear not to. And a dead woman
—my mother—was with her.

13. Perhaps groups of *rimatori* and rhymers' clubs are popular throughout literary history because they speak to the social confederation of poets as a kind of rhyme, or echo chamber, of compatible sounds. The imagists' identification by a visual phenomenon is far more unusual than the recurrence of groups of rhymers and rhymesters. The term has a derogatory ring, based in Aristotle's denigration of "mere verse," that also becomes a badge of modesty—this resonance can be detected in the earliest use of the word in English print: John Dennis's 1719 "But as Poets are not capable, so neither are they impartial Judges. I speak of those who are only Rhimesters" (*OED*). When William Butler Yeats, Ernest Rhys, Lionel Johnson, and others formed the Rhymer's Club in London in 1890, their goal was to recite and publish works together that would follow a new aesthetic of becoming closer to speech. A useful contrasting example of poetic confederation and what might be called "disfederation" is Edward Pen's contention in "Free Verse Movement: Its Reception in Japan and China," in *Tokyo 1991: The Force of Vision; Proceedings of the International Comparative Literature Association Meetings* (Tokyo: University of Tokyo Press, 1995), 61–67, that free verse arose in Japanese poetry as a consequence of the deprofessionalization of the role of the poet.

14. There is an intriguing and uncanny connection between this poem and the argument Allen Grossman makes in his *Summa Lyrica* about the relation of rhyme to the prelinguistic chora of the mother:

> *Scholium on rhyme and the mother tongue*. The mother is present wherever in the poem language is specialized toward sound, as in rhyme which arrests the word in the ear, requiring that it delay in the realm of the body, before passing to sensory extinction as mere notation in the brain. Rhyme like all phonic or merely structural repetition (as in grammatical rhyme) summons to common membership at the level of the species, tending to extinguish difference as transcendence and establish difference at the level of substance. The difference/no difference ambiguity in rhyme functions as the repetition of the sufficient con-

> ditions of sensing (the rule of texture), and as the substantiation of the parallel ambiguity at the level of meaning. Sound as silence (rhyme as sensation) articulates silence as sound (the meaning of words and sentences).

Allen Grossman, "Summa Lyrica," in *The Sighted Singer: Two Works on Poetry for Readers and Writers* (Baltimore: Johns Hopkins University Press, 1992), 362.

15. John Milton, *Complete Poems and Major Prose*, ed. Merritt Y. Hughes (New York: Odyssey, 1957), 210.

16. It is striking that couplets are dominant even earlier. Andrew Marvell, for example, seems to have had some knowledge of Dante. In "Tom May's Death" (line 62) he mentions the Guelphs and "Ghib'llines" and refers to the "basket" used to receive votes in Florentine elections. See Nigel Smith's note to line 62 of the poem in *The Poems of Andrew Marvell* (London: Longman, 2003), 123. Marvell's travels in Italy in the 1640s may have exposed him to Italian editions of the *Commedia*. Yet there is no use of terza rima in his poetry—he occasionally uses song forms of *abab* and *abcabc*, but the end-line rhyming couplet dominates his verse.

17. Ralph Waldo Emerson, "The Poet," in *Essays: First and Second Series*, Library of America (New York: Vintage Books, 1990), 229.

18. Reuven Tsur, *What Makes Sound Patterns Expressive?* (Durham, NC: Duke University Press, 1992), 5–35.

19. Emanuel Swedenborg, *An Hieroglyphic Key to Natural and Spiritual Mysteries by Way of Representations and Correspondences*, trans. from the Latin by R. Hindmarsh (London: R. Hindmarsh, 1792), 15. Hindmarsh writes in his preface to this work, "Correspondence in general may be defined, the relation subsisting between the essence of a thing and its form, or between the cause and its effect; thus the whole natural world corresponds to the spiritual world; the body of a man, with all its parts corresponds to his soul; and the literal sense of Word corresponds to its spiritual sense." He contrasts this to the arbitrary choices of speakers and writers who are using figures and metaphors—it is the interior, intrinsic connection that he emphasizes, in accordance with the doctrines of Swedenborg, concluding that "the language of correspondences is the language of God himself" (3–4). In this sense, the sounds of words are more intrinsic and spiritual than the arbitrary meanings that are conferred upon them by human beings. Baudelaire's deep interest in the doctrines of Swedenborg is evident even before his "Correspondances" of 1861, in his 1860 essay "Le poëm du haschisch," where he writes, "Fourier et Swedenborg, l'un avec ses *analogies*, l'autre avec ses *correspondances*, se sont incarnés dans le végétal et l'animal qui tombent sous votre regard, et, au lieu d'enseigner par la voix, ils vous endoctrinent par la forme et par la couleur" (Fourier and Swedenborg, one with his *analogies*, the other with his *correspondences*,

have incarnated themselves within the vegetable and animal domains that come into your view, and instead of instructing you with their voices, they indoctrinate you through form and color) (in Charles Baudelaire, *Oeuvres complètes*, ed. Y.-g. Le Dantec [Paris: Gallimard, 1961], 376). "Correspondances" itself emphasizes the transposition of odors as strongly as the visual senses: "Les parfums, les couleurs et les sons se répondent" (Perfumes, colors, and sounds respond to one another). For Swedenborg a theology of the Word underlies rhyme; for Baudelaire correspondences are synesthetic but their "longs échos" are effected through the medium of poetic language.

20. Ralph Waldo Emerson, "Swedenborg," in *Representative Men* (Boston: Phillips, Sampson, 1850), 111.

21. As mentioned in my first chapter, in his *Physics* Aristotle suggests that the maker partly imitates nature and partly carries to completion what nature has left incomplete. *Physics*, trans. R. P. Hardie and R. K. Gaye, in *Basic Works of Aristotle*, bk. 2, pp. 236–39. And in the *Nicomachean Ethics* he also emphasizes the conceptual origins of art, writing, "All art is concerned with coming into being . . . and considering how something may come into being which is capable of either being or not being and whose origin is in the maker and not in the thing made." *Nicomachean Ethics*, trans. W. D. Ross, in *Basic Works of Aristotle*, 6.4, p. 1025.

22. See Dante's discussion of rhyming practices by his contemporaries in 2.12.8; 2.13.4; and 2.13.6. Michael Hurley's essay "Interpreting Dante's *Terza Rima*," *Forum for Modern Language Studies* 41, no. 3 (2005): 320–30, discusses Dante's adaptation of metaphors from the Florentine wool industry to individual words and phrases (328–30).

23. William Wordsworth, "Preface to *Lyrical Ballads* and Appendix" (1850 version), in *Selected* Prose, ed. John Hayden (Harmondsworth, UK: Penguin, 1988), 296.

24. Arthur Schopenhauer, *The World as Will and Idea*, bk. 3, reprinted in *Critical Theory since Plato*, ed. Hazard Adams (New York: Harcourt Brace Jovanovich, 1971), 483.

25. See Ruth Weir, *Language in the Crib* (The Hague: Mouton, 1966). Clare Kirtley, Peter Bryant, Morag MacLean, and Lynette Bradley, in "Rhyme, Rime, and the Onset of Reading," *Journal of Experimental Child Psychology* 48 (1989): 224–45, argue that English-speaking children divide syllables into opening consonants or consonant clusters and the remainder (the rhyme). This predilection may make children more sensitive to rhyme and lead to heightened phonological awareness around the time of learning to read. In "A Deficit in Rime Awareness in Children with Down Syndrome," Margaret Snowing, Charles Hulme, and Robin Mercer discovered that children with Down syndrome did fairly well on tests of identifying allit-

eration but could not score above chance recognition in determining end rhymes. See *Reading and Writing: An Interdisciplinary Journal* 15 (2002): 471–95.

26. For a discussion of how nonsense choruses in lullabies encode the vowel preferences of the singer's language, see Bess Lomax Hawes, "Form and Function: Some Thoughts on the American Lullaby," *Journal of American Folklore* 87 (1974): 140–48.

27. Bruna de Cara and Usha Goswami, "Phonological Neighbourhood Density: Effects in a Rhyme Awareness Task in Five-Year-Old Children," *Journal of Child Language* 30 (2003): 697.

28. Marjorie Perloff, in her essay "The Linear Fallacy," *Georgia Review* (Winter 1981): 855–68, points out that the free verse line works as poetry only when it involves "both recurrence and suspension" (866). It is striking that these principles also characterize rhyme, even in its most "traditional" uses, and we might ask whether the most successful free verse, in absolving rhyme, has taken on rhyme's most fundamental formal gestures (which I would rephrase inversely as suspension and recurrence) without its particular manifestation in sound.

29. Paul Bauschatz, "Rhyme and the Structure of English Consonants," *English Language and Linguistics* 7, no. 1 (2003): 29–56, 52.

30. Henri Meschonnic brings this connection forward in "Rhyme and Life," trans. Gabriella Bedetti, *Critical Inquiry* 15, no. 1 (Autumn 1988): 90–107: "[Rhyme] participates in *paronomasia* . . . what only its restrictive identification to a final position masked. Rhyme cheats the way destiny would cheat if it played cards. Because it would know ahead of time. Rhyme knows ahead of time . . . because rhyme is a principle of listening" (96).

31. This tension between rhyme and syntax seems inevitable, despite various attempts by theorists of poetics to contradict it. Dryden, for example, in his dedication to his 1664 play *The Rival Ladies*, claimed that rhyme could be successfully included in "ordinary speaking" so readily, and be such a helpful aid to memory, that it "has all the advantages of prose beside its own." See the dedication to the earl of Orrery in *The Rival Ladies* (London: W.W. for Henry Herringman, 1664), 5–7. An illuminating contemporary position on this issue of poetry's relation to ordinary speaking is the contemporary French poet Jacques Roubaud's argument that the free verse practiced in France in the 1970s had only an "illusion" of liberty because it had not yet freed itself from the demands of ordinary syntax: the freedom of free verse should not be expressed in relation to metrics but in relation to the language. See Andrew Eastman, "Jacques Roubaud et le 'vers libre' américain," *Revue française d'études américaines* 80 (1999): 24.

32. Louis Simpson wrote in a 1982 article, "Irregular Impulses," *Ohio Review* 28:54–57, that "writing in regular form leads to writing light verse." If adjacent

rhymes occur today most often in advertising, perhaps it is because advertising is designed to stamp its impression on the wax of our disbelief.

33. T. S. Eliot uses close rhyme and related devices of sound repetition extensively in his "Four Quartets," where he writes, "My words echo / Thus, in your mind." Close rhyme and rhymes separated by only one word appear in *unseen eyebeam, white light, receipt for deceit, sea anemone, hardly barely, grief into relief, Mars converse, horoscope haruspicate, observe disease, tea leaves, riddle the inevitable, the womb or tomb, daemonic chthonic, budding nor fading, dark lake, flood and drouth, done and been, faces and places, all shall be well*. He also plays with transposed letters in *deliberate hebetude* and the several-times-repeated *dawn wind* and *winter lightning*. The overall effect is regeneration by echo. *Collected Poems*, 173–209.

34. Ian K. Lilly, "On Adjacent and Nonadjacent Russian Rhyme Pairs," *Slavic and East European Journal* 29, no. 2 (Summer 1985): 195.

35. At the same time, there is evidence that fifteenth-century scribes, when copying manuscripts, would change words into their own dialects but would rarely change the spelling of a rhyming word—the rhyme thereby was a way of transmitting pronunciation intact. See Stefania Maria Maci, "The Language of *Mary Magdalene* of the Bodleian MS Digby 133," *Linguistica e Filologia: Quaderni del Dipartimento di Linguistica, Università degli Studi di Bergamo* 10 (1999): 135. For studies of poetic rhymes as a record of dialect pronunciation in American poetry, see Gene Russell, "Dialectal and Phonetic Features of Edward Taylor's Rhymes," *American Literature* 43, no. 2 (1971): 165–80, and Kathryn Anderson McEuen, "Whittier's Rhymes," *American Speech* 20, no. 1 (1945): 51–57.

36. Philip Sidney, *A Defence of Poetry*, ed. J. A. Van Dorsten (Oxford: Oxford University Press, 1966). Sidney argues famously as well that "verse" serves as a mnemonic (50–51). At the very end of his treatise, he discusses the differences between English verse and ancient verse on the one hand and French and Italian rhyming practices on the other. He sees English verse "before any other vulgar language I know" as best suited for carrying forward the ancient tradition of the "well-weighed syllable" and the possibilities of rhyme for "the sweet sliding" necessary for musical effects (73).

37. See Kristin Hanson's "Vowel Variation in English Rhyme" and "A Note on the History of the Rhetoric of Rhymes" in *Studies in the History of the English Language: A Millennial Perspective*, ed. Donka Minkova and Robert Stockwell (Berlin: Mouton de Gruyter, 2002), 207–29. Hanson is particularly interested in the expressive possibilities of partial rhymes. For an analogous argument about iconic uses of rhyme, as in George Herbert's use of "rhyme" and "chime" in "Deniall" and Dryden's use of "alone," "grown," and "none" to signify negation, see Max Nänny, "Iconic Uses of Rhyme," in *Outside-In-Inside-Out: Iconicity in Language and Liter-*

ature, ed. Costantino Maeder, Olga Fischer, and William Herlofsky (Amsterdam: Benjamins, 2005), 195–215. Following Marjorie Perloff's pathbreaking *Rhyme and Meaning in the Poetry of Yeats* (The Hague: Mouton, 1970), Michael McKie's "Semantic Rhyme: A Reappraisal" (*Essays in Criticism* 46, no. 4 [1996]: 342–43) discusses Yeats's composition process, which often would begin with a prose analysis of a set of rhymes and what could be made of them.

38. Krystina Pomorska, "Semiotic Implications of Rhymes: Pushkin's Poems of the Erzerum Period," *Canadian-American Slavic Studies* 22, nos. 1–4 (1988): 377–81. All the primary rhymes in these poems are of Turkic origin, are feminine, and are placed at the end of the stanza, in the accusative case. Rhyme words end the stanza and end the sentence, for each stanza is a sentence (378). In a suggestive comparison to the subtle changes in action worked by Skelton's rhyming adverbs, Pushkin rejected a popular proscription against using verbs as rhyme words. J. Thomas Shaw, "Parts of Speech in Puškin's Rhymewords and Nonrhymed Endwords," *Slavic and East European Journal* 37, no. 1 (Spring 1993): 1–3.

39. Aristotle, "De somniis," in *Parva naturalia* 459a-b, trans. J. I. Beare, in *Basic Works*, 620 (re a projectile moving in space): "For in the case of these the movement continues even when that which set up the movement is no longer in contact [with the things that are moved]." He goes on to discuss the aftereffects of sense perception with regard to the transition from sunlight to darkness, the transference of colors, and observations of moving water. See the discussion of the legacy of Aristotle's observations of motion effects in Frans A. J. Verstraten, "On the Ancient History of the Direction of the Motion Aftereffect," *Perception* 25 (1996): 1177–87. Verstraten's discussion of motion aftereffects, sometimes called "the waterfall effect," whereby watching the descent of water over a fall will lead the viewer to see the reverse effect of water ascending once the eyes are turned away, provides a nice gloss on the effect of the Henry Vaughan poem on a waterfall that I discuss in the chapter on moods—Vaughan's turn, at the poem's closure, away from the phenomenon to consider heavenly ascent enacts the "waterfall effect" on a metaphysical level.

40. See Hurley, "Interpreting Dante's *Terza Rima*," for a discussion of terza rima's pattern as like "the juggler's three-ball cascade" (323).

41. See also the discussion of clapping, ululation, and other ways of marking line endings in Ode S. Ogede, "Oral Performance as Instruction: Aesthetic Strategies in Children's Play Songs from a Nigerian Community," *Children's Literature Association Quarterly* 19, no. 3 (Fall 1994): 114–15, and the role of clicks in nursery rhymes used by nursing mothers in China, Geoffrey S. Nathan, "Clicks in a Chinese Nursery Rhyme," *Journal of the International Phonetic Association* 31, no. 2 (2001): 223–28.

42. George Santayana, *Skepticism and Animal Faith* (New York: Charles Scribner's, 1923), 153.

43. In *The Art of the Poetic Line* (St. Paul, MN: Graywolf, 2008), James Longenbach suggests that in the twentieth century free verse has not been only a development for its own ends but a means of refinement in rhyming practices. Discussing the period in 1917 when Pound and Eliot returned to a practice of rhymed quatrains as a "counter-current" to the free verse they had been practicing, Longenbach writes of Pound's "Hugh Selwyn Mauberley": "The extraordinary rhythmic delicacy, which depends on the control of the line, could not have been achieved without an ongoing devotion to the craft of free verse" (48).

CHAPTER SEVEN

1. Hannah Arendt, "What Is Freedom?" in *Between Past and Future: Eight Exercises in Political Thought* (New York: Viking), 148.

2. Percy Shelley, "A Defence of Poetry," in *Shelley's Poetry and Prose*, ed. Donald H. Reiman and Neil Fraistat (New York: W. W. Norton, 2002), 526.

3. Translation by Michael Alexander, *The Earliest English Poems* (London: Penguin, 1977), 42.

4. The social status of professional wandering minstrels was so low that they were outside of the ties and responsibilities of medieval society—even their status as members of the universal church could come into question—but from the eleventh century forward, troubadours and *trouveres* attached to courts could range from aristocrats to renegades. In the Welsh code of laws, the *penkerd* or "chief of song" was given free land and a seat next to the king. Other bards also had free land and a horse from the king and a harp and gold ring from the queen. In return the bards were expected to sing the praises of their benefactors. John Southworth, *The English Medieval Minstrel* (Woodbridge, Suffolk, UK: Boydell and Brewer, 1989), 4–5, 22–23. For a discussion of the intersections of the roles of messengers, heralds, and minstrels in fourteenth- and fifteenth-century England, see 135.

5. Dante, *Convivio* (Florence: Le Lettere, 1995), 3.2, 7–9: "l'anima umana essere vuole naturalmente con tutto desiderio; e però che 'l suo essere dipende da Dio e per quello si conserva, naturalmente disia e vuole a Dio essere unita per lo suo essere fortificare. . . . E però che nelle bontadi della natura [e] della ragione si mostra la divina, vène che naturalmente l'anima umana con quelle per via spirituale sé unisce. . . . E questo unire è quello che noi dicemo amore. . . ."

6. In David Campbell, ed. and trans., *Greek Lyric: Sappho and Alcaeus*, Loeb Classical Library (Cambridge, MA: Harvard University Press, 1982), 279. The Horace citation is discussed on 229.

7. The source of this much-anthologized poem and its less-known accompanying musical score is British Museum Royal MS 58 f.5. Robert E. Jungman, "'Western Wind' and Tibullus I, 45–48," *English Language Notes* 27, no. 2 (December 1989): 19–26. Jungman argues that Tibullus's work was known to Chaucer and would have been available to a sixteenth-century writer.

8. See the discussion of Ariosto's debt to Dante, and the departure of Renaissance humanism from previous ideas of liberty and faith, in Giuseppe Mazzotta, "Italian Renaissance Epic," in *The Cambridge Companion to Epic*, ed. Catherine Bates (Cambridge: Cambridge University Press, 2010), 105–11. Mazzotta explores the relations Ariosto's characters bear to Lutheran notions of liberty and atheism, as well as the binary relations between freedom and captivity in the epic's plot.

9. "The *Divina Commedia* must not be considered as an epic; to compare it with epic poems is usually unprofitable. It is in a sense lyric, the tremendous lyric of the subjective Dante; but the soundest classification of the poem is Dante's own, 'as a comedy which differs from tragedy in its content.'" Pound concludes that the work is "a great mystery play, or better, a cycle of mystery plays." This 1910 essay was reprinted in Pound's *The Spirit of Romance* (New York: New Directions, 1968) and in part in Peter S. Hawkins and Rachel Jacoff, eds., *The Poet's Dante: Twentieth-Century Responses* (New York: Farrar, Straus and Giroux, 2001), 3–11.

10. "Io te sovra te corono e mitrio," says Virgil: I crown and miter you over yourself.

11. The other side of this process of revision is a willingness to leave works unfinished or suspended. See Robert Hollander, *Dante: A Life in Works* (New Haven, CT: Yale University Press, 2001), 114, for a discussion of Dante's decision to leave the *Convivio* and *De vulgari eloquentia* incomplete in order to begin the *Commedia*, as he had left the *Convivio* incomplete while he began *De vulgari eloquentia* (55). For a discussion of how *De monarchia* clarifies Dante's positions on the relative power of the pope and emperor, see 161–63. Hollander (9, 43) also discusses Dante's shifts between various lyric modes, which he characterizes as "his inclination to experiment."

12. Osip Mandelstam, "Conversation about Dante," in *The Selected Poems of Osip Mandelstam*, trans. Clarence Brown and W. S. Merwin (New York: New York Review of Books, 2004), 103–62. The essay, which dates to 1933, is reprinted from a 1971 translation by Clarence Brown and Robert Hughes (140). A 1979 translation by Jane Gray Harris and Constance Link of the essay appears as well in Hawkins and Jacoff, eds., *Poet's Dante*, 40–93.

13. For a discussion of the treatment of poets more generally in the *Commedia*, see Teodolinda Barolini, "Bertran de Born and Sordello: The Poetry of Politics in

Dante's *Comedy*," *PMLA* 94, no. 3 (1979): 395–405. Barolini points out that "only the epic poets are permitted to move in the *Comedy* while the lyric poets remain fixed in their respective circles, terraces or heavens. And yet Sordello moves . . . [he is] the only lyric poet to move at all" (402). Barolini concludes that this may be because other poets, particularly Bertran de Born, who now stands holding his own head as a lantern, created division rather than unity—for Dante, "the larger the audience, the greater the poet."

14. Hawkins and Jacoff in *The Poet's Dante* discuss these various interpretations of the effects of terza rima in the introduction to their reader (xxi–xxii). Terza rima is sometimes described as a matter of either two steps forward and one step backward or, changing the perspective, two steps backward and one step forward. Either account emphasizes the tense relations between progress and delay, anticipation and memory, and blessing and contrition, all at work in the poem.

15. Ezra Pound emphasizes this fairy-tale form of harsh favor at the beginning of his *Cantos* when he describes Odysseus's path as "aforesaid by Circe"—Circe has given Odysseus guidance in his journey to the underworld, and after that he is on his own. Canto 1 (line 18) in *The Cantos of Ezra Pound* (New York: New Directions, 1975), 3.

16. *The Aeneid of Virgil*, trans. Rolfe Humphries (New York: Scribner's, 1951), bk. 1, 18.

17. At the end of Canto 21 of the *Inferno* Malacoda gives Virgil and Dante what turn out (at the end of Canto 23) to be deliberately misleading directions.

18. *Aeneid*, bk. 6: Describing those punished in Hell, the Sibyl advises, "Seek not to know too much about their doom" (165).

19. "Ad ascoltarli er' io del tutto fisso, / quando 'l maestro mi disse: 'Or pur mira, / che per poco che teco non mi risso!' " (30, lines 130–32).

20. *Purgatorio* Canto 5, line 45: "però pur va, e in andando ascolta."

21. Canto 2, lines 1–3, of *Paradiso*: "O voi che siete in piccioletta barca / desiderosi d'ascoltar, seguiti / dietro al mio legno che cantando varca, . . ."

22. *Inferno*, Canto 4, lines 103–5: "Così andammo infino a la lumera, / parlando cose che 'l tacere è bello, / sì com' era 'l parlar colà dov'era."

23. *Inferno* 10, lines 63–73. In his encounter with the shade of Guido's father, Cavalcante de' Cavalcanti, Dante uses the past tense when referring to Guido, to the horrified surprise of Cavalcanti, who asks, "Non viv' elli ancora? / non fiere li occhi suoi lo dolce lume?" Dante hesitates in his answer and the father falls back, but later in the Canto (109–11) Dante asks Virgil whether he cannot assure the father that the son is still living. Virgil is in a hurry and it's not clear whether or not the correction is made.

24. Canto 33, lines 10–12: "Io non so chi tu se' né per che modo / venuto se' qua giù; ma fiorentino / mi sembri veramente quand' io t'odo."

25. *Purgatorio*, Canto 30, lines 62–63: "quando mi volsi al suon del nome mio, / che di necessità qui si registra, . . ."

26. Given Wordsworth's evident debt to Dante for this structure, it is fascinating to trace his ambivalence toward Dante's influence. In an October 1805 letter to Sir George Beaumont, he complains about the difficulty of "construing" Michelangelo's poems and writes, "There is a mistake in the world concerning the Italian language; the poetry of Dante and Michael Angelo provides that if there be little majesty and strength in Italian verse, the fault is in the authors, and not in the tongue. I can translate, and have translated, two books of Ariosto at the rate, nearly, of 100 lines a day." (2:206); in a May 1817 letter to Samuel Rogers he jokingly mentions that poets can follow Dante and place their enemies in "h—ll" (2:99); in a letter of September 1821 to Walter Savage Landor he mentions a Latin translation of Dante, implying that he has read it and Landor has not (2:153); and in another letter to Landor in January 1824, he asks Landor what he thinks of Dante, who has become "the fashion" thanks to the "example of Schlegel": "I have not read him [Dante] for many years, his style I used to think admirable for conciseness and vigor, without abruptness; but I own that his fictions often struck me as offensively grotesque and fantastic, and I felt the poem tedious from various causes" (2:216). All quotes are from *Letters of the Wordsworth Family*, ed. William Knight, 3 vols. (Boston: Ginn, 1907).

27. Thomas De Quincey, "William Wordsworth," in *Literary Reminiscences* (Boston: Ticknor and Fields, 1861), 1:314–15.

28. Gray's poem, with its poet who encounters the villagers in the churchyard only by means of the marked absence of their tombs, reaches closure when, via his imagination, the poet speaks a dramatic monologue in the voice of his own eulogist. This strikingly tautological structure of call and response makes all the more poignant the sense of the poet as stranded wanderer. *Complete Poems*, 37–43.

29. My discussion of Wordsworth in this chapter is deeply indebted to Allen Grossman's essay "Figuring the Real: Wordsworth's 'The Solitary Reaper,'" in *True-Love: Essays on Poetry and Valuing* (Chicago: University of Chicago Press, 2009), 127–43. Grossman contends of "The Solitary Reaper" that it is a poem that enacts Wordsworth's interest in theatricalizing consciousness by formal representations that often are built out of strange, indigenous, or untranslatable languages—"the poetic interest that he adds to the interest of the world as it is represented in prose, principally by his sister Dorothy" (131). He emphasizes that in "Resolution and Independence" the Leech-Gatherer exemplifies the nonreciprocity between per-

sons. Specifically "his work is not to make poems—he is not a poet—but to mediate the relation between the practice of poetry and vital life" (133).

30. Frederick Garber, *Wordsworth and the Poetry of Encounter* (Urbana: University of Illinois Press, 1972), 14. Garber includes in his book a rich account of the obligation Wordsworth's reliance on singularity bears to the Hebrew scriptures' concerns with singularity and purity: "Being alone, unique, and single, then, comes to signify having about oneself an association with hidden powers which are difficult to know and never completely knowable. The powers seem tied in with the state of singularity itself, so that something that is alone can, at least potentially, have an immensely potent capacity to reveal the might of hidden forces connected with the insights afforded by imaginative vision" (42–43).

31. *The Notebooks of Samuel Taylor Coleridge*, vol. 1, *1794–1804*, ed. Kathleen Coburn (New York: Pantheon/Bollingen, 1957), *Notes*, 170. Coburn adds that Coleridge also mentioned "the gloomy imagination of Dante" in *The Watchman* (4:102), March 23, 1796. Coleridge, in "This Lime-Tree Bower My Prison" and many of his poems to Sara Hutchinson, reminds us that there is also a poetry of missed meetings, one that perhaps culminates in Thomas Hardy's 1912–13 poems. We can think of elegy as that poetry's most common mode, though there is also the poetry of regret and mischance that speaks to relations between the living as well as those between the living and the dead.

32. Beverly Taylor, "Byron's Use of Dante in 'The Prophecy of Dante,'" *Keats-Shelley Journal* 28 (1979): 105.

33. Dante's influence on Shelley's "Triumph of Life" is central to T. S. Eliot's appreciation of Dante in his second essay on Dante, his 1950 address "What Dante Means to Me," to the Italian Institute in London. The address is reprinted in Hawkins and Jacoff, *The Poet's Dante*, 28–39. See also Eliot's earlier 1929 essay "Dante," in *Selected Essays of T. S. Eliot* (New York: Harcourt Brace, 1964), 199–237. Here Eliot emphasizes the universality of Dante's images and visual metaphors and suggests that allegory makes the poem more comprehensible not only theologically but also poetically. He also makes some incisive remarks on the role of surprise in the effectiveness of Dante's images (208).

34. Here is a translation:

To a passerby
A deafening din, the street around me roared.
Long, slender, in deep mourning, regal sadness,
A woman went past, with a haughty hand,
Lifting, flouncing her ribbons and hem.

Agile and graceful, with her leg like a statue's.
Twitching like a madman, I drank in
Her eye, livid sky where storms come to life.
The fascinating sweetness and the killing joy.

Lightning . . . then night! Fleeting beauty
Whose glance made me feel all at once reborn.
Will I see you again only in eternity?

Elsewhere, far from here! too late! maybe never!
Since I don't know where you go, you don't know where I go,
O you I could have loved, O you who knew it, too!

35. Of course, Eliot's own note to *The Waste Land* suggests that these lines "were stimulated by the account of one of the Antarctic expeditions (I forget which, but I think of Shackleton's): it was related that the party of explorers, at the extremity of their strength, had the constant delusion that there was *one more member* than could actually be counted." This information occludes, but cannot make invisible, the presence of other allusions—here the cowled medieval figure who does not in fact appear in Shackleton's account of three explorers who somehow seemed to be four, as well as the supper at Emmaus (Luke 24:30–31) and the fourth figure among the three Hebrew youths thrown into the furnace in Daniel 3:25.

36. Nadezhda Mandelstam, *Hope against Hope*, trans. Max Hayward (New York: Modern Library, 1999), 231.

37. The exception to her isolation is the famous story of the November evening and night she spent speaking with Isaiah Berlin in Leningrad in 1945, when he was working for the British Foreign Office and came to her apartment to meet her. György Dalos, in *The Guest from the Future: Anna Akhmatova and Isaiah Berlin*, trans. Antony Wood (New York: Farrar, Straus and Giroux, 1996), like many other biographers, makes a case that this meeting was the initiation of a "love story," but he also includes some documentation of the serious consequences the meeting had for Akhmatova's fate under the Stalinist regime. The meeting is suggestively discussed in a recent book by Svetlana Boym, *Another Freedom: The Alternative History of an Idea* (Chicago: University of Chicago Press, 2010), 94–98. Boym concludes that "the meeting with Akhmatova was fundamental for Berlin's conception of liberty and pluralism of "'the ends of life'" (98). Boym mistakenly writes that the initial meeting took place in 1946; November 1945 is the date given in all other sources, including Isaiah Berlin himself in "Anna Akhmatova: A Memoir," in *The Complete Poems of Anna Akhmatova*, ed. Judith Hemschemeyer (Boston: Zephyr, 1992), 35–55. In fact, there was a second brief farewell meeting, in January 1946,

and one day after Akhmatova's living space was wired for sound surveillance. See Roberta Reeder, *Anna Akhmatova: Poet and Prophet* (New York: St. Martin's, 1990), 286–88. And by September Akhmatova was publically expelled from the Writers' Union and her work was banned.

38. Reeder, *Anna Akhmatova*, 31–77. I am indebted to this monumental biography, and also to Elaine Feinstein's *Anna of All the Russias: The Life of Anna Akhmatova* (London: Weidenfeld and Nicolson, 2005), 1–9, 119–27, and Konstantin Polivanov, ed., *Anna Akhmatova and Her Circle*, trans. Patricia Beriozkina (Fayetteville: University of Arkansas Press, 1994). I also thank the staff at the Akhmatova Museum in St. Petersburg, who kindly helped me in the summer of 2005. The Kunitz-Hayward translation is Boston: Little, Brown, 1973.

39. See the entry on Dante's treatise, "Questio de aqua et terra," in *The Dante Encyclopedia*, ed. Richard Lansing (New York: Garland, 2000),734–35. I am also indebted in the following discussion of Dante's water imagery to Daniel J. Donno, "Moral Hydrography: Dante's Rivers," *MLN* 92, no. 1 (1977): 130–39.

40. *Inferno* 14, lines 76–84. This canto also includes the explanation of the Old Man of Crete's role in the river system (lines 103–20).

CHAPTER EIGHT

1. Nadezhda Mandelstam discusses the poem throughout her memoir *Hope against Hope*, trans. Max Hayward (New York: Modern Library, 1999), and records that even Genrikh Grigorievich Yagoda, the head of Stalin's secret police from 1934 to 1936, had memorized the poem; he was executed himself after the last show trial in 1938 (83). See also Emma Gerstein's *Moscow Memories: Memories of Anna Akhmatova, Osip Mandelstam and Literary Russia under Stalin*, trans. John Crowfoot (Woodstock, NY: Overlook, 2004), 341–56.

2. Osip Mandelstam, *Stone*, trans. Robert Tracy (Princeton, NJ: Princeton University Press, 1981), 12. See also Osip Mandelstam, *Selected Poems*, trans. David McDuff (Cambridge: Rivers Press, 1973), 130–31. Both Tracy and McDuff date the poem to November 1933.

3. These and other allusions in the poem are discussed and explained in José Manuel Prieto, "Reading Mandelstam on Stalin," trans. Esther Allen, *New York Review of Books* 72, no. 10 (June 10, 2010): 70.

4. Gerstein, *Moscow Memories*, 340–41.

5. Nadezhda Mandelstam, *Hope Abandoned*, trans. Max Hayward (New York: Atheneum, 1974).

6. Donald Davie, foreword to *Osip Mandelstam: Poems*, ed. and trans. James Greene (London: Elek, 1980), 9–11.

7. Osip Mandelstam, "Octets," trans. Donald Davie, *Agenda* 14, no. 2 (1976): 11–14. Here are transliterations of these two octets:

73
V īgol'chatykh chumnykh bokalakh
My p'em navazhden'e prīchīn,
Kasaemsia kriuch'iamī malykh,
Kak legkaia smert,' velīchīn.
Ī tam, gde stsepīlīs' bīriul'kī,
Rebenok molchan'e khranīt—
Bol'shaia vselennaia v liul'ke
U malen'koĭ vechnostī spīt.

75
Preodolev zatverzhennost' prīrody,
Golubotverdyĭ glaz pronīk v ee zakon:
V zemnoĭ kore iurodstvuiut porody,
Ī, kak ruda, īz grudī rvetsia ston.
Ī tianetsia glukhoĭ nedorazvītok
Kak by dorogoĭ, sognutoiu v rog,—
Poniat' prostranstva vnutrenniĭ īzbytok,
Ī lepestka, ī kupola zalog.

I am deeply grateful to Leeore Schnairsohn for making these transliterations when none were available in the printed literature.

8. Kenneth Burke, "The Calling of the Tune," in *The Philosophy of Literary Form* (Berkeley: University of California Press, 1973), 221; W. H. Auden, "Criticism in a Mass Society," in *The Intent of the Critic*, ed. D. A. Stauffer (Princeton, NJ: Princeton University Press, 1941), 125–47. In a poem from September 1953, "The Truest Poetry Is the Most Feigning," Auden played with the notion that the poet's freedom is a matter of strategic adaptability, not transcendence, thereby ironically transcending the need for transcendent claims. He mockingly suggests that the poet who finds the political climate changing while writing a love poem might change course and instead celebrate the figure in and of power:

If half-way through such praises of your dear,
Riot and shooting fill the streets with fear,
And overnight as in some terror dream
Poets are suspect with the New Regime,
Stick at your desk and hold your panic in,
What you are writing may still save your skin.

He describes how the poem's subject can readily be adapted to these new conditions:

. . . in an hour your poem qualifies
For a State pension or His annual prize,
And you will die in bed (which He will not:
that public nuisance will be hanged or shot).

The poem ends by proclaiming the poet's facility with fiction and independence from reality: "What but tall tales, the luck of verbal playing, / Can trick his lying nature into saying / That love, or truth in any serious sense, / Like orthodoxy, is a reticence?" The deeply comic, resurrecting flexibility of self-making described by Auden has its roots in earlier philosophical arguments about the freedom of art making and forms of work that in contrast proceed under the pressure of necessity.

9. Immanuel Kant, *Critique of the Power of Judgment*, trans. and ed. Paul Guyer (Cambridge: Cambridge University Press, 2000), 186.

10. Karl Marx, *Economic and Philosophic Manuscripts of 1844*, trans. Martin Milligan, ed. Dirk Struik (New York: International Publishers, 1964), 110–11.

11. Percy Bysshe Shelley, "A Defence of Poetry," in *Shelley's Poetry and Prose*, ed. Donald H. Reiman and Neil Fraistat (New York: W. W. Norton, 2002), 503.

12. Ibid., 496–97.

13. Plato, *Theaetetus*, ed. Bernard Williams, trans. M. J. Levett, rev. Myles Burnyeat (Indianapolis: Hackett, 1992), 1–13.

14. Adriana Cavarero, *In Spite of Plato* (New York: Routledge, 1995), 107.

15. Ibid., 106.

16. Étienne Gilson, *The Arts of the Beautiful* (New York: Charles Scribner, 1965, repr. New York: Dalkey Archive, 2000), 81.

17. Conversely, since the advent of modernization and a decline in the need for child labor, for many in the upper classes this division of tasks has resulted in an aestheticization of children themselves. And in those areas of the economy still structured around migrant, seasonal, home-based, and other forms of unorganized labor, the exploitation of children's bodies continues even in the richest nations.

18. Gilson, *Arts of the Beautiful*, 130–32.

19. Henri Bergson, *Creative Evolution*, trans. Arthur Mitchell (New York: Henry Holt, 1911, repr. Mineola, NY: Dover Books, 1988), 13.

20. Euripides, *Andromache*, trans. Susan Stewart and Wesley Smith (Oxford: Oxford University Press, 2001), 31. P. T. Stevens's note to the Greek text (Oxford: Clarendon, 1998) suggests, following work by Max Pohlenz, that Euripides might be

thinking of Aristophanes and Eupolis collaborating on *The Knights*, a play we now attribute to Aristophanes (154n476).

21. A suggestive exception is the collaboration from 1984 to 1986 between Andy Warhol and Jean Michel Basquiat in the paintings *Ten Punching Bags (Last Supper)*, which preserved in both their forms and themes a sense of agonism. See Victor Bockris, *Warhol: The Biography* (Cambridge, MA: Da Capo, 2003), 61–62. The collaborative works of Mike Kelley and Paul McCarthy, saturated with adolescent fantasy, also present a form of "playing" that borders on aggression. Fantasy is revealed as privative and shared at once, and the burden of reconciling its forces is in turn foisted upon the viewer. Philip Monk, *Mike Kelley and Paul McCarthy: Collaborative Works* (Toronto: Power Plant, 2000).

22. Pierre Bourdieu, "The Historical Genesis of a Pure Aesthetic," in *The Field of Cultural Production*, ed. Randal Johnson, no trans. (New York: Columbia University Press, 1993), 259–60. For a far more detailed historical examination of the classical origins of the rise of aesthetics, see James I. Porter, "Is Art Modern? Kristeller's 'Modern System of the Arts' Reconsidered," *British Journal of Aesthetics* 49, no. 1 (January 2009): 1–24. Porter makes a plea in the tradition of John Dewey for a consideration of not only how aesthetic features of works of art are embedded in cultural and social practices but how they are experienced (23–24).

23. I discuss these ideas more extensively in "On the Art of the Future," in *The Open Studio: Essays on Art and Aesthetics* (Chicago: University of Chicago Press, 2005), 15–28.

24. In a prescient argument in her essay "The Concept of History," in *Between Past and Future: Eight Exercises in Political Thought* (New York: Viking, 1961), 41–90, Hannah Arendt writes of the difference between fabrication, or building material by means of human artifice and defending it against the elements, on the one hand, and technology, the acquisition of means of intervention into nature that begins natural processes of our own, on the other (60). She writes, "To act into nature, to carry human unpredictability into a realm where we are confronted with elemental forces which we shall perhaps never be able to control reliably, is dangerous enough. Even more dangerous would it be to ignore that for the first time in our history the human capacity for action has begun to dominate all others—the capacity for wonder and thought in contemplation no less than the capacities of *homo faber* and the human *animal laborans*" (62).

25. Hannah Arendt, *The Life of the Mind* (New York: Harcourt, 1971), 127. Similarly, in "What Is Freedom?" she writes that "the Greek word ἀρχειν, which covers beginning, leading, ruling, that is, the outstanding qualities of the free man, bears witness to an experience in which being free and the capacity to begin something

new coincided. Freedom, as we would say today, was experienced in spontaneity" (in *Between Past and Future*, 166).

26. In *Between Past and Future*, 165. Here Arendt seems to rely on the distinction Kant makes in his "Metaphysics of Morals" between *Wille* (the form of self-legislation that is inwardly binding, hence a kind of conscience) and *Willkür* (the faculty of choice that ensues from legal freedoms), yet she also strives to show the interdependence of the inward and external constraints.

27. Arendt, *Human Condition*, 29.

28. For a more positive account of Arendt's philosophy of politics and creativity than the one I offer here, see Linda Zerilli, *Feminism and the Abyss of Freedom* (Chicago: University of Chicago Press, 2005).

29. Hannah Arendt, "Introduction into Politics" (trans. of "Was ist Politik?"), in *The Promise of Politics*, ed. Jerome Kohn (New York: Schocken, 2005), 104.

30. Arendt, "What Is Freedom?" 151–53.

31. Ibid., 153–54.

WORKS CITED

Adan, Ana. "Mood Rhythmicity and Individual Differences." In *Causes, Role and Influences in Mood States*, edited by Anita V. Clark, 33–56. New York: Nova, 2005.

Addison, Joseph and Richard Steele, and others. *The Spectator in 4 volumes*. London: J. M. Dent, 1913.

Adorno, Theodor. *Aesthetic Theory*. Translated by Robert Hullot-Kentor, Minneapolis: University of Minnesota Press, 1997.

Akehurst, F. R. P. "Incantatory Value of Words in the Provençal Troubadours." In *Court and Poet*, edited by Glyn S. Burgess, 59–68. Liverpool: Cairns, 1981.

Akhmatova, Anna. *Anna Akhmatova and Her Circle*. Compilation and notes by Konstantin Polivanov, translated by Patricia Beriozkina. Fayetteville: University of Arkansas Press, 1994.

———. *The Complete Poems of Anna Akhmatova*. Edited by Judith Hemschemeyer. Boston: Zephyr, 1992.

———. *Poems of Akhmatova*. Translated by Stanley Kunitz and Max Hayward. Boston: Little, Brown, 1973.

Alberti, Leon Battista. *On Painting*. Translated by John R. Spencer. New Haven, CT: Yale University Press, 1967.

Aldington, Richard. "Free Verse in England." *Egoist*, September 15, 1914, 351–52.

Alexander, Michael, ed. *The Earliest English Poems*. London: Penguin, 1977.

Alighieri, Dante. *Convivio*. Florence: Le Lettere, 1995.

———. *De vulgari eloquentia*. Edited by Pio Rajna. Florence: Società Dantesca Italiana, 1960.

———. *De vulgari eloquentia*. Translated by Stephen Botterill. Cambridge: Cambridge University Press, 1996.

———. *Dante's Lyric Poetry*. Translated by K. Foster and P. Boyde. Oxford: Clarendon, 1967.

Anderson, Bernhard, ed. *Creation in the Old Testament*. Philadelphia: Fortress Press, 1984.

Anderson, Gary A. *Sacrifices and Offerings in Ancient Israel*. Harvard Semitic Monographs. Atlanta: Scholars Press, 1987.

Arendt, Hannah. "The Concept of History." In *Between Past and Future: Eight Exercises in Political Thought*, 41–90. New York: Viking, 1961.

———. *The Human Condition*. 2nd ed. Chicago: University of Chicago Press, 1988.

———. "Introduction into Politics" (translation of "Was ist Politik?"). In *The Promise of Politics*, edited by Jerome Kohn, 93–200. New York: Schocken, 2005.

———. *The Life of the Mind*. New York: Harcourt, 1971.

———. "What Is Freedom?" In *Between Past and Future: Eight Exercises in Political Thought*, 143–72. New York: Viking, 1961.

Aristotle. *The Basic Works of Aristotle*. Edited by Richard McKeon. New York: Random House, 1941.

Arnauld, Antoine. *The Art of Thinking: Port Royal Logic*. Translated by James Dickoff and Patricia James. Library of Liberal Arts. New York: Bobbs-Merrill, 1964.

Arnim, Achim von, and Clemens Brentano, comps. and eds. *Des Knaben Wunderhorn: Alte deutsche Lieder*. 3 vols. Stuttgart: Philipp Reclam, 2006. (Reprint of Heidelberg: Mohr und Zimmer, 1806.)

Athanassakis, Apostolos N. *The Homeric Hymns*. Baltimore: Johns Hopkins University Press, 1976.

Auden, W. H. "Criticism in a Mass Society." In *The Intent of the Critic*, edited by D. A. Stauffer, 125–47. Princeton, NJ: Princeton University Press, 1941.

———. *Collected Poems*. Edited by Edward Mendelson. New York: Modern Library, 2007.

Augustine of Hippo. *The City of God against the Pagans*. Edited and translated by R. W. Dyson. Cambridge: Cambridge University Press, 1998.

———. *Confessions*. Translated by R.S. Pine-Coffin. London: Penguin, 1961.

Ballard, Bruce. *The Role of Mood in Heidegger's Ontology*. London: University Press of America, 1991.

Barolini, Teodolinda. "Bertran de Born and Sordello: The Poetry of Politics in Dante's *Comedy*." PMLA 94, no. 3 (1979): 395–405.

Bataille, Georges. *The Accursed Share*, vol. 1, *Consumption*. Translated by Robert Hurley. New York: Zone Books, 1991. (Translation of *La part maudite*. Paris: Les Éditions de Minuit, 1949.)

Baudelaire, Charles. *Oeuvres complètes*. Edited by Y.-G. Le Dantec. Paris: Gallimard, 1961.

Bauschatz, Paul. "Rhyme and the Structure of English Consonants." *English Language and Linguistics* 7, no. 1 (2003): 29–56.

Beardsley, Monroe. "The Metaphorical Twist." *Philosophy and Phenomenological Research* 22, no. 3 (March 1962): 293–307.

Beauchamp, Paul. *Création et separation*. Paris: Desclée de Brouwer, 1969.

Beer, Andrew. "Tradition and Originality in Callimachus's 'Hymn to Apollo.' " *Frankfurter elektronische Rundschau zur Altertumskunde* 1 (2006): 1–7, http://.fera-journal.eu.

Benthall, R. A. "New Moons, Old Ballads and Prophetic Dialogues in Coleridge's 'Dejection: An Ode.'" *Studies in Romanticism* 37 (Winter 1998): 591–614.

Bergson, Henri. *Creative Evolution*. Translated by Arthur Mitchell. New York: Henry Holt, 1911; reprint Mineola, NY: Dover Books, 1988.

Berlin, Isaiah. *Concepts and Categories: Philosophical Essays*. London: Hogarth, 1980; reprint Oxford: Oxford University Press, 2002.

———. "Two Concepts of Liberty." In *Four Essays on Liberty*, 118–72. London: Oxford University Press, 2002.

Blake, William. *The Complete Poetry and Prose of William Blake*. Edited by David V. Erdman. Berkeley: University of California Press, 1982.

Boas, George. *History of Ideas*. New York: Scribner's, 1969.

Boethius. *The Consolation of Philosophy*. Translated by Victor Watts. London: Penguin, 1999.

Bockris, Victor. *Warhol: The Biography*. Cambridge, MA: Da Capo, 2003.

Bonnefoy, Yves. "On the Translation of Form in Poetry." In *Companion to Contemporary World Literature from the Editors of "World Literature Today,"* edited by Pamela A. Genova, 5–11. New York: Twayne / Thompson Gale, 2003.

Bourdieu, Pierre. "The Historical Genesis of a Pure Aesthetic." In *The Field of Cultural Production*, edited by Randal Johnson, no trans., 254–66. New York: Columbia University Press, 1993.

Boym, Svetlana. *Another Freedom: The Alternative History of an Idea*. Chicago: University of Chicago Press, 2010.

Bulloch, A. W. *Callimachus: The Fifth Hymn*. Cambridge: Cambridge University Press, 1985.

Bullock, C. H. *An Introduction to Old Testament Poetic Books*. Chicago: Moody Press, 1985.

Bundy, Elroy. "The 'Quarrel' between Kallimachus and Apollonius." *California Studies in Classical Antiquity* 5 (1972): 39–92.

Burke, Kenneth. "The Calling of the Tune." Reprinted in *The Philosophy of Literary Form*, 221–33. Berkeley: University of California Press, 1973.

Callimachus. *Hymns and Fragments*. Translated by A. W. Mair. Loeb Classical Library. Cambridge, MA: Harvard University Press, 1969.

Camhi, Leslie. "Did Duchamp Deceive Us?" *Art News* 98 (February 1999): 98–102.

Campbell, David, ed. and trans. *Greek Lyric: Sappho and Alcaeus*. Loeb Classical Library. Cambridge, MA: Harvard University Press, 1982.

Carew, Thomas. *Poems by Thomas Carew Esquire, one of the gentlemen of the priviechamber and Sewer in Ordinary to His Majesty*. London: I.D. for Thomas Walkley, 1640.

Cavarero, Adriana. *In Spite of Plato*. New York: Routledge, 1995.

Cavell, Stanley, *Philosophy the Day after Tomorrow*. Cambridge, MA: Harvard University Press, 2005.

Celant, Germano. *Art Povera*. New York: Praeger, 1969.

Clark, Timothy. *The Theory of Inspiration: Composition as a Crisis of Subjectivity in Romantic and Post-Romantic Writing*. Manchester: Manchester University Press, 1997.

Clay, Jenny. *The Politics of Olympus: Form and Meaning in the Major Homeric Hymns*. Princeton, NJ: Princeton University Press, 1989.

Cleanthes. "Hymn to Zeus." Translated by James Adams in *The Stoic and Epicurean Philosophers*, edited by Whitney J. Oates, 591–92. New York: Random House, 1940.

Clinton, Kevin. "The Author of the Homeric *Hymn to Demeter*." *Opuscula Atheniensia* 16, no. 4 (1986): 43–49.

Coleridge, Samuel Taylor. *Aids to Reflection*. Edited by John Beer. Princeton, NJ: Princeton University Press, 1997.

———. *Biographia Literaria*. Edited by James Engell and Walter Jackson Bate. 2 vols. in one. Princeton, NJ: Princeton University Press, 1983.

———. *Coleridge's Dejection: The Earliest Manuscripts and the Earliest Printings*. Edited by Stephen M. Parrish. Ithaca, NY: Cornell University Press, 1988.

———. *Collected Letters*. Edited by Earl Leslie Griggs. Oxford: Clarendon, 1956.

———. *The Collected Works*, vol. 5, *Lectures 1808–1818*. Edited by R. A. Foake. London: Routledge, 1987.

———. *The Collected Works*, vol. 16, *Poetical Works, Poems*, pts. 1–2, *Reading Text and Variorum Text*. Edited by J. C. C. Mays. Princeton, NJ: Princeton University Press, 2001.

———. *The Complete Poems*. Edited by William Keach. London: Penguin, 1997.

———. *Complete Works*. Edited by W. G. Shedd. New York: Harper, 1856.

———. *Marginalia*. Edited by George Whalley. Princeton, NJ: Princeton University Press, 1980.

———. *The Notebooks of Samuel Taylor Coleridge*. Edited by Kathleen Coburn. Princeton, NJ: Princeton University Press; New York: Pantheon/Bollingen, 1957.

Connelly, Joan Breton. *Portrait of a Priestess: Women and Ritual in Ancient Greece*. Princeton, NJ: Princeton University Press, 2007.

Cook, Eleanor. *A Reader's Guide to Wallace Stevens*. Princeton, NJ: Princeton University Press, 2007.

Dalos, György. *The Guest from the Future: Anna Akhmatova and Isaiah Berlin*. Trans. Antony Wood. New York: Farrar, Straus and Giroux, 1996.

Davie, Donald. Foreword to *Osip Mandelstam: Poems*. Edited and translated by James Greene. London: Elek, 1980.

de Cara, Bruna and Usha Goswami, "Phonological Neighbourhood Density: Effects in a Rhyme Awareness Task in Five-Year-Old Children." *Journal of Child Language* 30 (2003): 695–710.

De Quincey, Thomas. *Literary Reminiscences*. Boston: Ticknor and Fields, 1861.

Deleuze, Gilles, and Félix Guattari. *What Is Philosophy?* Translated by Hugh Tomlinson and Graham Burchell. New York: Columbia University Press, 1991.

Dickinson, Emily. *The Poems of Emily Dickinson*. Edited by R. W. Franklin. Cambridge, MA: Harvard University Press, 1998.

Donno, Daniel J. "Moral Hydrography: Dante's Rivers." *Modern Language Notes* 92, no. 1 (1977): 130–39.

Dryden, John. *The Rival Ladies*. London: W. W. for Henry Herringman, 1664.

Eastman, Andrew. "Jacques Roubaud et le 'vers libre américan.'" *Revue française d'études américaines* 80 (1999): 23–32.

Eliot, T. S. *Collected Poems, 1909–1962*. New York: Harcourt, 1970.

———. *Selected Essays*. New York: Harcourt Brace, 1964.

Ellenbogen, Mark A. "Stress, Psychopathology and the Regulation of Mood and Cortisol Levels." In *Causes, Role and Influence of Mood States*, edited by Anita V. Clark, 1–32. New York: Nova, 2005.

Emerson, Ralph Waldo. "The Poet." In *Essays: First and Second Series*, 215–38. Library of America. New York: Vintage Books, 1990.

———. "Swedenborg." In *Representative Men*, 95–145. Boston: Phillips, Sampson, 1850.

Epictetus, *The Discourses, as Reported by Arrian*. Edited and translated by W. A. Oldfater. New York: Grove, 2007.

Färber, Hans. *Die Lyrik in der Kunsttheorie der Antike*. Munich: Neuer Filser Verlag, 1936.

Euripides. *Alcestis*. Translated by Richard Aldington. London: Chatto and Windus, 1930.

———. *Andromache*. Edited by P. T. Stevens. Oxford: Clarendon, 1998.

———. *Andromache*. Translated by Susan Stewart and Wesley Smith. Oxford: Oxford University Press, 2001.

———. *Cyclops; Alcestis; Medea*. Translated by D. Kovacs. Loeb Classical Library. Cambridge, MA: Harvard University Press, 1994.

Feeney, Denis. "Horace and the Greek Lyric Poets." In *Horace 2000: A Celebration; Essays for the Bimillennium*, edited by Niall Rudd, 41–63. London: Duckworth, 1993.

———. *Literature and Religion at Rome: Cultures, Contexts and Beliefs*. Cambridge: Cambridge University Press, 1998.

Feinstein, Elaine. *Anna of All the Russias: The Life of Anna Akhmatova*. London: Weidenfeld and Nicolson, 2005.

Feuerbach, Ludwig. *The Essence of Christianity*. Translated by Marian Evans. London: Trübner, 1881.

Fineman, Joel. *Shakespeare's Perjured Eye: The Invention of Subjectivity in the Sonnets*. Berkeley: University of California Press, 1986.

Foley, Helene P., ed. *The Homeric Hymn to Demeter*. Princeton, NJ: Princeton U. Press, 1994.

Ford, Andrew. *Homer: The Poetry of the Past*. Ithaca, NY: Cornell University Press, 1992.

François, Anne-Lise. *Open Secrets: The Literature of Uncounted Experience*. Stanford, CA: Stanford University Press, 2007.

Friend, A. M. "The Portraits of the Evangelists in Greek and Latin Manuscripts." Part 1: *Art Studies* 5 (1927): 115–50; part 2: *Art Studies* 7 (1929): 3–29.

Fry, Paul. *The Poet's Calling in the English Ode*. New Haven, CT: Yale University Press, 1980.

Garber, Frederick. *Wordsworth and the Poetry of Encounter*. Urbana: University of Illinois Press, 1972.

Gell, Alfred. "The Technology of Enchantment and the Enchantment of Technology." In *Anthropology, Art and Aesthetics*, edited by J. Coote and A. Shelton, 40–63. Oxford: Clarendon, 1992.

Gerstein, Emma. *Moscow Memories: Memories of Anna Akhmatova, Osip Mandelstam and Literary Russia under Stalin*. Translated by John Crowfoot. Woodstock, NY: Overlook, 2004.

Gilson, Étienne. *The Arts of the Beautiful*. New York: Charles Scribner, 1965, reprint New York: Dalkey Archive, 2000.

———. *Forms and Substance in the Arts*. Translated by Salvator Attanasio. Normal, IL: Dalkey Archive, 2001.

Ginsberg, Allen. *Kaddish and Other Poems, 1958–1960*. San Francisco: City Lights Books, 1961.

Goethe, Johann Wolfgang von, and Friedrich Schiller. *Correspondence between Goethe and Schiller*. Translated by Liselotte Dieckmann. New York: Peter Lang, 1994.

Gray, Thomas. *The Complete Poems*. Edited by H. W. Starr and J. R. Hendrickson. Oxford: Clarendon, 1966.

Grossman, Allen. "Figuring the Real: Wordsworth's 'The Solitary Reaper.'" In *True-Love: Essays on Poetry and Valuing*, 127–43. Chicago: University of Chicago Press, 2009.

———. "Summa Lyrica." In *The Sighted Singer: Two Works on Poetry for Readers and Writers*, edited by Allen Grossman and Mark Halliday, 205–374. Baltimore: Johns Hopkins University Press, 1992.

Grote, Simon. "Pietistische *Aisthesis* und moralische Erziehung bei Alexander Gottlieb Baumgarten." *Aufklärung* 20 (2008): 175–98.

Guiette, Robert. *D'une poésie formelle en France au Moyen Âge*. Paris: A.-G. Nizet, 1972.

Guyer, Paul. *Kant and the Experience of Freedom: Essays on Aesthetics and Morality*. Cambridge: Cambridge University Press, 1993.

Hampshire, Stuart. *Freedom of the Individual*. New York: Harper and Row, 1965.

Hanson, Kristin. "Vowel Variation in English Rhyme: A Note on the History of the Rhetoric of Rhymes." In *Studies in the History of the English Language: A Millennial Perspective*, edited by Donka Minkova and Robert Stockwell, 207–29. Berlin: Mouton de Gruyter, 2002.

Harmon, William "Rhyme in English Verse: History, Structures, Functions." *Studies in Philology* 84, no. 4 (Fall 1987): 365–93.

Hawes, Bess Lomax. "Form and Function: Some Thoughts on the American Lullaby." *Journal of American Folklore* 87 (1974): 140–48.

Hawkins, Peter S. and Rachel Jacoff, eds. *The Poet's Dante: Twentieth-Century Responses*. New York: Farrar, Straus and Giroux, 2001.

Hazlitt, William. *Selected Essays of William Hazlitt, 1778–1830*. Edited by Geoffrey Keynes. New York: Random House, 1948.

Hegel, G.W. F. *Aesthetics: Lectures on Fine Art*. Translated by T. M. Knox. 2 vols. Oxford: Clarendon, 1975.

———. *Phenomenology of Spirit*. Translated by A. V. Miller. Oxford: Oxford University Press, 1977.

Heidegger, Martin. *Basic Writings*. Edited and translated by David F. Krell. New York: Harper Collins, 1997.

———. *Being and Time*. Translated by John Macquarrie and Edward Robinson. New York: Harper and Row, 1962.

———. *The Essence of Human Freedom*. Translated by Ted Sadler. London: Continuum, 2005.

Hesiod. *Theogony*. Translated by M. L. West. Oxford: Oxford University Press, 1988.

Hollander, Robert. *Dante: A Life in* Works. New Haven, CT: Yale University Press, 2001.

Holmes, Richard. *Coleridge: Early Visions, 1772–1804*. New York: Pantheon, 1989.

———. *Shelley: The Pursuit*. New York: Penguin, 1987.

Hudak, Thomas John. "Internal Rhyme Patterns in Classical Thai Poetry." *Crossroads* 3, nos. 2–3 (1987): 94–105.

Hume, David. *Essays and Treatises on Several Subjects*. London: A. Millar, 1758.

———. *A Treatise of Human Nature*. London: John Noon, 1739.

Hurley, Michael. "Interpreting Dante's *Terza Rima*." *Forum for Modern Language Studies* 41, no. 3 (2005): 320–30.

Hyppolite, Jean. *Genesis and Structure of Hegel's "Phenomenology of Spirit."* Evanston, IL: Northwestern University Press, 1974.

Janeway, Christopher. "Arts and Crafts in Plato and Collingwood." *Journal of Aesthetics and Art Criticism* 50, no. 1 (Winter 1992): 45–54.

———. "Craft and Fineness in Plato's *Ion*." In *Oxford Studies in Ancient Philosophy*, vol. 10, edited by Julia Annas, 1–23. Oxford: Clarendon, 1992.

Jonas, Hans. "Jewish and Christian Elements in Philosophy: Their Share in the Emergence of the Modern Mind." In *Philosophical Essays: From Ancient Creed to Technological Man*. Englewood Cliffs, NJ: Prentice Hall, 1974.

Jonson, Ben. *The Complete Poems*. Edited by George Parfitt. New Haven, CT: Yale University Press, 1975.

JPS Torah Commentary. Edited with commentary by Nahum M. Sarna. Philadelphia: Jewish Publication Society, 1989.

Jungman, Robert E. "'Western Wind' and Tibullus I, 45–48." *English Language Notes* 27, no. 2 (December 1989): 19–26.

Kant, Immanuel *Anthropology from a Pragmatic Point of View*. Edited by Robert B. Louden. Cambridge: Cambridge University Press, 2006.

———. *Critique of the Power of Judgment*. Translated and edited by Paul Guyer. Cambridge: Cambridge University Press, 2000.

———. *Lectures on Ethics*. Translated by Peter Lauchlan Heath, edited by Jerome B. Schneewind. New York: Cambridge University Press, 1997.

Keats, John. *The Complete Poems*. ed. John Barnard. London: Penguin, 1988.

———. *The Letters of John Keats*. 2 vols. Edited by Maurice Buxton Forman. Oxford: Oxford University Press, 1931.

Kehew, Robert. ed. *Lark in the Morning: The Verses of the Troubadours*. Chicago: University of Chicago Press, 2005.

Kirk, G. S. "Pitfalls in the Study of Greek Sacrifice." In *Le sacrifice dans l'antiquité*, edited by Jean Rudhardt and Olivier Reverdin, 41–80. Geneva: Fondation Hardt, 1981.

Kirtley, Clare, Peter Bryant, Morag MacLean, and Lynette Bradley. "Rhyme, Rime, and the Onset of Reading." *Journal of Experimental Child Psychology* 48 (1989): 224–45.

Knight, William, ed. *Letters of the Wordsworth Family*. 3 vols. Boston: Ginn, 1907.

Kockelmans, Joseph J. *Edmund Husserl's Phenomenology*. West Lafayette, IN: Purdue University Press, 1994.

Kubler, George. *The Shape of Time: Remarks on the History of Things*. New Haven, CT: Yale University Press, 1962.

Kurke, Leslie. *The Traffic in Praise: Pindar and the Poetics of Social Economy*. Ithaca, NY: Cornell University Press, 1991.

Langer, Susanne. *Feeling and Form*. New York: Charles Scribner's, 1953.

Lansing, Richard, ed. *The Dante Encyclopedia*. New York: Garland, 2000.

Leibnitz, Gottfried Wilhelm. "On the Ultimate Origin of Things." In *Philosophical Works of Leibnitz*, translated by George M. Duncan, 106–13. New Haven, CT: Tuttle, Morehouse and Taylor, 1908.

Levinas, Emmanuel. "Reality and Its Shadow." In *The Levinas Reader*, edited by Seán Hand, 129–43. London: Blackwell, 2001.

Lilly, Ian K. "On Adjacent and Nonadjacent Russian Rhyme Pairs." *Slavic and East European Journal* 29, no. 2 (Summer 1985): 188–97.

Longenbach, James. *The Art of the Poetic Line*. St. Paul, MN: Graywolf, 2008.

Maci, Stefania Maria. "The Language of *Mary Magdalene* of the Bodleian MS Digby 133." *Linguistica e Filologia: Quaderni del Dipartimento di Linguistica, Università degli Studi di Bergamo* 10 (1999): 105–39.

Mackie, Hilary. *Graceful Errors*. Ann Arbor: University of Michigan Press, 2003.

Mandelstam, Nadezhda. *Hope Abandoned*. Translated by Max Hayward. New York: Atheneum, 1974.

———. *Hope against Hope*. Translated by Max Hayward. New York: Modern Library, 1999.

Mandelstam, Osip. "Conversation about Dante." In *The Selected Poems of Osip Mandelstam*, translated by Clarence Brown and W. S. Merwin, 103–62. New York: New York Review of Books, 2004.

———. "Octets." Translated by Donald Davie. *Agenda* 14, no. 2 (1976): 11–14.

———. *Selected Poems*. Translated by David McDuff. Cambridge, UK: Rivers, 1973.

———. *Stone*. Translated by Robert Tracy. Princeton, NJ: Princeton University Press, 1981.

Marvell, Andrew. *The Poems of Andrew Marvell*. Edited by Nigel Smith. London: Longman, 2003.

Marx, Karl. *Economic and Philosophic Manuscripts of 1844*. Translated by Martin Milligan, edited by Dirk Struik. New York: International Publishers, 1964.

Marx, Werner, ed. *The Philosophy of F. W. J. Schelling*. Translated by Thomas Nenon. Bloomington: Indiana University Press, 1984.

Mazzotta, Giuseppe. "Italian Renaissance Epic." In *The Cambridge Companion to Epic*, edited by Catherine Bates, 93–118. Cambridge: Cambridge University Press, 2010.

McCarthy, Vincent. *The Phenomenology of Moods in Kierkegaard*. The Hague: Martinus Nijhoff, 1978.

McEuen, Kathryn Anderson."Whittier's Rhymes." *American Speech* 20, no. 1 (1945): 51–57.

McKie, Michael. "Semantic Rhyme: A Reappraisal." *Essays in Criticism* 46, no. 4 (1996): 340–58.

McShine, Kynaston, and Lynne Cooke, eds. *Richard Serra Sculpture: Forty Years*. New York: Museum of Modern Art, 2007.

Menander Rhetor. Edited by D. A. Russell and N. G. Wilson. Oxford: Oxford University Press, 1981.

Merleau-Ponty, Maurice. "Freedom." In *The Phenomenology of Perception*, translated by Colin Smith, 434–56. London: Routledge, 1989.

Meschonnic, Henri. "Rhyme and Life." Translated by Gabriella Bedetti. *Critical Inquiry* 15, no. 1 (Autumn 1988): 90–107.

Miller, Andrew, trans. and ed. *Greek Lyric: An Anthology in Translation*. Indianapolis: Hackett, 1996.

Milton, John. *Complete Poems and Major Prose*. Edited by Merritt Y. Hughes. New York: Odyssey, 1957.

Monk, Philip. *Mike Kelley and Paul McCarthy: Collaborative Works*. Toronto: Power Plant Contemporary Art Gallery, 2000.

Morris, William N. *Mood: The Frame of Mind*. New York: Springer-Verlag, 1989.

Mowinckel, Sigmund. *The Psalms in Israel's Worship*. Translated by D. R. Ap-Thomas. 2 vols. Nashville: Abingdon, 1962.

Nänny, Max. "Iconic Uses of Rhyme." In *Outside-In-Inside-Out: Iconicity in Language and Literature*, edited by Costantino Maeder, Olga Fischer, and William Herlofsky. Amsterdam: Benjamins, 2005.

Nathan, Geoffrey S. "Clicks in a Chinese Nursery Rhyme." *Journal of the International Phonetic Association* 31, no. 2 (2001): 223–28.

Nietzsche, Friedrich. *The Birth of Tragedy and Other Writings*. Edited by Raymond Geuss and Ronald Speirs. Cambridge: Cambridge University Press, 2004.

———. *The Gay Science: With a Prelude in Rhymes and an Appendix of Songs*. Translated by Walter Kaufmann. New York: Vintage Books, 1974.

Norden, Eduard. *Die Antike Kunstprosa: vom VI. jahrhundert v. Chr. bis in die zeit der Renaissance*. 2 vols. Leipzig: Teubner, 1898.

O'Brien, Peter. *Introductory Thanksgivings in the Letters of Paul*. Leiden: E. J. Brill, 1977.

Ogede, Ode S. "Oral Performance as Instruction: Aesthetic Strategies in Children's Play Songs from a Nigerian Community." *Children's Literature Association Quarterly* 19, no. 3 (Fall 1994): 113–17.

Otway, Thomas. *The Orphan*. Edited by Aline Mackenzie Taylor. Lincoln: University of Nebraska Press, 1976.

Ovid, *Metamorphoses*. Translated by A. D. Melville. Oxford: Oxford University Press, 1986.

———. *Metamorphoses*. Translated by Frank Justus Miller, revised by G. P. Goold. Loeb Classical Library. Cambridge, MA: Harvard University Press, 1984.

Pamuk, Orhan. *Snow*, Translated by Maureen Freely. New York: Alfred A. Knopf, 2004.

Patterson, Orlando. *Freedom*, vol. 1, *Freedom in the Making of Western Culture*. New York: Basic Books, 1991.

Pen, Edward. "Free Verse Movement: Its Reception in Japan and China." In *Tokyo 1991: The Force of Vision; Proceedings of the International Comparative Literature Association Meetings*, 61–67. Tokyo: University of Tokyo Press, 1995.

Perloff, Marjorie. "The Linear Fallacy." *Georgia Review*, Winter 1981, 855–68.

———. *Rhyme and Meaning in the Poetry of Yeats*. The Hague: Mouton, 1970.

Pico della Mirandola. "Oration on the Dignity of Man." In *The Renaissance Philosophy of Man*, edited by Ernst Cassirer, Paul Kristeller, and J. H. Randall, 223–25. Chicago: University of Chicago Press, 1948.

Pindar. *The Complete Odes*. Translated by Anthony Verity, edited by Stephen Instone. Oxford: Oxford University Press, 2007.

———. *Nemean Odes, Isthmian Odes, Fragments*. Translated by William H. Race. Cambridge, MA: Harvard University Press, Loeb, 1997.

———. *The Odes of Pindar*. Translated by C. M. Bowra. London: Penguin, 1969.

Plato. *Gorgias and Phaedrus*. Translated by James H. Nichols. Ithaca, NY: Cornell University Press, 1998.

———. *Ion, Hippias Minor, Laches, Protagoras*. Translated by R. E. Allen. New Haven, CT: Yale University Press, 1996.

———. *Republic*. Translated by G. M. A. Grube. Indianapolis, Hackett, 1992.

———. *Symposium*. Translated by Alexander Nehamas and Paul Woodruff. Indianapolis: Hackett, 1989.

———. *"The Symposium" of Plato: The Shelley Translation*. Edited by David K. O'Connor. South Bend, IN: St. Augustine's, 2002.

———. *Theaetetus*. Edited by Bernard Williams, translated by M. J. Levett, revised by Myles Burnyeat. Indianapolis: Hackett, 1992.

Plotinus. *The Enneads*. Translated by Stephen McKenna. London: Penguin, 1991.

Podro, Michael. *The Critical Historians of Art*. New Haven, CT: Yale University Press, 1982.

Pomorska, Krystina. "Semiotic Implications of Rhymes: Pushkin's Poems of the Erzerum Period." *Canadian-American Slavic Studies* 22, nos. 1–4 (1988): 377–81.

Porter, James I. "Is Art Modern? Kristeller's 'Modern System of the Arts' Reconsidered." *British Journal of Aesthetics* 49, no. 1 (January 2009): 1–24.

Pound, Ezra. *The Cantos of Ezra Pound*. New York: New Directions, 1975.

———. *The Spirit of Romance*. New York: New Directions, 1968.

Preminger, Alex, and T. V. F. Brogan, eds. *Princeton Encyclopedia of Poetry and Poetics*. Princeton, NJ: Princeton University Press, 1993.

Prieto, José Manuel. "Reading Mandelstam on Stalin." Translated by Esther Allen. *New York Review of Books* 72, no. 10 (June 10, 2010): 68–72.

Princeton Encyclopedia of Poetry and Poetics. Edited by Alex Preminger and T. V. F. Brogan. Princeton, NJ: Princeton University Press, 1993.

Quintilian. *The Orator's Education, Books 6–8*. Edited by and translated by Donald A. Russell. Cambridge, MA: Harvard University Press, 2001.

Reeder, Roberta. *Anna Akhmatova: Poet and Prophet*. New York: St. Martin's, 1990.

Revard, Stella P. *Pindar and the Renaissance Hymn-Ode, 1450–1700*. Tempe: Arizona Center for Medieval and Renaissance Studies, 2001.

Richards, I. A. *The Philosophy of Rhetoric*. Oxford: Oxford University Press, 1936.

Ricoeur, Paul. *Philosophie de la volonté*. Paris: Aubier, 1950. Translated by Erazim V. Kohák as *Freedom and Nature: The Voluntary and the Involuntary*. Evanston, IL: Northwestern University Press, 1966.

———. *The Rule of Metaphor: Multi-disciplinary Studies of the Creation of Meaning in Language*. Translated by Robert Czerny with Kathleen McLaughlin and John Costello. Toronto: University of Toronto Press, 1977.

Rilke, Rainer Maria. *The Selected Poetry of Rainer Maria Rilke*, edited and translated by Stephen Mitchell. New York: Random House, 1984.

Robinson, Jenefer. "Emotional Responses to Music: What Are They? How Do They Work? And Are They Relevant to Aesthetic Appreciation?" In *The Oxford Handbook of the Philosophy of Emotion*, edited by Peter Goldie, 651–80. New York: Oxford University Press, 2010.

Rush, Fred. "Literature and Politics." in *Handbook of Philosophy and Literature*, edited by Richard Eldridge, 496–516. London: Oxford University Press, 2009.

Russell, Gene. "Dialectal and Phonetic Features of Edward Taylor's Rhymes." *American Literature* 43, no. 2 (1971): 165–80.

Ryle, Gilbert. *The Concept of Mind*. New York: Barnes and Noble, 1949.

Santayana, George. *Skepticism and Animal Faith*. New York: Charles Scribner's, 1923.

Sappho. *If Not, Winter: Fragments of Sappho*. Translated by Anne Carson. New York: Vintage, 2002.

Sarna, Nahum S. *On the Book of Psalms: Exploring the Prayers of Ancient Israel*. New York: Schocken, 1993.

———. *Understanding Genesis*. New York: Jewish Theological Seminary of America and McGraw-Hill, 1966.

Sartre, Jean-Paul. *The Psychology of Imagination*. New York: Citadel, 1966.

Scarry, Elaine. *The Body in Pain: The Making and Unmaking of the World*. New York: Oxford University Press, 1987.

Schaeffer, Jean-Marie. *Art of the Modern Age*. Translated by Steven Rendall. Princeton, NJ: Princeton University Press, 2000.

Schelling, Friedrich Wilhelm Joseph. *Philosophical Investigations into the Essence of Human Freedom*. Translated by Jeff Love and Johannes Schmidt. Albany: State University of New York Press, 2006.

———. "Philosophical Investigations into the Essence of Human Freedom and Related Matters." In *Philosophy of German Idealism*, edited by Ernst Behler, translated by Priscilla Hayden-Roy, 217–84. New York: Continuum, 1987.

———. "Three Essays." In *Idealism and the Endgame of Theory*, translated and edited by Thomas Pfau. Albany: State University of New York Press, 1994.

Schiller, Friedrich von. "Naïve and Sentimental Poetry." In *"Naïve and Sentimental Poetry" and "On the Sublime": Two Essays*, translated by Julius A. Elias. New York: Frederick Ungar, 1967.

Schipper, Mineke. "Stories of the Beginning: Origin Myths of Africa South of the Sahara." In *Imagining Creation*, edited by Markham Geller and Mineke Schipper, 103–8. Leiden: E. J. Brill, 2008.

Schopenhauer, Arthur. *The World as Will and Idea*. Translated by R. B. Haldane and J. Kemp. 4th ed. London: Kegan Paul, 1896.

———. *The World as Will and Idea*, bk. 3. In *Critical Theory since Plato*, edited by Hazard Adams, 475–89. New York: Harcourt Brace Jovanovich, 1971.

Sennett, Richard. *The Craftsman*. New Haven, CT: Yale University Press, 2008.

Shaw, J. Thomas. "Parts of Speech in Puškin's Rhymewords and Nonrhymed Endwords." *Slavic and East European Journal* 37, no. 1 (Spring 1993): 1–22.

Shearer, Rhonda Roland. "Marcel Duchamp's Impossible Bed and Other 'Not' Readymade Objects: A Possible Route of Influence from Art to Science." *Art and Academe* 10, no. 1 (Fall 1997): 28–62, and 10, no. 2 (Winter 1998): 76–94.

Shelley, Percy Bysshe. "A Defence of Poetry." In *Shelley's Poetry and Prose*, edited by Donald H. Reiman and Neil Fraistat, 509–35. New York: W. W. Norton, 2002.

———. *Shelley's Poetry and Prose*. Edited by Donald Reiman and Neil Fraistat. New York: W. W. Norton, 2002.

———. *Shelley's Prose and Poetry*. Edited by Donald Reiman and Sharon B. Powers. New York: W. W. Norton, 1977.

Shuster, George. *The English Ode from Milton to Keats*. New York: Columbia University Press, 1940.

Sidney, Philip. *A Defence of Poetry*. Edited by J. A. Van Dorsten. Oxford: Oxford University Press, 1966.

Simmel, Georg. *The Philosophy of Money*. Edited by David Frisby, translated by Tom Bottomore and David Frisby. London: Routledge, 2004.

Simpson, Louis, "Irregular Impulses: Some Remarks on Free Verse." *Ohio Review* 28 (1982): 54–57.

Smith, David. "Report on Voltri." In *David Smith*, edited by Garnett McCoy, 156–63. New York: Praeger, 1973.

Smith, D. Vance. *The Book of the Incipit: Beginnings in the Fourteenth Century*. Minneapolis: University of Minnesata Press, 2001.

Snowing, Margaret, Charles Hulme, and Robin Mercer. "A Deficit in Rime Awareness in Children with Down Syndrome." *Reading and Writing: An Interdisciplinary Journal* 15 (2002): 471–95.

Southworth, John. *The English Medieval Minstrel*. Woodbridge, Suffolk, UK: Boydell and Brewer, 1989.

Speiser, E. A., ed. *Genesis*. The Anchor Bible 1. New York: Doubleday, 1964.

Spender, Stephen. "The Making of a Poem." In *Creativity*, edited by P. E. Vernon, 61–76. London: Penguin, 1970.

Spenser, Edmund. *The Poetical Works of Edmund Spenser*. Edited by J. C. Smith and E. De Selincourt. London: Oxford, 1960.

Spitzer, Leo. *Classical and Christian Ideas of World Harmony: Prolegomena to an Interpretation of the Word "Stimmung."* Edited by Anna Granville Hatcher. Baltimore: Johns Hopkins University Press, 1963.

Starkie, Enid. *Arthur Rimbaud*. New York: New Directions, 1961.

Stevens, Wallace. *Complete Poetry and Prose*. New York: Library of America, 1997.

Stolnitz, Jerome. "On the Origins of 'Aesthetic Disinterestedness.'" *Journal of Aesthetics and Art Criticism* 20 (1961): 131–43.

Stewart, Susan. *The Open Studio: Essays on Art and Aesthetics*. Chicago: University of Chicago Press, 2005.

Stuart, Moses. *Hebrew Grammar*. Andover, MA: Codman, 1823.

Swedenborg, Emanuel. *An Hieroglyphic Key to Natural and Spiritual Mysteries by*

Way of Representations and Correspondences. Translated by R. Hindmarsh. London: R. Hindmarsh, 1792.

Szczeklik, Andrzej. *Catharsis: on the Art of Medicine*. Translated by Antonia Lloyd-Jones. Chicago: University of Chicago Press, 2005.

Taylor, Beverly. "Byron's Use of Dante in 'The Prophecy of Dante.'" *Keats-Shelley Journal* 28 (1979): 102–19.

Thayer, Robert E. *The Origin of Everyday Moods*. New York: Oxford University Press, 1996.

Tresmontant, Claude. *La préscience de Dieu, la prédestination et la liberté humaine*. Paris: François-Xavier de Guibert, 1996.

Tsur, Reuven. *What Makes Sound Patterns Expressive?* Durham, NC: Duke University Press, 1992.

Valéry, Paul. *The Art of Poetry*. Edited by Jackson Mathews. Princeton, NJ: Princeton University Press, 1989.

Vaughan, Henry. *The Complete Poems*. Edited by Alan Rudrum. London: Penguin, 1976.

Vernant, J.-P. *Mythe et société en Grèce ancienne*. Paris: F. Maspero, 1974.

Verstraten, Frans A. J. "On the Ancient History of the Direction of the Motion Aftereffect." *Perception* 25 (1996): 1177–187.

Vico, Giambattista. *New Science*. Translated by David Marsh. London: Penguin, 2001.

Virgil. *The Aeneid of Virgil*. Translated by Rolfe Humphries. New York: Scribner's, 1951.

von Hallberg, Robert. *Lyric Powers*. Chicago: University of Chicago Press, 2008.

Waddell, Helen, ed. *Medieval Latin Lyrics*. New York: Henry Holt, 1929.

Warnock, Mary. *Imagination*. Berkeley: University of California Press, 1978.

Weir, Ruth. *Language in the Crib*. The Hague: Mouton, 1966.

Wesling, Donald. "The Prosodies of Free Verse." In *Twentieth-Century Literature in Retrospect*, edited by Reuben Brower, 155–87. Cambridge, MA: Harvard English Studies, 1971.

Williams, G. W. *Tradition and Originality in Roman Poetry*. Oxford: Clarendon, 1968.

Wordsworth, Dorothy. *The Grasmere and Alfoxden Journals*. Edited by Pamela Woof. Oxford: Oxford University Press, 2002.

Wordsworth, William. *Poems*. Edited by John O. Hayden. London: Penguin, 1977.

———. *The Prelude: The Four Texts (1798, 1799, 1805, 1850)*. Edited by Jonathan Wordsworth. London: Penguin, 1995.

———. *Selected Prose*. Edited by John Hayden. Harmondsworth, UK: Penguin, 1988.

Wordsworth, William, and Samuel Taylor Coleridge. *Lyrical Ballads, 1798*. Edited by W. J. B. Owen. Oxford, Oxford University Press, 1969.

Worthen, John. *The Gang: Coleridge, the Hutchinsons, and the Wordsworths in 1802*. New Haven, CT: Yale University Press, 2001.

Young, Edward. *Conjectures on Original Composition in a Letter to the Author of Sir Charles Grandison*. 2nd ed. London: Millar and Dodsley, 1759.

———. *The Works of Dr. Edward Young*. 6 vols. London: Mallard, Durfey, Nelson, et al. 1779.

Zerilli, Linda. *Feminism and the Abyss of Freedom*. Chicago: University of Chicago Press, 2005.

Žižek, Slavoj. *The Abyss of Freedom / Ages of the World: An Essay by Slavoj Žižek with the Text of Schelling's "Die Weltalter" (Second Draft, 1813)*. Translated by Judith Norman. Ann Arbor: University of Michigan, 1997.

Zuckerkandl, Victor. *Sound and Symbol: Music and the External World*. Translated by Willard R. Trask. Bollingen Series 44. New York: Pantheon, 1956.

INDEX

NOTES

NOTES

NOTES

NOTES

NOTES